CERTIFICATION CIRCLE™

MOUS

Microsoft Excel 2002

Barbara Clemens

Handwritten notes:

F2 Edit

Ctrl G Go To

=SUM(Sheet1: Sheet4!A6) adds cells A6 on sheets 1 through 4

=SUM(Sheet1! A5, Sheet2! B6,)

relative reference - adjusts
absolute reference
($A$1) (always A4) $A3 always A

F4 cycles through the absolute reference possibility

F9 - Date and Time update (Now Function)

page 167
F3 Paste Name Dialog Box
Ctrl S = Save

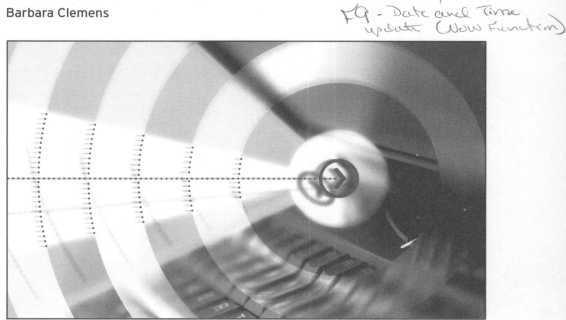

EXPERT

MICROSOFT OFFICE USER SPECIALIST
APPROVED COURSEWARE

D1465922

THOMSON
COURSE TECHNOLOGY™

Australia • Canada • Mexico • Singapore • Spain • United Kingdom • United States

MOUS Microsoft Excel 2002

CERTIFICATION CIRCLE™ *EXPERT*

Barbara Clemens

Managing Editor:
Nicole Jones Pinard

Product Managers:
Debbie Masi
Julia Healy

Editorial Assistant:
Christina Kling Garrett

Production Editor:
Debbie Masi

Contributing Author:
Carol Cram

Developmental Editors:
Helen Clayton, Kim Crowley

Composition House:
GEX Publishing Services

QA Manuscript Reviewers:
Nicole Ashton, John Freitas,
Jeff Schwartz, Alex White

Book Designers:
Joseph Lee, black fish design

COPYRIGHT © 2002 Course Technology, a division of Thomson Learning. Thomson Learning is a trademark used herein under license.

ISBN 0-619-05717-3

Printed in Canada

1 2 3 4 5 6 7 8 9 WC 06 05 04 03 02

For more information, contact Course Technology, 25 Thomson Place, Boston, Massachusetts, 02210.

Or you can visit us on the World Wide Web at www.course.com

Thank You, Advisory Board!

This book is a result of the hard work and dedication by authors, editors, and more than 30 instructors focused on Microsoft Office and MOUS certification. These instructors formed our Certification Circle Advisory Board. We looked to them to flesh out our original vision and turn it into a sound pedagogical method of instruction. In short, we asked them to partner with us to create *the* book for preparing for a MOUS Exam. And, now we wish to thank them for their contributions and expertise.

ADVISORY BOARD MEMBERS:

Linda Amergo	Old Westbury
Shellie Besharse	Mississippi County Community College
Margaret Britt	Copiah Lincoln Community College
Becky Burt	Copiah Lincoln Community College
Judy Cameron	Spokane Community College
Elizabeth T. De Arazoza	Miami-Dade Community College
Susan Dozier	Tidewater Community College
Dawna Dewire	Babson College
Pat Evans	J. Sargent Reynolds
Susan Fry	Boise State University
Joyce Gordon	Babson College
Steve Gordon	Babson College
Pat Harley	Howard Community College
Rosanna Hartley	Western Piedmont Community College
Eva Hefner	St. Petersburg Junior College
Becky Jones	Richland College
Mali Jones	Johnson and Wales University
Angie McCutcheon	Washington State Community College
Barbara Miller	Indiana University
Carol Milliken	Kellogg Community College
Maureen Paparella	Monmouth University
Mike Puopolo	Bunker Hill Community College
Kathy Proietti	Northern Essex Community College
Pamela M. Randall	Unicity Network
Theresa Savarese	San Diego City College
Barbara Sherman	Buffalo State
Kathryn Surles	Salem Community College
Beth Thomas	Hagerstown Community College
Barbara Webber	Northern Essex Community College
Jean Welsh	Lansing Community College
Lynn Wermers	North Shore Community College
Sherry Young	Kingwood College

Preface

elcome to the
*CERTIFICATION CIRCLE
SERIES*. Each book in this
series is designed with one
thing in mind: preparing you to
pass a Microsoft Office User
Specialist (MOUS) exam. This
strict focus allows you to target
the skills you need to be suc-
cessful. You will not need to
study anything extra—it's like
getting a peek at the exam
before you take it! Read on to
learn more about how the book
is organized and how you will
get the most out of it.

Table of Contents
This book is organized around
the MOUS exam objectives.
Each Skill on the exam is
taught on two facing pages
with text on the left and figures on the right. This also
makes for a terrific reference;
if you want to brush up on a
few skills, it's easy to find the
ones you're looking for.

Getting Started Chapter
Each book begins with a
Getting Started Chapter.
This Chapter contains skills
that are *not* covered on the
exam but the authors felt
were vital to understanding
the software. The content
in this chapter varies from
application to application.

Skill Set 8
Integrating with Other Applications

Import Data to Access
Import Data from an Excel Workbook

You can import data into an Access database from several file formats, including an Excel workbook or another Access, FoxPro, dBase, or Paradox database.
It is not uncommon for a user to enter a list of data into Excel and later decide
to convert that data into an Access database, because the user wants to use
Access's extensive form or report capabilities or wants multiple people to be able
to use the data at the same time. (An Access database is inherently **multi-user**;
many people can enter and update data at the same time.) Since the data in an
Excel workbook is structured similarly to data in an Access table datasheet, you
can easily import data from an Excel workbook into an Access database by
using the **Import Spreadsheet Wizard**.

Skill Overview
Each skill starts with a paragraph
explaining the concept and how
you would use it. These are
clearly written and concise.

File Open Icon
We provide a realistic
project file for every
skill. And, it's in the
form you need it in
order to work through
the steps; there's no
wasted time building
the file before you can
work with it.

Skill Steps
The Steps required
to perform the skill
appear on the left
page with what you
type in green text.

tip

Step 4
You can also
import Excel
workbook data
into an existing
table if the field
names used in the
Excel workbook
match the field
names in the
Access table.

Activity Steps
ClassesO1.mdb

1. Click File on the menu bar, point to Get External Data, then
   click Import
2. Navigate to the drive and folder where your Project Files are
   stored, click the Files of type list arrow, click Microsoft Excel,
   click Instructors, then click Import to start the Import
   Spreadsheet Wizard
   See Figure 8-1.
3. Select the First Row Contains Column Headings check box,
   then click Next
4. Click Next to indicate that you want to create a new table, then
   click Next to not specify field changes
5. Click the Choose my own primary key option button to set
   InstructorID as the primary key field, then click Next
6. Type Instructors in the Import to Table box, click Finish, then
   click OK
7. Double-click Instructors to open it in Datasheet View
   See Figure 8-2. Imported data works the same way as any other table
   of data in a database.
8. Close the Instructors table

Tips
We provide tips
specific to the skill
or how the skill is
tested on the exam.

98   Certification Circle

Additional Projects

For those who want more practice applying the skills they've learned, there is a project for each skill set located at the back of each book. The projects ask you to combine the skills you've learned to create a meaningful document – just what you do in real life.

Project for Skill Set 1
Working with Cells and Cell Data

Sales Projection for Alaska Adventures

You work for Alaska Adventures, a small company based in Juneau, Alaska, that offers sea kayaking, mountain biking, and hiking tours. You've received a workbook containing a sales projection for the sea kayaking tours that the company hopes to sell in the busy summer months of June, July, and August. In this project, you will complete and format this worksheet. The workbook also contains a second worksheet that includes a list of the guests who purchased sea kayaking tours on a single day during the previous summer. You'll use the AutoFilter features on this list to determine the number of customers who came from countries other then the United States and Canada.

Activity Steps

open EC_Project1.xls

1. Clear the contents and formats of cell A3, drag cell A4 up to cell A3, then delete cell D14 and shift the cells left
2. Merge cell A3 across cells A3 to E3, then check the spelling in the worksheet and correct any errors
3. Enter Total in cell E5, use the Go To command to navigate to cell C13, then change the value in cell C13 to 1200
4. Use the SUM function in cell E12 to add the values in cells B12 through D12, then copy the formula to cells E13 through E15
5. Select cells B12 through B16, then use the AutoSum button to calculate the totals required for cells B16 through E16
6. In cell B18, enter the formula required to subtract the value in cell B16 from the value in cell B9, then copy the formula to cells C18 through E18
7. Use Find and Replace to locate all instances of 1500 and replace them with 500
8. Format cells B7 through E7, B9 through E9, B12 through E12, B16 through E16, and B18 through E18 with the Currency style, format cells B8 through E8 and cells B13 through E15 with the Comma style, then compare the completed worksheet to Figure EP 1-1
9. Switch to the Customers worksheet, then use AutoFilter to show only the international customers in the Category column The filtered list appears as shown in Figure EP 1-2

close EC_Project1.xls

Step 8
To save time, press and hold the [CTRL] key, select each group of cells, and then click the Currency Style button.

2   Certification Circle

Skill 1
Import Data to Access

Figure 8-1: Import Spreadsheet Wizard dialog box

Figure 8-2: Imported Instructors table in Datasheet View

Seven records were imported

Figures

There are at least two figures per skill which serve as a reference as you are working through the steps. Callouts focus your attention to what's important.

Extra Boxes

This will *not* be on the exam–it's extra–hence the name. But, there are some very cool things you can do with Office xp so we had to put this stuff somewhere!

extra!

Using delimited text files

You can import data from a **delimited text file**, a file of unformatted data where each field value is delimited (separated) by a common character, such as a comma or a tab. Each record is further delimited by a common character, such as a paragraph mark. A delimited text file usually has a **txt** (for text) file extension. You can use delimited text files to convert data from a proprietary software system (such as an accounting, inventory, or scheduling software system) into a format that other programs can import. For example, most accounting software programs won't export data directly into an Access database, but they can export data to a delimited text file, which can then be imported by Access.

Target Your Skills

At the end of each unit, there are two Target Your Skills exercises. These require you to create a document from scratch, based on the figure, using the skills you've learned in the chapter. And, the solution is provided– there's no wasted time trying to figure out if you've done it right.

Additional Resources

There are many resources available with this book—both free and for a nominal fee. Please see your sales representative for more information. The resources available with this book are:

INSTRUCTOR'S MANUAL

Available as an electronic file, the Instructor's Manual is quality-assurance tested and includes unit overviews, lecture topics, solutions to all lessons and projects, and extra Target Your Skills. The Instructor's Manual is available on the Instructor's Resource Kit CD-ROM, or you can download if from www.course.com.

FACULTY ONLINE COMPANION

You can browse this textbook's password protected site to obtain the Instructor's Manual, Solution Files, Project Files, and any updates to the text. Contact your Customer Service Representative for the site address and password.

PROJECT FILES

Project Files contain all of the data that students will use to complete the lessons and projects. A Readme file includes instructions for using the files. Adopters of this text are granted the right to install the Project Files on any stand-alone computer or network. The Project Files are available on the Instructor's Resource Kit CD-ROM, the Review Pack, and can also be downloaded from www.course.com.

SOLUTION FILES

Solution Files contain every file students are asked to create or modify in the lessons and projects. A Help file on the Instructor's Resource Kit includes information for using the Solution Files.

FIGURE FILES

Figure Files contain all the figures from the book in bitmap format. Use the figure files to create transparency masters or in a PowerPoint presentation.

SAM, SKILLS ASSESSMENT MANAGER FOR MICROSOFT OFFICE XP SAM^{xp}

SAM is the most powerful Office XP assessment and reporting tool that will help you gain a true understanding of your students' proficiency in Microsoft Word, Excel, Access, and PowerPoint 2002.

TOM, TRAINING ONLINE MANAGER FOR MICROSOFT OFFICE XP TOM

TOM is Course Technology's MOUS-approved training tool for Microsoft Office XP. Available via the World Wide Web and CD-ROM, TOM allows students to actively learn Office XP concepts and skills by delivering realistic practice through both guided and self-directed simulated instruction.

Certification Circle Series, SAM, and TOM: the true training and assessment solution for Office XP.

Preparing for the MOUS Exam

Studying for and passing the Microsoft Office User Specialist (MOUS) exams requires very specific test preparation materials. As a student and reviewer of MOUS exam materials, I am proud to be a part of a team of creators that produced a new series specifically designed with the MOUS exam test taker in mind.

The Certification Circle Series ™ provides a fully integrated test preparation solution for MOUS Office^XP with the powerful combination of its Core and Expert textbooks, testing software with Skills Assessment Manager (SAM^XP) and Training Online Manager (TOM^XP). This combination coupled with the Exam Reference Pocket Guide for quick test taking tips and Office^XP materials will provide the skills and confidence a student will need to pass the MOUS exams.

How does the Certification Circle Series provide the best test preparation materials? Here's how:

▶ Core and Expert texts are based entirely on MOUS exam objectives.

▶ Table of Contents in each book maps directly to MOUS exam objectives in a one to one correlation.

▶ "Target Your Skills" exercises in the end of unit material presents problem solving questions in similar fashion to the MOUS 2002 exams.

▶ Skills Assessment Manager (SAM ^XP) provides a simulated testing environment in which students can target their strengths and weakness before taking the MOUS exams.

If you are an experienced Excel user, you'll probably want to go directly to the Target Your Skills exercise at the end of the Skill Set and Test your mastery of the objectives in that Skill Set. If you are unsure about how to accomplish any part of the exercise, you can always go back to the individual lessons that you need to review, and practice the steps required for each MOUS objective.

If you are relatively new to Excel, you'll probably want to complete the lessons in the book in a sequential manner, using Target Your Skills exercise at the end of each Skill Set to confirm that you've learned the skills necessary to pass each objective on the MOUS test.

The Target Your Skills exercises simulate the same types of activities that you will be requested to perform on the test. Therefore, your ability to complete them in a timely fashion will be a direct indicator of your preparedness for the MOUS exam.

Judy Cameron, Spokane Community College
and the Certification Circle Series Team

SAM, Skills Assessment Manager for Microsoft Office XP

SAM XP–the pioneer of IT assessment.

How can you gauge your students' knowledge of Office XP? SAM XP makes teaching and testing Office XP skills easier. SAM XP is a unique Microsoft Office XP assessment and reporting tool that helps you gain a true understanding of your students' ability to use Microsoft Word, Excel, Access, and PowerPoint 2002, and coming soon Outlook 2002, Windows 2000 and Windows XP.

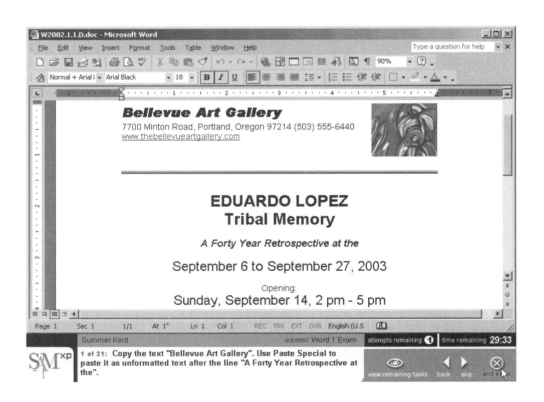

TOM, Training Online Manager for Microsoft Office XP

TOM—efficient, individualized learning when, where, and how you need it.

TOM is Course Technology's MOUS-approved training tool for Microsoft Office XP that works in conjunction with SAM XP assessment and your Illustrated Office XP book. Available via the World Wide Web or a stand-along CD-ROM, TOM allows students to actively learn Office XP concepts and skills by delivering realistic practice through both guided and self-directed simulated instruction.

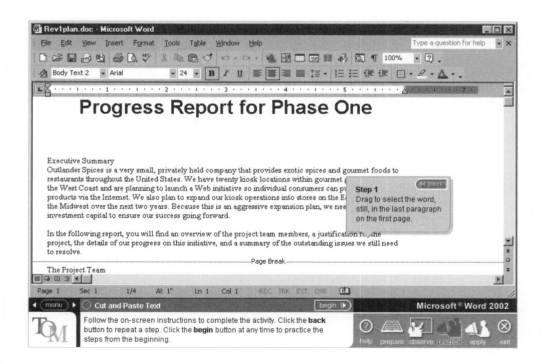

Certification Circle: Exam Reference Pocket Guide

The Microsoft Office ^{XP} Exam Reference Pocket Guide is a reference tool designed to prepare you for the Microsoft Office User Specialist (MOUS) exams. The book assumes that you are already familiar with the concepts that are the basis for the skills covered in this book. The book can therefore be used as a study companion to brush up on skills before taking the exam or as a desk reference when using Microsoft Office programs.

There are six chapters in this book. The first chapter in the book, *Exam Tips*, provides some background information on the MOUS Certification program, the general process for taking an exam, and some helpful hints in preparing and successfully passing the exams.

The remaining five chapters each cover a different Office program: Word, Excel, Access, PowerPoint, and Outlook. Each program-specific chapter begins by covering program basics in a brief *Getting Started* section. This section covers the basic skills that are not specifically covered in the MOUS exams, but that are essential to being able to work in the program. The *Getting Started* section is followed by the complete set of skills tested by the Microsoft MOUS Certification exams, starting with the Core or Comprehensive exam, and then followed by the Expert exam where applicable. These sections are labeled and ordered to exactly match the Skill Sets and Skill Activities tested in the MOUS Certification Exam. Clear, bulleted steps are provided for each skill.

Because there are often different ways to complete a task, the book provides multiple methods where appropriate for each skill or activity, including Menu, Button, Keyboard, Mouse, and Task Pane methods. The MOUS exams allow you to perform the skills using any one of these methods, so you can choose the method with which you are most comfortable to complete the task. It is the perfect companion to any of the Certification Circle Series textbooks or as a stand-alone reference book.

Contents

MOUS Microsoft Excel 2002

CERTIFICATION CIRCLE™ EXPERT

MOUS Microsoft Excel 2002

CERTIFICATION CIRCLE™ EXPERT

MOUS Microsoft Excel 2002

CERTIFICATION CIRCLE™ *EXPERT*

MOUS Microsoft Excel 2002

CERTIFICATION CIRCLE™ *EXPERT*

MOUS Microsoft Excel 2002

CERTIFICATION CIRCLE™ EXPERT

Skill List

1. Start and exit the Excel program
2. Explore the Excel window
3. Open and close an Excel Workbook
4. Navigate an Excel Workbook
5. Explore task panes
6. Copy workbook files
7. Save a workbook
8. Preview and print a worksheet
9. Get Help

Microsoft Excel 2002 is a **spreadsheet** program, which is a program that lets you organize and analyze numeric information using a grid of columns and rows. Once you have entered your information into an Excel file, called a **workbook,** you can analyze it by having Excel perform calculations. Excel has many types of **charts** that let you portray your data in graphic form. But the real power of Excel lies in its ability to rapidly recalculate formulas when you change basic information; because you can easily explore different outcomes, Excel can be a powerful decision-making tool. This Getting Started Skill Set familiarizes you with the main parts of the Excel window and basic Excel skills; it also gives you information on the conventions in this book to help you complete the activities correctly.

Getting Started

Getting Started with Excel 2002

Start and Exit the Excel Program
Start and Exit Excel

In order to use Excel tools, you need to start the program. When you start Excel, your computer reads the program from your hard disk and displays it on the screen. You start Excel the same way you would start any other Microsoft Office program, by using the Start menu on the Windows taskbar at the bottom of the screen. After you start the program, you can open and work with Excel workbooks. When you are finished, you close your workbooks and **exit**, or close, the program. *In this book, we assume that Excel will be running on your computer before you proceed with lesson steps and that you will exit Excel at the end of your work session.*

Depending on your computer system, your startup procedure could differ from these instructions. If you are working on a networked computer, you may need to check with your technical resource person.

Activity Steps

1. Make sure your computer is on and that you can see the Windows desktop on your screen

2. Click the **Start button**  on the Windows taskbar

3. Point to **Programs**

4. Point to **Microsoft Excel**
   See Figure GS-1.

5. Click **Microsoft Excel**
   The Excel program starts, displaying the program window and a blank worksheet on the screen.

6. If your window is not maximized, click the **Maximize button** 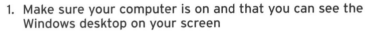 on the Excel title bar
   See Figure GS-2.
   The **New Workbook task pane** appears on the right side of the screen. The task pane window opens as you use the program to give you easy access to specific program features. In this case, it displays options for opening new Excel workbooks.

7. Click the **Close button** on the Excel program window title bar

8. If you see a dialog box asking if you want to save your changes, click **No**

Figure GS-1: Programs submenu

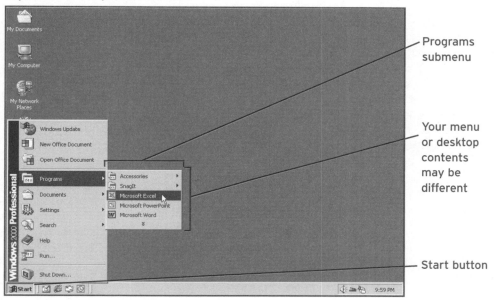

— Programs
submenu

— Your menu
or desktop
contents
may be
different

— Start button

Figure GS-2: Excel program window

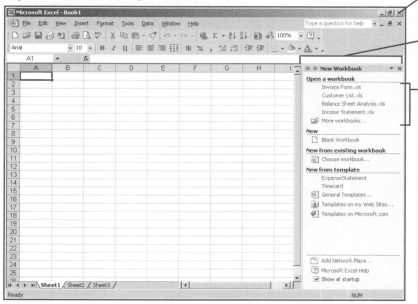

— Program window
Close button

— New Workbook
task pane

— Your workbook
list may vary

extra!

Another way to start Excel

You can also start Excel by opening a folder on the Windows desktop and double-clicking any Excel workbook icon, which will both start Excel and open that workbook.

Getting Started

Getting Started with Excel 2002

Explore the Excel Window
Explore Excel Window Elements

At the top of the Excel window you see the **title bar** containing the program and workbook name, as well as the **menu bar** and the **toolbars**, which you use to enter and work with information. The Excel program window contains the **worksheet**, which is the grid of columns and rows where you enter information. (Some people refer to a worksheet as a spreadsheet, although this also describes the software category.) An Excel workbook file can have multiple worksheets. In a worksheet, the intersection of each column and row is called a **cell**. One cell always has a black border surrounding it, which means it is the **active cell**; any numbers or words you type will appear in the active cell.

Activity Steps

1. **If you have not done so already, start the Microsoft Excel program**
   The program starts, and a new workbook automatically opens.

2. **Examine Figure GS-3 and Table GS-1 to identify the main parts of the Excel window and learn the function of each one**
   The cell at the intersection of column A and row 1 has a dark border around it, meaning that it is the active cell. The active cell is also called the **selected** or **highlighted cell**.

3. **Click the cell at the intersection of column D and row 15**
   Cell D15 is now the active cell. The column D heading and row 15 heading are now shaded. The Name box in the Formula bar reads "D15," which is the address of the active cell. A **cell address** is the combination of column number and row number that uniquely identifies each cell.

4. **Move the mouse to place the pointer over the toolbars, then slowly move the pointer, pausing over several buttons**
   As you point to each toolbar button, a yellow **ScreenTip** identifies it. While the steps in this book contain pictures of the buttons you click, you can use ScreenTips as you perform the steps to verify that you are selecting the correct button.

Step 1
The screens in this book show the Excel toolbars in two rows. If your screen shows only one toolbar instead of the two shown in the figure, click the Toolbar Options button on the right side of either toolbar, then click Show Buttons on Two Rows.

Figure GS-3: Excel window elements

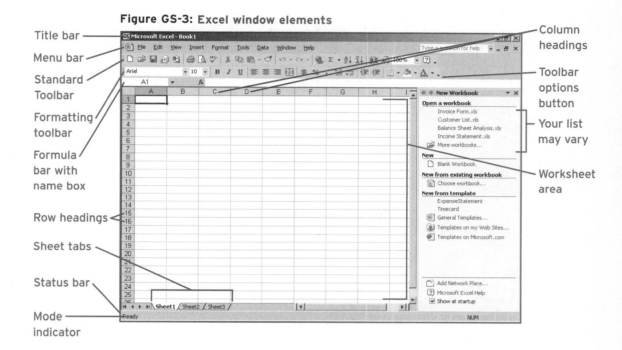

Title bar
Menu bar
Standard Toolbar
Formatting toolbar
Formula bar with name box
Row headings
Sheet tabs
Status bar
Mode indicator

Column headings
Toolbar options button
Your list may vary
Worksheet area

TABLE GS-1: Description of Excel window elements

element	description	element	description
Title bar	Displays program and workbook names	Column and row headings	Contain column letters and row numbers that identify worksheet cells
Menu bar	Contains names of menus with commands that let you interact with Excel	Worksheet area	Contains cells that will hold text and numbers you enter
Standard toolbar	Displays buttons you click to quickly open, save, and print worksheets	Sheet tabs	Let you display other worksheets in the workbook
Formatting toolbar	Displays buttons you click to change the appearance of worksheet text and numbers	Status bar	Gives information on status of program after certain actions
Formula bar with Name box	Formula Bar shows formula of active cell and buttons you use in creating formulas; Name box contains address of active cell or worksheet area	Mode indicator	Displays text such as "Enter" or "Edit" to indicate action taking place

Getting Started
Getting Started with Excel 2002

Open and Close an Excel Workbook
Open and Close an Excel Workbook

A **workbook** is an Excel file containing one or more worksheets. Worksheets contain information, usually a combination of text and numbers, that you analyze using Excel tools. After you start the Excel program, you either begin with a new workbook or open an existing one. When you open a workbook, your computer reads the file information from a disk, places it in your computer's temporary memory, and displays it on your screen. When you are finished with a workbook, you close it, which removes it from memory, but the workbook file remains on your disk. If you exit the Excel program while a workbook is open, the workbook will close also, but the program will ask if you want to save any changes you have made.

Activity Steps

1. If Excel is not already running, start it now
2. Click the **Open button** on the Standard toolbar
3. Click the **Look in list arrow**, then navigate to the location where your Project Files are stored
   See Figure GS-4.
   If your Project Files are stored in a folder, navigate to the folder by using the **Up One Level button** to move up in the disk structure, or by double-clicking folders to open them and move downward in the disk structure.
4. Click the filename **Income01**, then click **Open**
   See Figure GS-5.
   The Income01 workbook file opens on the screen. Its title appears in the title bar. The filename is Income01, and its file extension is .xls. A **file extension** contains a period followed by three letters and tells you what program created the file: .xls represents a Microsoft Excel file, .doc a Microsoft Word file, and .ppt a Microsoft PowerPoint file.
5. Click the **Close Window button** on the right side of the Menu bar to close the file but leave the Excel program open

Step 2
You can also click the More Workbooks hyperlink in the New Workbook task pane to display the Open dialog box.

Figure GS-4: Open dialog box

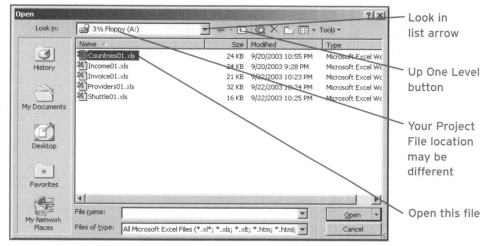

Look in
list arrow

Up One Level
button

Your Project
File location
may be
different

Open this file

Figure GS-5: Open document

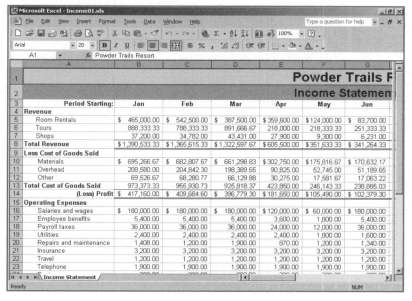

extra!

Displaying file extensions
This book assumes that your computer is set to display file extensions. To display them, go to the Windows desktop, then double-click any drive or folder icon. Click **OK**. Click **Tools**, click **Folder Options**, then click the **View tab**. Click to remove the check from **Hide file extensions for known file types**, then Click **OK**.

Getting Started
Getting Started with Excel 2002

Navigate an Excel Workbook
Navigate an Excel Workbook

As you enter and analyze data in an Excel workbook, you will need to move around the worksheet cells and, in many cases, switch among worksheets. You will save time if you use the most efficient ways of navigating in Excel. As you move the mouse pointer over different window areas, the pointer changes shape to indicate the type of action you can perform: the select pointer ⌖ lets you select open menus and click buttons; the normal pointer ✛ lets you select worksheet cells; the I-beam pointer I lets you insert text and formulas; the column pointer ↓ and row pointer → let you highlight an entire column or row. See Table GS-2 for a list of keyboard navigation tools.

Step 2
Scroll bars can help you navigate quickly, although they do not move the active cell. Click the scroll arrows to move one row or column at a time; click the gray areas on either side of the scroll box to move one screenful at a time; or drag the scroll box to move large distances.

Activity Steps

 open Countries01.xls

1. Click cell **B4**, press **[Tab]** five times, then look in the Formula bar
   The formula for the selected cell, cell G4, appears in the Formula bar; the selected cell address (G4) appears in the Name box.

2. Press **[↓]** three times, noticing that the cell addresses in the Name box change for each cell

3. Click the **down arrow** on the vertical scroll bar until the chart is visible on your screen
   See Figure GS-6.

4. Click the **Europe, Asia**, then the **North America sheet tabs**

5. Click the **International Guests sheet tab**, then press **[Pg Up]** (or **[Page Up]**)

6. Press **[Ctrl][Home]**
   The selected cell is now cell A1.

 close Countries01.xls

Figure GS-6: Chart on worksheet

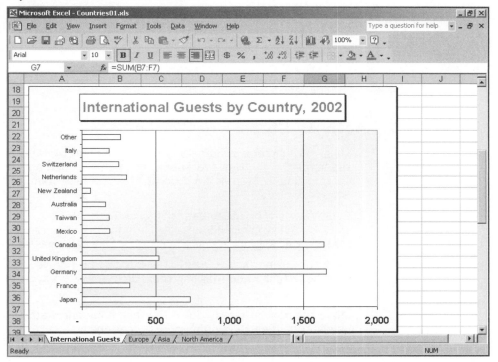

TABLE GS-2: Keyboard navigation tools

to move	press	to move	press
Up, down, left, or right by one cell	[↑] [↓] [←] [→]	Up one screen	[Pg Up] or [Page Up]
One cell to the right One cell to the left	[Tab] [Shift][Tab]	Down one screen To beginning of a row	[Pg Dn] or [Page Down] [Home]
One cell down	[Enter]	To cell A1 in the worksheet	[Ctrl][Home]

Getting Started

Getting Started with Excel 2002

Explore Task Panes

Explore the Excel Task Panes

As you perform Excel tasks, you will sometimes see **task panes**, windows that appear next to the worksheet to let you perform specific tasks. When you start Excel or when you select the New command from the File menu, the New Workbook task pane appears automatically. Table GS-3 describes the four Excel task panes. In the steps below, you learn how to display task panes and move among them.

Step 2
If the task pane was open on your screen at the start of this activity, Step 2 will close it; repeating the step will redisplay it.

Activity Steps

1. Make sure Excel is running and there is a blank workbook on the screen, if the New Workbook task pane is open on your screen, skip to Step 4; if a different task pane is open, skip to Step 3.

2. Click **View** on the menu bar, then click **Task Pane**
   The Task Pane command is a **toggle**, meaning that if you select it once, the task pane appears; if you select it again, the task pane closes.

3. Click the **Other Task Panes list arrow** ▼ on the New Workbook task pane title bar, then click **New Workbook**
   See Figure GS-7.

4. Move the pointer slowly down the task pane and watch how the pointer changes, depending on its location
   When the pointer turns to 🖑, the pointer is over a hyperlink that you can click to open that file.

5. Click the **Other Task Panes list arrow** on the New Workbook task pane title bar, then click **Clipboard**

6. Click the **Back arrow** ◀ on the task pane title bar

7. Click the **Other Task Panes list arrow** in the new Workbook task pane title bar, then click **Search**

8. Click the **Other Task Panes list arrow**, then click **Insert Clip Art**

9. Click the **Close button** ✕ on the task pane title bar

Figure GS-7: New Workbook task pane

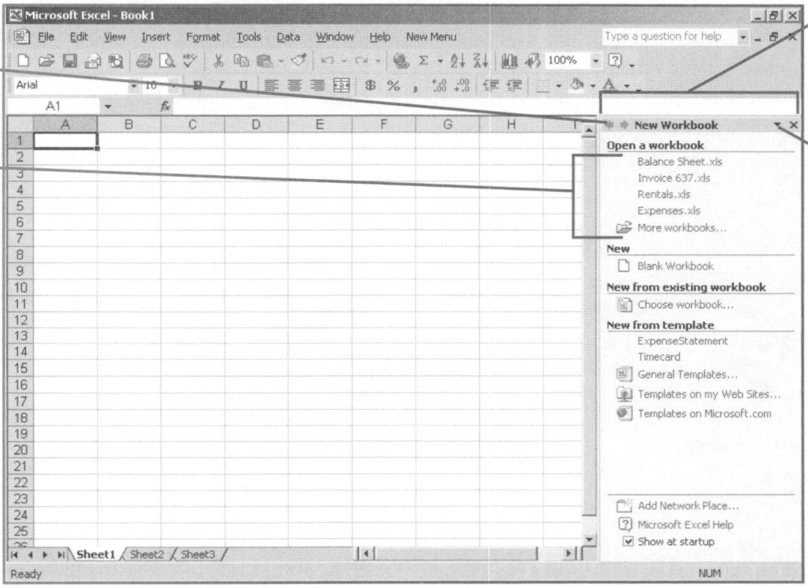

Back arrow

Your list
may vary

New
Workbook
task pane

Other Task
Panes list
arrow

TABLE GS-3: Excel task panes

task pane	what it does
New Workbook	Shows hyperlinks you can click to open a new Excel workbook, which can be blank a copy of an existing workbook; or to open dialog boxes with more options for opening workbooks.
Clipboard	Shows items on the Office Clipboard, a temporary holding area in your computer's memory that holds up to 24 items you have cut or copied in any Office program; click a clipboard item to paste it in the active cell of the open worksheet.
Search	Search for Excel files on your disks by entering a file type, part of a name, and/or a location; has Basic and Advanced options
Insert Clip Art	Lets you search for graphics related to a topic you type, then insert a graphic into your worksheet
Document Recovery	In case the Excel program encounters problems and stops responding, this task pane appears automatically and lists the workbooks (also called **documents**) that were open at the time and the versions it has recovered; click the version you want to open. *The Document Recovery task pane appears only after you restart Excel due to program difficulties or an unexpected computer shutdown.*

Getting Started

Getting Started with Excel 2002

Copy Workbook Files
Copy Project Files

This book instructs you to open and close each project file without saving changes at the end of each activity. Before starting the activities in this book, you should copy all Excel Project Files so you have an original and intact set of files, in case you inadvertently accept your changes as you complete the activities. You can copy your workbooks to a folder, or you can copy them to another disk.

The location of the folder copy will depend on the View menu option you have selected to arrange your files. You may need to scroll to see the folder copy. You can also use the Copy and Paste commands on the Edit menu to copy files or folders.

Activity Steps

1. If the Excel program is running, click the **Minimize button** on the title bar to display the Windows desktop

2. If you have any other programs running, repeat Step 1 to minimize them

3. On the Windows desktop, double-click **My Computer**, then double-click folders and use the **Address list arrow** and the **Up arrow** to display the folder where your Project Files are stored
   The files may be stored in a folder named 5670-3, the last 5 digits of the ISBN number for this book.

4. Click **File** on the menu bar, point to **New**, then click **Folder**

5. Type **Backups**, then press **Enter**

6. Right-click the **Project Files folder**, then click **Copy**

7. Double-click the **Backups folder**, right-click in the folder window, then click **Paste**
   See Figure GS-8, which assumes that the Project Files folder is named for the last five digits of the ISBN number for this book. Windows places a copy of your Project Files folder in the Backups folder. You can use these Project File copies in case you should inadvertently save your changes as you work through the lessons. Then you can always return to the original versions of the files.

Figure GS-8: Copy of Project Files folder

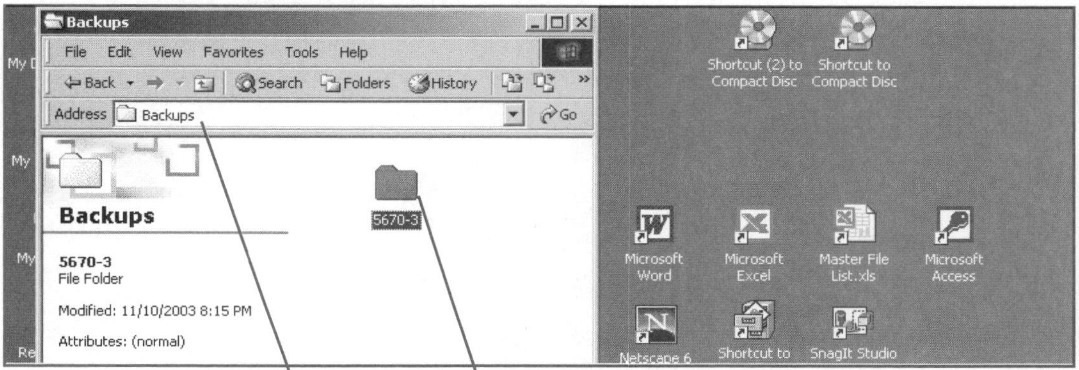

Your storage location and contents will differ

Project File folder

Microsoft Excel 2002   **13**

extra!

Naming copied folders

If you copy a folder to a location that has a folder of the same name, Windows assigns the copied folder the name Copy of [foldername]. You can change it to a more meaningful name to help you distinguish it from the originals. Click the folder, click the folder name, then type a new name.

Getting Started

Getting Started with Excel 2002

Save Workbooks

Save an Excel Workbook with a New Name

Although this book assumes you will close your workbooks without saving at the end of each activity, you will usually want to save your Excel workbooks on a disk. (You will learn more about saving workbooks in Skill Set 2.) You can save your workbooks in the My Documents folder, but if you have many different workbooks, it might be difficult to find the one you need later on. It's good practice to save each workbook with a unique and descriptive name in a folder you name. To save a workbook using its existing name in its present location, you can use the Save button on the Standard toolbar. But to change a workbook's name or its save location, you use the Save As command on the File menu.

Step 1
To create a new Excel workbook, click the New button on the Standard toolbar or click File on the menu bar, then click New. Using the File menu command will open the New Workbook task pane; you then click Blank Workbook in the task pane.

Activity Steps

 open Shuttle01.xls

1. Click **File** on the menu bar, then click **Save As**

2. Click the **Save in list arrow**, then navigate to the drive or folder where you store your Project Files

3. Drag to select the text in the File name box (if it's not already selected), then type **Schedule**
   See Figure GS-9.

4. Click **Save** to save the workbook with the new name in the location you selected
   The saved file named Schedule remains open on the screen. The original file, Shuttle01, closes and remains unchanged on your disk.

5. Observe the total in cell **D18**, click cell **D14**, type **3**, then press **[Enter]**
   The total in cell D18 changes from 52 to 51.

6. Click the **Save button** on the Standard toolbar
   See Figure GS-10.

 close Schedule.xls

Figure GS-9: Save As dialog box with new File name

Your storage location may differ

Save in list arrow

New File name

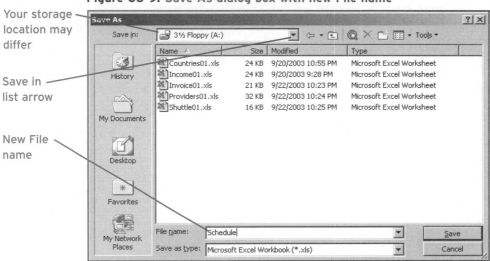

Figure GS-10: Saving the modified file

New filename in title bar

Save button

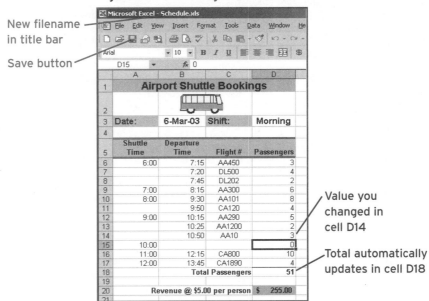

Value you changed in cell D14

Total automatically updates in cell D18

Getting Started

Preview and Print a Worksheet
Preview and Print a Worksheet

The activities in this book do not instruct you to print your worksheets, but you can print a worksheet any time you want a hard copy. Before printing, you should always preview your worksheet to make sure it looks the way you want. That way you can make any necessary changes in its appearance without wasting paper and toner. If you print your workbooks at a shared printer, you may want to place your name in a worksheet cell to help you identify your copy.

Activity Steps

 open Invoice01.xls

1. Click cell **B6**, type **your name**, press **[Enter]**, then click the **Print Preview button** 🔍 on the Standard toolbar
   The workbook appears in the Preview window, showing how the worksheet will look when you print it. When you move the pointer over the worksheet image, it becomes the **Zoom pointer** 🔍.
   See Figure GS-11.

2. Click near the word "invoice" at the top of the image, then click again
   You "zoom in" to get a closer look at the image, then "zoom out."

3. Click **Print** on the Preview toolbar
   See Figure GS-12.

4. Under Print what, click the **Active sheet(s) option button**, if it's not already selected

5. Make sure the Number of copies box reads 1

6. Click **OK**

 close Invoice01.xls

Step 1
To print a worksheet without previewing, click the Print button 🖨 on the Standard toolbar.

Figure GS-11: Worksheet in Print Preview with zoom pointer

Preview
toolbar

Zoom
pointer

Preview
of printed
document

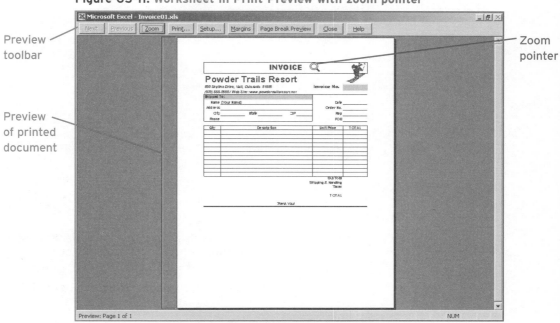

Figure GS-12: Print dialog box

Your printer
information
and options
may be
different

Indicate number
of copies here

Select this
option

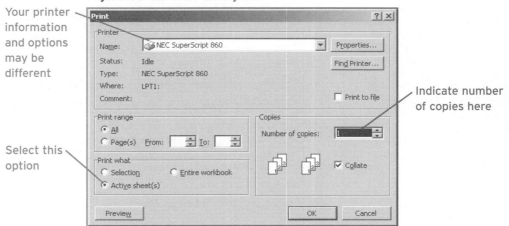

Getting Started

Getting Started with Excel 2002

Get Help
Use Online Help

Whenever you don't know how to proceed as you use Excel, you can always use its **online help system** to find answers to your questions. (The term "online" in "online help" means that you can find help on the screen instead of referring to a book.) There are several ways to get help in Excel. The fastest way is to use the "Type a question for help" box in the Excel menu bar, which will display topic hyperlinks. You click a hyperlink to open the help system and view help information on the topic you clicked. You can also use the Contents, Index, and Answer Wizard tabs in the Help window to search in different ways. You can use the **Print button** 🖨 at the top of the Help window to print any Help topic for future reference.

Step 1
To get help, you can also use the Office Assistant, an animated character in the shape of a paper clip that appears on your screen. Click Help, then click Show the Office Assistant; click the Assistant, type a question in the question balloon, then click a topic. The Help window opens.

Activity Steps

1. Make sure the Excel program is open with a blank workbook on the screen; to display a blank workbook, click the **New button** 🗋 on the Standard toolbar

2. Click the **Type a question for help** box on the right side of the menu bar

3. Type **save workbooks**, press [Enter], then click the **Save a workbook** hyperlink in the topic list that appears

4. Click **Show All** in the instructions window
   See Figure GS-13.

5. If your window does not display the tabs shown in Figure G-13, click the **Show button** 🔂 in the Help window toolbar

6. Click the **Index tab** in the Help window (if it's not already selected)

7. Click in the **Type keywords box**, type **print**, then press [Enter]

8. Under Choose a topic, click **About printing**, then click the **Show All link** in the information pane
   See Figure GS-14. Topics and terms that have definitions appear in blue text; when you click them or click Show All, the definition appears in green text.

9. Click the **Close button** ☒ on the Help window

Figure GS-13: Microsoft Excel Help dialog box

Show button becomes Hide button

Help information on saving a workbook

If necessary, drag this border to make your Help window size match this figure

This link is a toggle to show or hide details

Click this link to display only an outline of the Help information

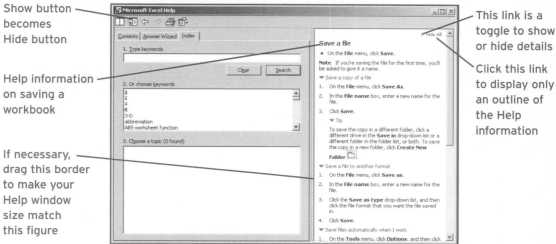

Figure GS-14: Help information on printing

Search text

Topics that relate to your search text

Click blue terms to see definitions; click again to hide definitions

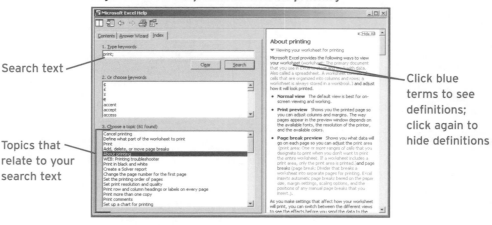

TABLE GS-4: Microsoft Excel Help window tabs

help window tab	how to use
Contents	Click plus signs next to topics to display further topics; click question mark icons to display help in right section
Answer Wizard	Type a question in the What would you like to do? Box, click Search, then click a topic to display information in right section
Index	Type text in Type keywords box, click Search, click topic at bottom, read explanation in right section

Getting Started

Getting Started with Excel 2002

Target Your Skills

 open Providers01.xls

1 Refer to Figure GS-15. Use the navigation keys to move around the worksheet and examine the cells and cell contents. Display the first four task panes shown in Table GS-3, ending with the Clipboard. Preview the worksheet, zoom in and out, then print the worksheet. Save the workbook as Analysis in the drive and folder where you store your files.

2 Open a blank workbook. Use the Office Assistant to search on "help window." Select "About getting help while you work." Click the Assistant character to hide the balloon. Click the topic **"Ask a Question box,"** then click it again. Click Show All, then scroll the window contents. See Figure GS-16. Use the Index tab to search on the word "print," then click the topic of your choice.

Figure GS-15

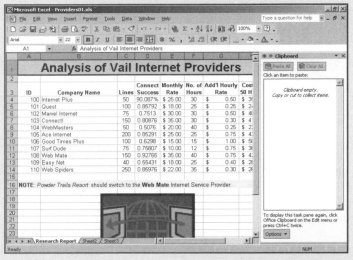

Figure GS-16

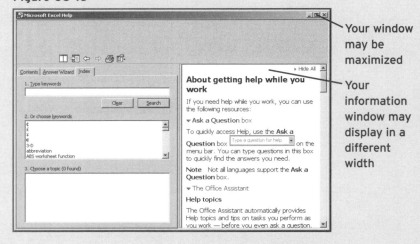

Your window may be maximized

Your information window may display in a different width

Skill Set 1

Working with Cells and Cell Data

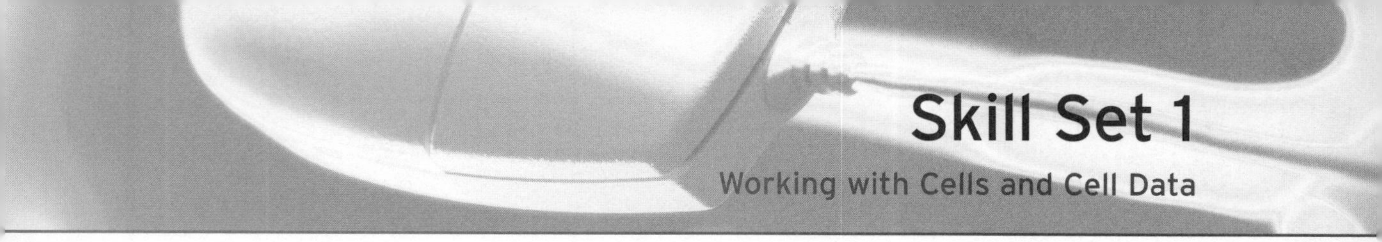

Skill List

1. Insert, delete, and move cells
2. Enter and edit cell data including text, numbers, and formulas
3. Check spelling
4. Find and replace cell data and formats
5. Work with a subset of data by filtering lists

In Skill Set 1, you learn how to enter and change cell data in Microsoft Excel 2002. Excel is an electronic spreadsheet program that lets you create and use workbooks. A **workbook** is an Excel file that contains **worksheets**, or electronic ledgers made up of rows and columns of cells. **Cells** are the intersections of worksheet rows and columns, and they can contain text, numbers, or formulas. You can add new data, delete, move, or edit existing data, or filter data to work on specific data in a large worksheet.

Skill Set 1

Working with Cells and Cell Data

Insert, Delete, and Move Cells
Insert and Delete Cells

As you build worksheets in Excel, you will need to add and delete information. You may find you forgot to add an item, or information may become obsolete. You can insert or delete cells, a block of cells, or entire rows or columns in any area of a worksheet. When you insert one or more cells, Excel adds them above the selected horizontal cell range or to the left of the selected vertical cell range. When you delete cells, Excel removes them from the worksheet. *After you insert or delete cells, be very careful to check the alignment of your data and the accuracy of your formulas. Also be sure columns or rows you want to delete don't contain any necessary data in an area not visible on the screen.*

Step 6
You can also right-click a selected range, or any row or column heading, then select Insert or Delete on the shortcut menu.

Activity Steps

 open Expenses01.xls

1. Select the range B11:E11

2. Click **Insert** on the menu bar, then click **Cells**
   See Figure 1-1.

3. Click **Shift cells down** (if it's not already selected), then click **OK**

4. Select cells **D7:D14**

5. Click **Edit** on the menu bar, then click **Delete**

6. Click the **Shift cells left** option button (if it's not already selected), then click **OK**
   See Figure 1-2.

 close Expenses01.xls

Figure 1-1: Insert dialog box

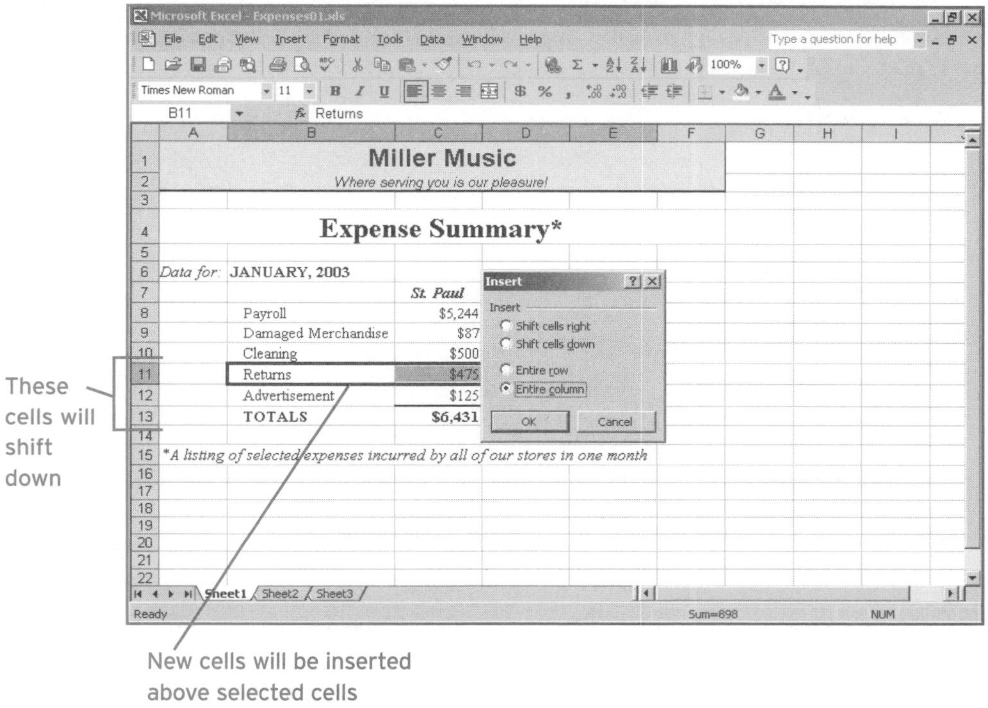

These cells will shift down

New cells will be inserted above selected cells

Figure 1-2: Worksheet after deleting cells

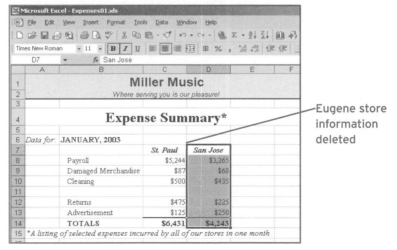

Eugene store information deleted

Skill Set 1

Working with Cells and Cell Data

Insert, Delete, and Move Cells
Merge and Split Cells

As you create worksheets, you will often want to create a title that spans several columns above your data. To do this, you can **merge**, or combine, contiguous cells into one large cell. You may also want to both merge cells and center a title in the new, larger cell. To do this you can use the Merge and Center button on the Formatting toolbar. You can **split** the cells into their original component cells using the same button. Like most formatting buttons, the Merge and Center button is a **toggle**, meaning that you click it once to apply the format to the selected cell or range, then click it again to remove the format. A merged cell takes the format of the leftmost cell in the range.

Step 2
To merge cells without centering, click Format on the menu bar, click Cells, click the Alignment tab, click to select the Merge Cells check box, then click OK.

Activity Steps

 open Update01.xls

1. Select the range **B6:E6**

2. Click the **Merge and Center button** 🔲 on the Formatting toolbar

3. Click the heading **Miller Music**
   This is a merged and centered cell. Its cell reference in the Name Box is A1.

4. Click the **Merge and Center button** 🔲 on the Formatting toolbar to split the cells

5. Click a blank area of the worksheet to deselect the cells
   See Figure 1-3.

 close Update01.xls

Figure 1-3: Merged and centered text

Merge and Center button

Split cells no longer merged

Text is centered in merged cell

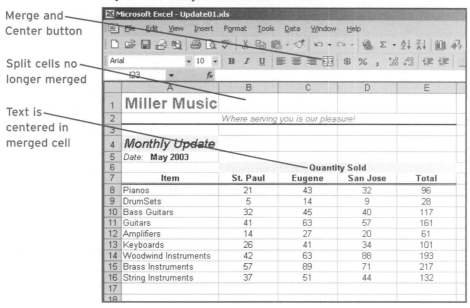

Skill Set 1

Working with Cells and Cell Data

Insert, Delete, and Move Cells
Move Cells

You can easily move worksheet cells to another area of the same worksheet, to another worksheet in the same workbook, or to a different workbook altogether. To move information short distances, you can drag the cells. To move cells to a different part of the worksheet or to another sheet or workbook, use the Copy and Paste buttons. Pasted information replaces any cell data in the paste range. When you move cells, the cells' contents, formulas, format, and comments move with them.

Step 5
To move data to a different work-sheet, cut the data, click the sheet tab of the destination worksheet, click the upper left cell of the paste range, then click the Paste button on the Standard toolbar.

Activity Steps

 open Summary01.xls

1. Select the range A17:F17

2. Place the mouse pointer over the edge of the selected range until it becomes

3. Drag the range down until the shaded outline is on row 19, then release the mouse button

4. Select the range A6:F15, then click the **Cut button** ✂ on the Standard toolbar
   See Figure 1-4.

5. Click cell **A8**
   You only need to select the upper left cell of the paste range.

6. Click the **Paste button** 📋 on the Standard toolbar, then click any blank cell
   The range you cut is now pasted in a new location: the range starting in cell A8.
   See Figure 1-5.

 close Summary01.xls

Figure 1-4: Cut range

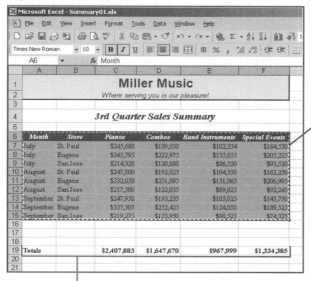

Dotted line around range indicates information has been cut

Range moved to new location

Figure 1-5: Moved ranges

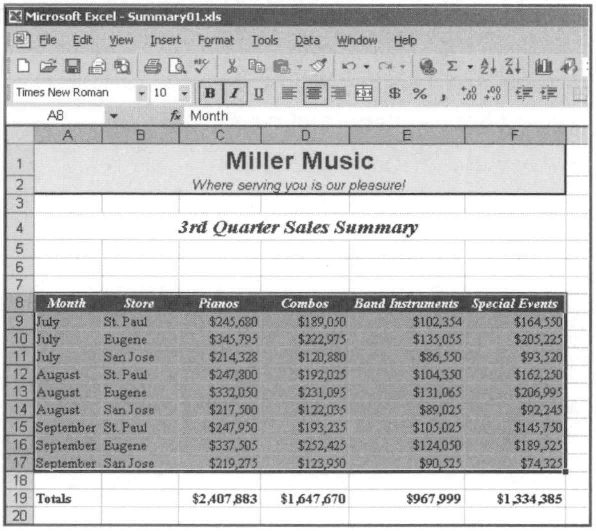

extra!

Using the Office Clipboard

When you cut information from an Office document, Office temporarily stores the data in the **Office Clipboard**, which appears in the task pane. The Office Clipboard stores up to 24 items in your computer's memory. All Clipboard items are available for you to paste as long as an Office program is open. To open the Clipboard task pane, click **View** on the menu bar, click **Task Pane**, click the **Other Task Panes list arrow** (the triangle in the Task Pane title bar), then select **Clipboard**. To paste any item, click the destination cell, then click the Clipboard item you want to paste.

Skill Set 1

Working with Cells and Cell Data

Enter and Edit Cell Data Including Text, Numbers, and Formulas

Enter Text and Numbers

You enter text and numbers in the **active cell**, which is the selected cell on your worksheet. You usually use text for **labels**, which are worksheet headings that identify the **values**, or numbers, that you may want to use in calculations. After you type a label or value, you can **enter**, or accept it, by using the mouse or the keyboard. Excel automatically left-aligns labels and right-aligns values. You can navigate around the worksheet using the mouse or the keyboard. See Table 1-1. To display other areas of a worksheet without moving the active cell, use the scroll bars.

Step 2
Occasionally you will want Excel to treat certain numbers (such as zip codes) as text instead of amounts to be used in calculations. To do this, place an apostrophe ('), also called the label prefix, before the number, as in '02174.

Activity Steps

 open Advertising01.xls

1. Click cell A10

2. Type **Newspapers**, then press [Tab]
   If you make a typing error, press [Backspace] and retype the character, or click the Cancel button ⊠ on the Formula bar and begin again.

3. Type **1800**, press [Tab], type **1300**, then press [Tab]

4. Type **1200**, then click the Enter button ✓ on the Formula bar

5. Enter the following data into the range A11:D11, using the same techniques you used in Steps 3 and 4:

   Radio Spots   600   800   700

6. Enter the following data in cells A12:D12:

   Subway Ads   300   400   250
   See Figure 1-6.

 close Advertising01.xls

Figure 1-6: Worksheet with labels and values entered

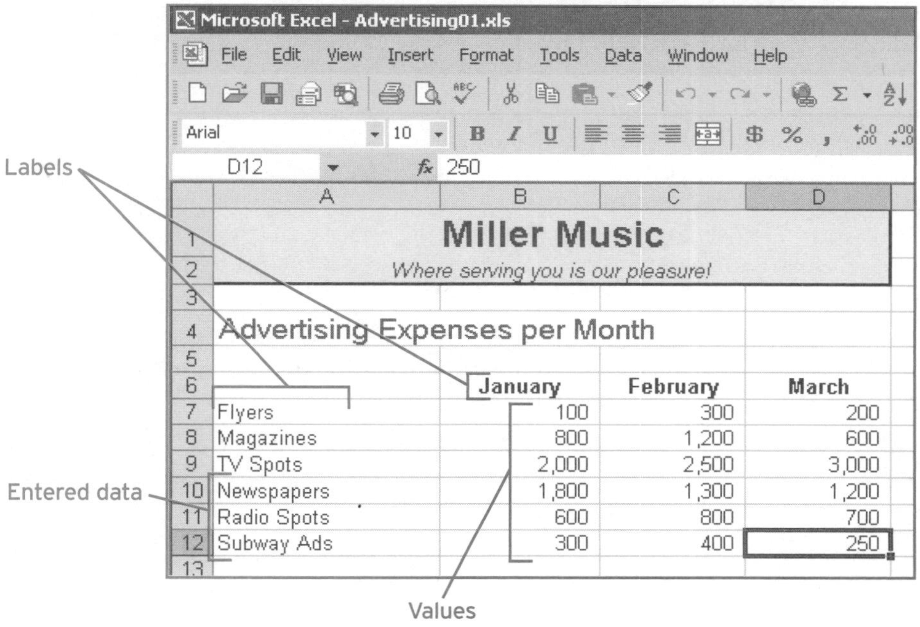

Labels →

Entered data →

Values

TABLE 1-1: Navigating within a worksheet using the keyboard

press	to move to	press	to move to
[Ctrl][Home]	Cell A1	[Page Up]	One screen up
[Tab]	Cell to right	[Page Down]	One screen down
[Enter]	Cell below	[Alt][Page Up]	One screen left
[up arrow], [down arrow], [left arrow] or [right arrow]	Cells above, below, to left or right	[Alt][Page Down]	One screen right

Skill Set 1

Working with Cells and Cell Data

Enter and Edit Cell Data Including Text, Numbers, and Formulas

Edit Text and Numbers

After you enter labels and values in a worksheet, you can easily edit them to correct errors or reflect new information. You can select a cell and edit data using the Formula bar, or you can use **in-cell editing**, which lets you modify the data directly in a selected cell.

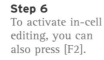

Step 6
To activate in-cell editing, you can also press [F2].

Activity Steps

 open Advertising02.xls

1. Click cell **C11**

2. Click in the Formula bar after the number, then press **[Backspace]** three times

3. Type **750** then click the **Enter button** ☑ in the Formula bar

4. Click cell **D9**, then in the Formula bar drag to select the **3**
   See Figure 1-7.

5. Type **2**, then click ☑ in the Formula bar
   Next, you'll use in-cell editing.

6. Double-click cell **A9** to the left of TV, press **[Delete]** twice, type **Television**, then click ☑ in the Formula bar

7. Double-click cell **D11**, if necessary, use ← to move the insertion point before the 7, press **[Delete]**, then type **6**

8. Press **[Enter]**
   See Figure 1-8.

 close Advertising02.xls

Figure 1-7: Editing in the Formula bar

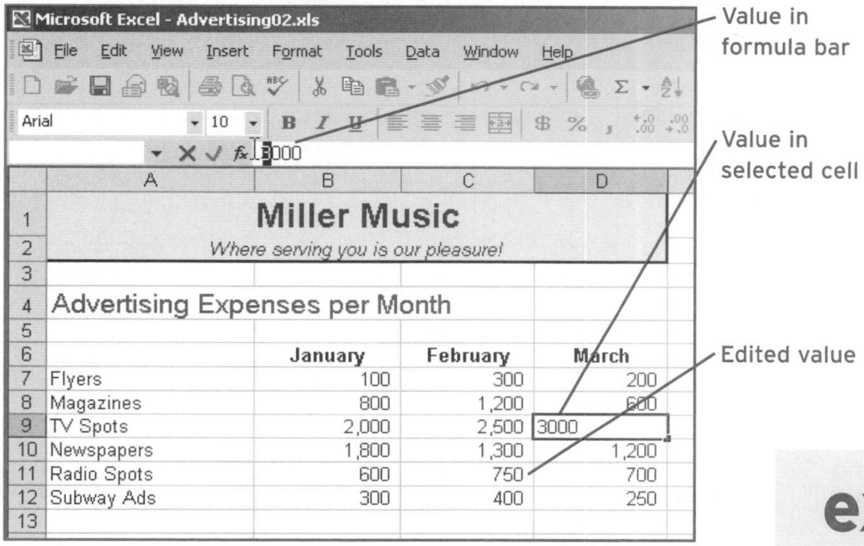

Value in formula bar

Value in selected cell

Edited value

Figure 1-8: Edited values

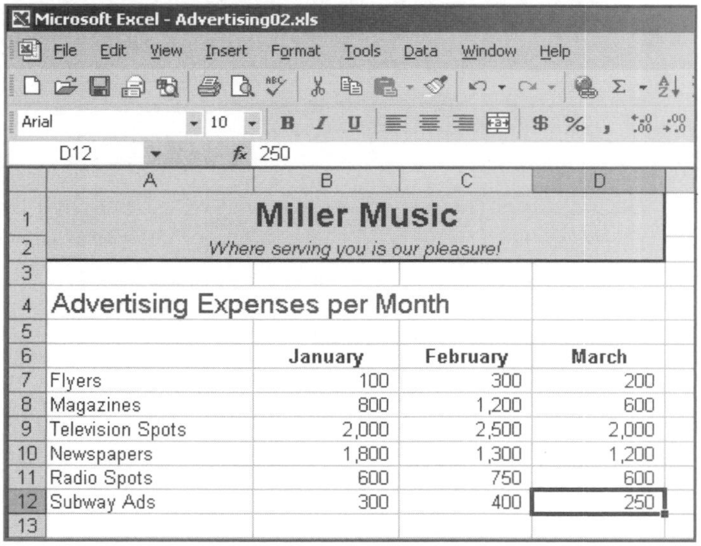

Skill Set 1

Working with Cells and Cell Data

Enter and Edit Cell Data Including Text, Numbers, and Formulas

Apply Number Formats

Depending on the purpose of your worksheet, your data values will need a specific look. When you **format** numeric values, you customize their appearance so they communicate the worksheet content and purpose easily. For example, a budget usually shows values with dollar signs; a timesheet often shows times of the day. Quantity information in an inventory appears without decimal places or dollar signs. Excel lets you quickly apply common formats using the Formatting toolbar or the Format Cells dialog box.

Step 8
You can use the Alignment, Font, Border, and Patterns tabs in the Format Cells dialog box to apply a wide array of formats to both labels and values.

Activity Steps

 open Markdowns01.xls

1. Select the range E8:E14
2. Click the **Currency Style button** $ on the Formatting toolbar
3. Click the **Decrease Decimal button** on the Formatting toolbar twice
4. Select the range F8:F14
5. Click the **Percent Style button** % on the Formatting toolbar
6. Select the range D8:D14
7. Click **Format** on the menu bar, click **Cells**, then click the **Number tab** (if it's not already selected)
   See Figure 1-9.
8. Click **General** in the Category list box, then click **OK**
   The **General** format displays values centered, with no specific number format.
   See Figure 1-10.

 close Markdowns01.xls

Figure 1-9: Format Cells dialog box

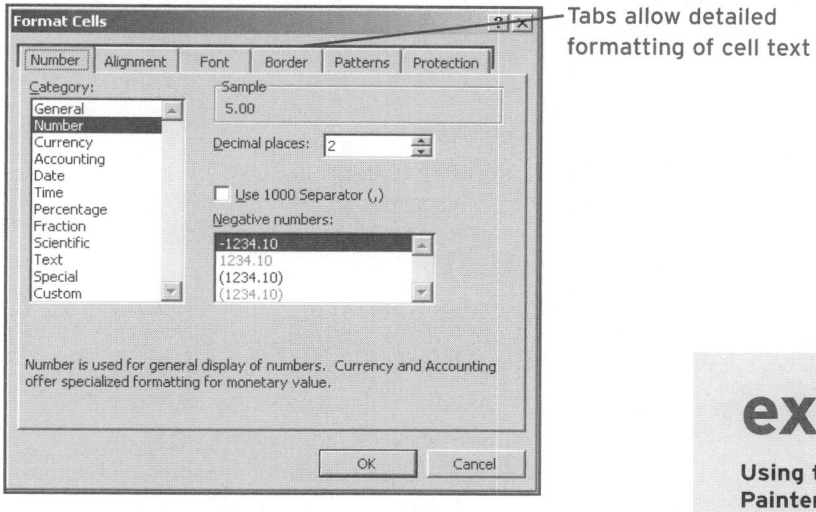

Tabs allow detailed formatting of cell text

Figure 1-10: Cell formats applied to values

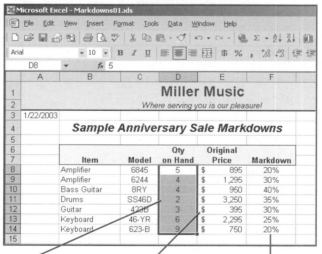

General format   Currency format   Percentage format

Skill Set 1

Working with Cells and Cell Data

Enter and Edit Cell Data Including Text, Numbers, and Formulas

Clear Cell Contents and Formats

When you want to delete only cell contents while leaving the cell in place, you can **clear** the cell. You can choose to clear cell contents, formats, comments, or all of these. It's important to understand the difference between clearing and deleting cells: Clearing empties the cell of its contents only, while deleting removes both the cell and its contents from the worksheet.

Step 6
Pressing [Delete] is another way of clearing only cell contents while leaving the cell format intact.

Activity Steps

 open Sales01.xls

1. Click cell **B7**

2. Click **Edit** on the menu bar, point to **Clear**, then click **All**

3. Type **75000**, then press **[Enter]**
   The new value does not have the comma and font format because you cleared both contents and formats. It is now in General format, the Excel default.
   See Figure 1-11.

4. Select the range **C7:C13**

5. Click **Edit** on the menu bar, point to **Clear**, then click **Formats**
   The values remain, but their formatting is removed.

6. Click cell **D7**, click **Edit** on the menu bar, point to **Clear**, then click **Contents**

7. Type **7**, then press **[Enter]**
   The formatting remained because you cleared only the cell contents.
   See Figure 1-12.

 close Sales01.xls

Figure 1-11: Clearing formats displays values in General format

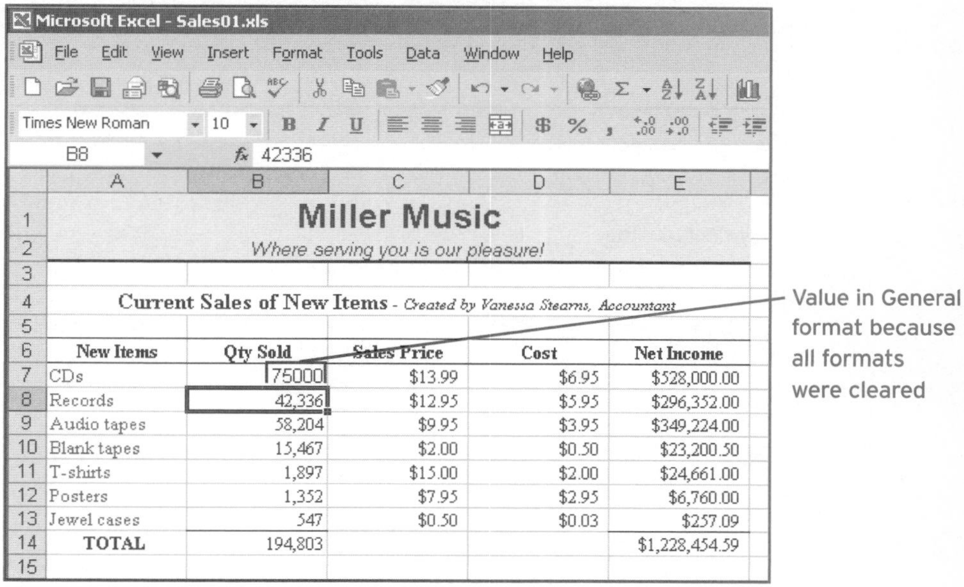

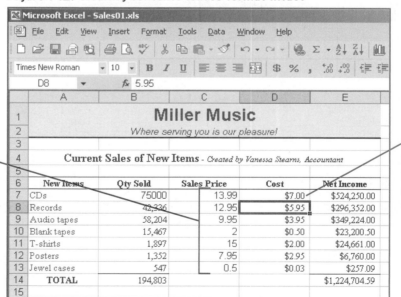

Value in General format because all formats were cleared

Figure 1-12: Clearing contents leaves format intact

Formats cleared from these values

New value retains original format because only contents were cleared

Skill Set 1

Working with Cells and Cell Data

Enter and Edit Cell Data Including Text, Numbers, and Formulas
Enter and Edit Formulas

Formulas are equations containing values and cell references that calculate a result. Formulas let you transform a simple list of labels and values into a powerful calculation and analysis tool; they contain values, cell references and **operators**, such as + and -. A **cell reference** is a cell address that tells Excel to use a value in a specific cell. A cell reference can be a single cell, such as A6 or C13, or a **cell range**, a group of two or more adjacent cells, such as A3:C6. An Excel formula always starts with = (an equal sign) and may not contain spaces. The formula =1+2 adds the values 1 and 2, and displays the value 3 as the result. The formula =A4*6 multiplies the value in cell A4 by 6. To enter cell addresses in formulas, you can type, point and click, drag, or a combination of the three. As with entering values, you must **enter** the formula, which instructs Excel to accept the formula and perform the calculation. If you edit a cell value that is used in a formula, or edit the formula itself, Excel automatically recalculates the formula. Table 1-2 lists common formula operators.

tip

If you see the formula itself in a cell after you enter it, you might have forgotten to type the equal sign before the formula. If you see an error message such as #VALUE, you might have mistyped an operator or a cell reference.

Activity Steps

 open Employee01.xls

1. Click cell **B9**

2. Type **=B7+B8**
   See Figure 1-13.

3. Click the **Enter button** ☑ on the **Formula bar**
   The total appears in cell B9.

4. Click cell **B10**
   You will intentionally enter an error in the formula, then correct it.

5. Type **=**, click cell **B9**, then type ***15**

6. Press **[Enter]**

7. Click cell **B10**, click in the Formula bar before the 15, type **.** (a period), then press **[Enter]**
   Excel recalculates the formula results using the edited formula.

8. With cell **B11** selected, type **=**, click cell **B9**, type **+**, click cell **B10**, then press **[Enter]**

9. Click cell **B7**, type **40**, then click the **Enter button** ☑ on the Formula bar
   The formulas are automatically recalculated using the new value.
   See Figure 1-14.

 close Employee01.xls

Figure 1-13: Formula cell references and operator before entering

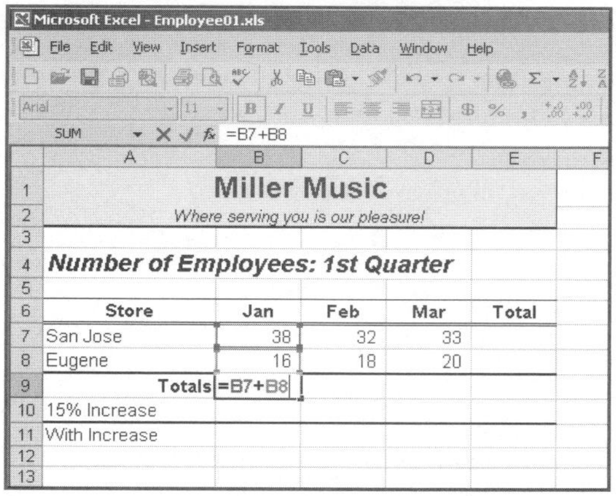

Figure 1-14: Recalculated formulas using edited values and formula

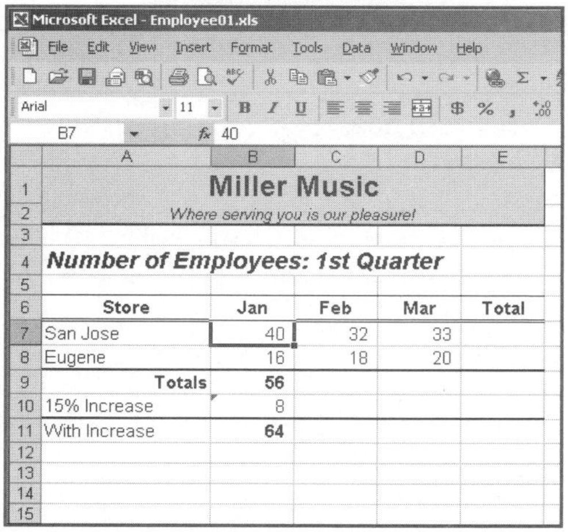

Table 1-2: Formula operators

operand	use to	operand	use to
=	Begin all formulas	*	Multiply values
+	Add values	/	Divide values
-	Subtract values	(and)	Enclose operations that should be performed first

Skill Set 1
Working with Cells and Cell Data

Enter and Edit Cell Data Including Text, Numbers, and Formulas
Add Functions to Formulas

Excel supplies many worksheet **functions**, which are presupplied formulas that calculate values. Some common functions are SUM, AVERAGE, and MAX. Each function has its own name and special **syntax**, or arrangement of elements. All functions start with = (an equal sign), followed by the function name, followed by **arguments**, which are cell or range references in parentheses that tell Excel which values to use to calculate the function result.

Step 8
To change the types of errors Excel checks for, click the smart tip list arrow, click Error Checking Options, select the options you want, then click OK.

Activity Steps

 open Inventory01.xls

1. Click cell **E18**

2. Type **=4*(E8+E9+E10+E11)** then press **[Enter]**

3. Click cell **E21**

4. Type **=4*** and click the **Insert Function button** 𝑓𝑥 on the Formula bar to open the Insert Function dialog box and the Excel Function Wizard
   See Figure 1-15.

5. In the Insert Function dialog box, click **SUM** in the Select a function list, then click **OK**

6. In the Function Arguments dialog box, click the **Collapse dialog box button** next to Number1, select the range **E12:E15** on the worksheet, then click the **Redisplay dialog box button**
   See Figure 1-16.

7. Click **OK**
   An error button smart tip offers help, noting that the formula omits adjacent cells and flagging this possible error. The formula is correct as written.

8. Click the **Error button Smart Tip**, then click **Ignore Error**

 close Inventory01.xls

Figure 1-15: Insert Function dialog box

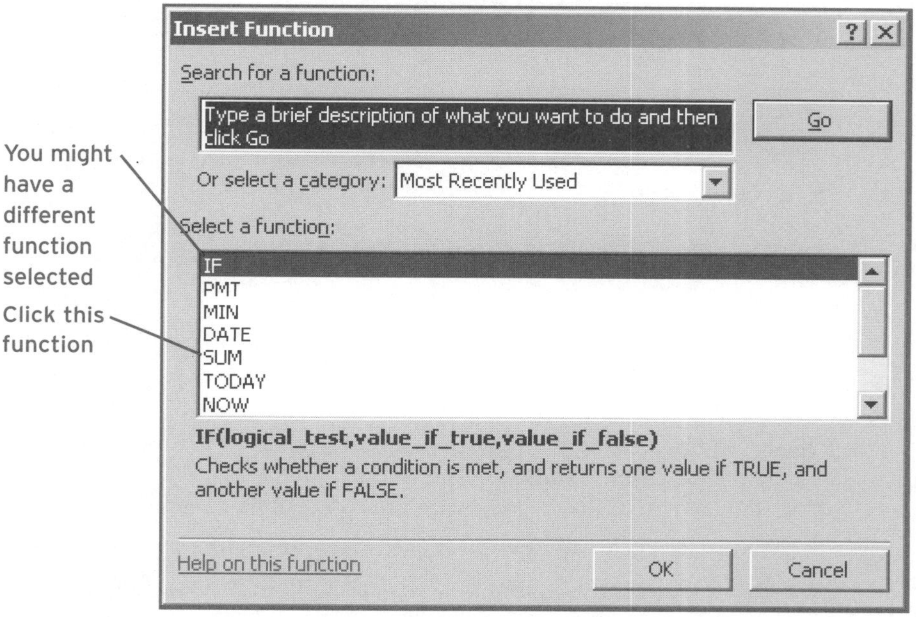

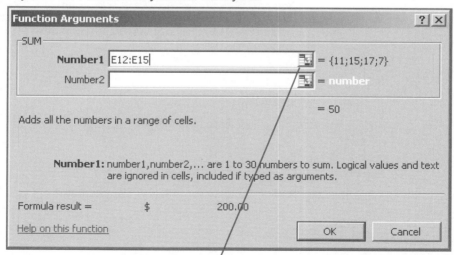

You might have a different function selected

Click this function

Figure 1-16: Function Arguments dialog box

Clicking Collapse dialog box button lets you drag to insert range

Skill Set 1
Working with Cells and Cell Data

Check Spelling
Check Worksheet Spelling

Even if you have a professional-looking spreadsheet with accurate data and attractive formatting, spelling errors can cast doubt on the reliability of your work. Excel provides a spelling checker that automatically compares each word in your worksheet against an internal spelling dictionary and flags errors. You can accept or reject suggested corrections or you can add the word in question to your own custom dictionary so Excel will not flag it again.

Step 1
Excel flags words that are not in its dictionary, such as your company name. You can click Add to Dictionary to include those words in your custom dictionary. Excel will recognize those words the next time you check spelling.

Activity Steps

 open Workshop01.xls

1. Click the **Spelling button** 📝 on the Standard toolbar
   Excel flags the incorrect spelling of "through" and suggests the correct spelling.
   See Figure 1-17.

2. Click **Change**
   Excel flags "perperson" and suggests a correction.

3. Click **Change**, then click **Change** again to correct "Beginning"

4. In the Suggestions box, click **Woodwinds**, then click **Change**
   The Spelling Checker flags "fture" and suggests only "future".

5. Click in the Not in Dictionary box to place the insertion point between the "f" and "t" of "fture", type **ea**, then click **Change**
   The Spelling Checker flags the name "Okimoto" and offers several suggestions.
   See Figure 1-18.

6. Click **Ignore All**

7. Click **OK**

 close Workshop01.xls

Figure 1-17: Incorrect spelling highlighted

Spell checker flags incorrect spelling

Spell checker suggests a possible correction

Click to accept displayed change

Click to change all occurrences in worksheet

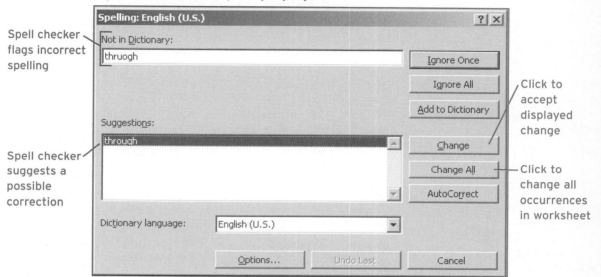

Figure 1-18: Corrected entry

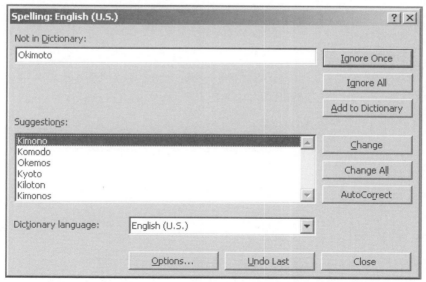

Skill Set 1

Working with Cells and Cell Data

Find and Replace Cell Data and Formats
Use Find and Replace to Replace Cell Contents

Correcting a few worksheet cells is not difficult, but if there are many occurrences of the same correction, you can use the Excel Find and Replace feature. For example, if you want to change the use of "Payroll" to "Salaries," the Find and Replace feature lets you do this quickly; it also lets you change only certain occurrences of an entry. You can also specify whether you want the found text or the replacement text to use upper- and lowercase letters. If you want to search only part of a worksheet, select the range before selecting the Find and Replace command.

Step 6
To have Excel search all sheets in a workbook, click Options in the Find and Replace dialog box, click the Within list arrow, then click Workbook.

Activity Steps

 open Report01.xls

1. Click **Edit** on the menu bar, click **Replace**, then click the **Replace tab** (if it's not already selected)

2. In the Find what box, select any existing text (if it's not already selected), type **Lodging**, then press **[Tab]**

3. In the Replace with box, type **Hotels**
   See Figure 1-19.

4. Click **Find Next**

5. Click **Replace**

6. Click **Replace** four more times

7. Click **Find Next**, then click **OK** in the message box

8. Click **Close**
   See Figure 1-20.

 close Report01.xls

Skill 4

Find and Replace Cell Data and Formats

Figure 1-19: Find and Replace dialog box

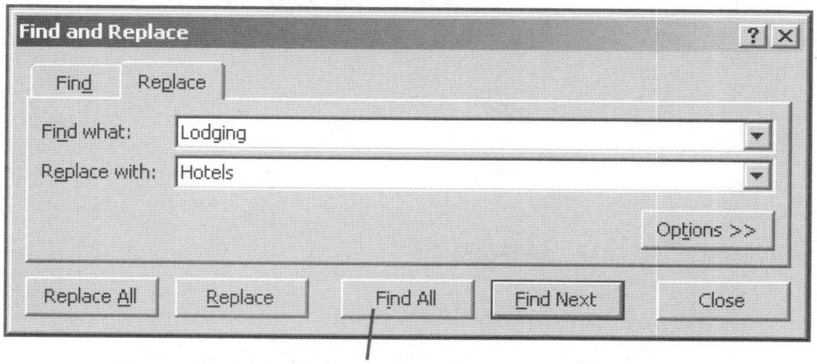

Click to view list of occurrences and their locations

Figure 1-20: Find and Replace results

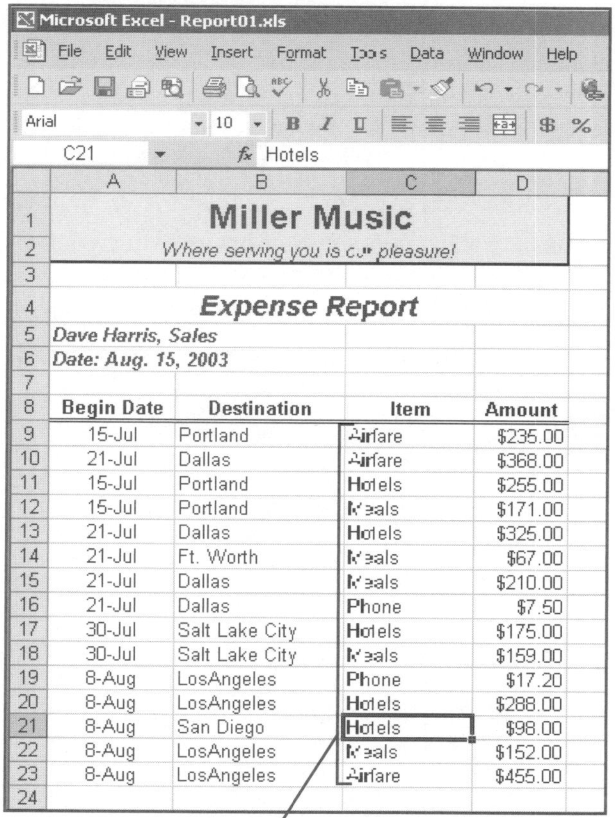

All occurrences of "Lodging" replaced with "Hotels"

extra!

Using wildcards in your search

If you are not sure how to spell the word you are looking for, you can use wildcard characters in your search text. The wildcard character * can represent any letter or group of letters: mart* will find Marty, Martin, martial, or Martinelli. Use the wildcard character ? to represent any single character: cu? will locate cup, cut, or cub, but not cube or cutter.

Skill Set 1

Working with Cells and Cell Data

Find and Replace Cell Data and Formats
Go to a Specific Cell

When you work in large worksheets, you often need to find a specific area or a particular type of cell. Instead of scrolling through the worksheet and trying to find the cells visually, you can use the Excel **Go To** command. It lets you select (or "go to") any cell address, a range of cells, objects, all cells with formulas, and so forth.

Activity Steps

 open Projected01.xls

1. Click **Edit** on the menu bar, then click **Go To**

2. In the Reference box of the Go To dialog box, type **D14**, compare your screen to Figure 1-21, then click **OK**
   Cell D14 is selected.

3. Click **Edit** on the menu bar, click **Go To**, then click **Special**
   See Figure 1-22.

4. Click the **Last Cell option button**, then click **OK**
   The lower right worksheet cell is selected.

5. Click **Edit** on the menu bar, click **Go To**, then click **Special**

6. Click the **Formulas option button**, then click **OK**
   See Figure 1-23.

7. Click **Edit** on the menu bar, click **Go To**, then click **Special**

8. Click the **Objects option button**, then click **OK** to select the chart object

 close Projected01.xls

Step 1
You can also press [Ctrl][G] to open the Go To dialog box.

Figure 1-21: Go To dialog box

Cell address you want to go to

Figure 1-22: Go To Special dialog box

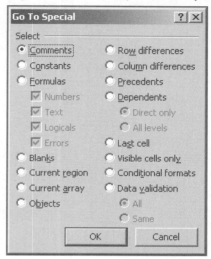

Figure 1-23: Worksheet with all formulas selected

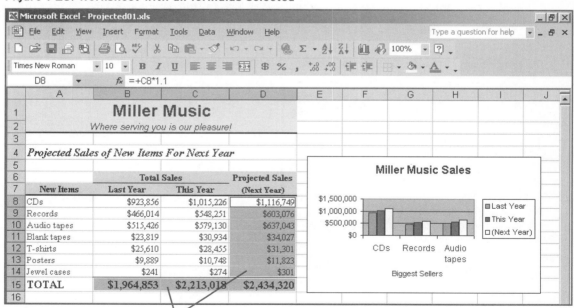

Cells with formulas highlighted

Skill Set 1

Working with Cells and Cell Data

Find and Replace Cell Data and Formats
Use Find and Replace to Change Cell Formats

You can use the Excel Find and Replace feature to replace not only cell contents but cell formats as well. This can save you a great deal of time in formatting worksheet headings and values, and it gives your worksheet a consistent look. For example, if you want to change all the worksheet values that are now in bold to unbolded italic, you could use the Find and Replace feature to do this in a few steps.

Step 8
If Excel does not find the format, clear any text from the Find what and Replace with text boxes. To clear any previously set formats, click the Format list arrow and click Clear Find Format and Clear Replace Format.

Activity Steps

 open Budget01.xls

1. Click **Edit** on the menu bar, then click **Replace**

2. If the Options button has » next to it, click **Options** to display the format options; if it does not, skip to Step 3

3. Click the topmost **Format button** (on the Find what line), then click the **Font tab**, if it's not already selected
   See Figure 1-24.

4. Under Font Style, click **Italic**, then click **OK**

5. Click the lower **Format button** (on the Replace with line)

6. Click **Bold** then click **OK**; select and delete any text in the "Find what" or "Replace with" boxes

7. Click **Find Next** until *Sales*, in cell A5, is highlighted, then click **Replace**
   See Figure 1-25.

8. Use the **Find Next** and **Replace buttons** to apply bold to only the indented italic labels, then click **Close**

 close Budget01.xls

Figure 1-24: Find Format dialog box

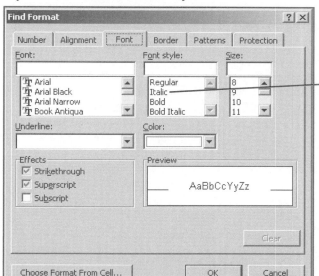

Click to specify that Excel should find italic text

Figure 1-25: Find and Replace Format dialog box

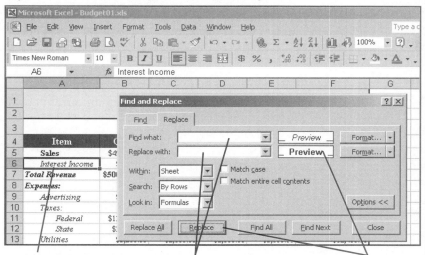

Excel has found italic text

To find and replace formats only, clear any text from these text boxes

Click Replace to replace the italic with bold text

extra!

Replacing by example
If there is a cell already formatted the way you want other cells to appear, you can use that as an example, rather than respecifying it in the Find Format or Replace Format dialog box. On the Format menu in the Find and Replace dialog box, choose Choose Format From Cell. When the pointer changes, and the dialog box temporarily closes, click the cell with the format you want to transfer. The Find and Replace dialog box reappears with the format of the cell you clicked selected.

Skill Set 1

Working with Cells and Cell Data

Work with a Subset of Data by Filtering Lists

Filter Lists using AutoFilter

In Excel, a collection of information is called a **list**. A list has columns with specific types of information, such as first name, address, or purchase amount, called **fields**. The individual items in each row are called **records**. You can easily **filter** the list to display only a **subset** of the data that matches certain conditions called **criteria**. For example, you could display only customers with "TX" in the State field, or sales reps with an amount greater than $50,000 in the Sales field. The simplest way to filter list information is to use the Excel **AutoFilter** feature, which displays list arrows for each field. After you filter on one field, you can click another list arrow to filter the list further. After filtering the list, you can print, chart, or analyze the information.

Step 5
To display all list records, click each blue list arrow, then click (All). To display all records in all fields, click Data on the menu bar, point to Filter, then click Show All.

Activity Steps

 open Report02.xls

1. Click any cell in the list range **A8:D23**

2. Click **Data** on the menu bar, point to **Filter**, then click **AutoFilter**
   A list arrow indicating that AutoFilter is on appears on each of the field names in the list.

3. Click the **Destination list arrow**, then click **Los Angeles**
   The Destination list arrow (and the row numbers where there is a sequence break) is now blue, indicating that a filter is in effect.
   See Figure 1-26.

4. Click the **Amount list arrow**, then click **Custom**

5. Click the **operator list arrow** in the Custom AutoFilter dialog box (next to equals), click **is greater than**, click in the amount box, type **200**, then click **OK**.
   See Figure 1-27.

 close Report02.xls

Figure 1-26: Filtered list

Blue list arrow shows that list is filtered

Blue row numbers indicate a filtered list with a break in numbering sequence

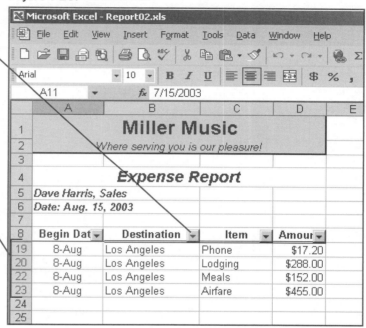

Figure 1-27: List with two filters applied

Destination and Amount list arrows are blue, indicating information is filtered on two fields

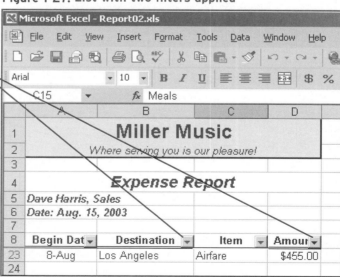

Skill Set 1

Working with Cells and Cell Data

Target Your Skills

 open Update02.xls

1 Use Figure 1-28 as a guide to modifying the Update02 worksheet file. Correct worksheet items as necessary, then spell check it. Format headings as shown. Create a formula in cell F9 that divides the total number of pianos by 3. Use a function in cell B17.

Figure 1-28

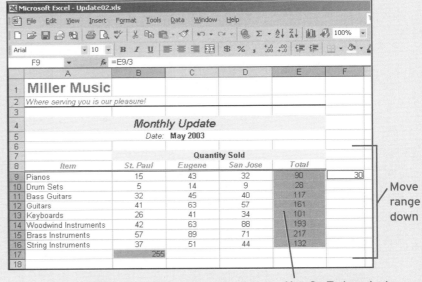

Move range down

Use Go To to select all cell with formulas

 open Travel 01.xls

2 Use Figure 1-29 as a guide for modifying the Travel01 file. Clear the contents and formats from all cells containing travel data for 11/30/03. Lastly, filter the data to display only travel to San Francisco for Lodging.

Figure 1-29

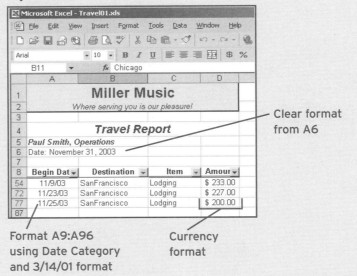

Clear format from A6

Format A9:A96 using Date Category and 3/14/01 format

Currency format

Skill Set 2

Managing Workbooks

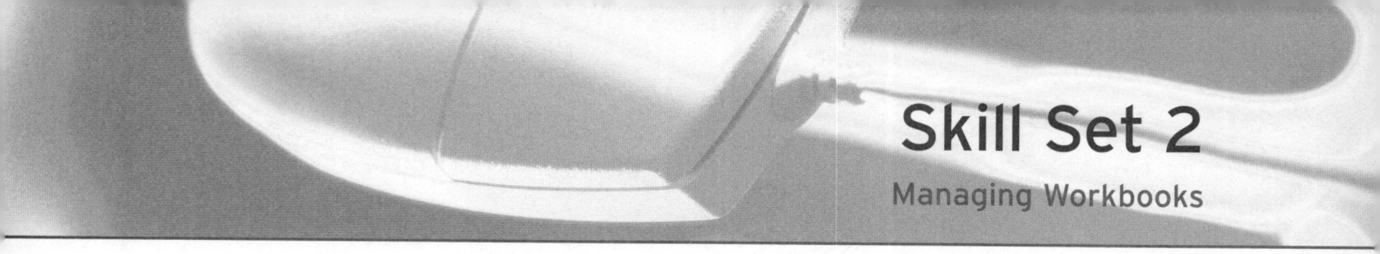

Skill List

1. Manage workbook files and folders
2. Create workbooks using templates
3. Save workbooks using different names and file formats

As you know, a workbook is a collection of worksheets in a single file. As you use Excel to present and analyze data, you will store workbooks in different locations on your computer. To use them, you will need to understand the way files and folders are organized on your computer and how to move among them. Then, as you create new workbooks or use existing ones, you'll be able to find and save them easily, using names and file formats that will meet your needs.

Skill Set 2
Managing Workbooks

Manage Workbook Files and Folders
Locate and Open Existing Workbooks

When you open a workbook file, your computer reads the file information from your disk and places it into its temporary memory, allowing you to see it on the screen. To locate a file on your computer, you use the Look in list arrow and the Up One Level buttons in the Open dialog box. Files are usually stored in **folders**, which are named storage locations on your disk that let you group and organize files as you would the physical folders in your file cabinet.

Step 2
The New Workbook task pane lists recently-opened workbooks. If the workbook you want is listed there, click it once to open it. To open a blank workbook, click the New button on the Standard toolbar, or the Blank Workbook hyperlink in the New Workbook task pane.

Activity Steps

1. Start Excel
2. Click the **Open button** on the Standard toolbar
3. Click the **Look in list arrow** in the Open dialog box
   See Figure 2-1.
   You can use the Look in list arrow to navigate between the levels and locations in the disk structure, or you can use the Up One Level button to move up in the disk structure. You can double-click a folder in the Open dialog box to move down in the disk structure.
4. Navigate to the location where your Project Files are stored
5. Click the filename **Staffing01**, then click **Open**
   See Figure 2-2.
   In the rest of the activities in this book, you will not see instructions for opening each workbook. Instead, each activity that requires a workbook file will display an Open File icon before its steps, with the name of the file you should open. After the last step, the Close File icon is your signal to close the file. Do not save your changes.

 close Staffing01.xls

Figure 2-1: Using the Open dialog box to locate files

Look in
list arrow

Up one level
button

Your
contents
will differ

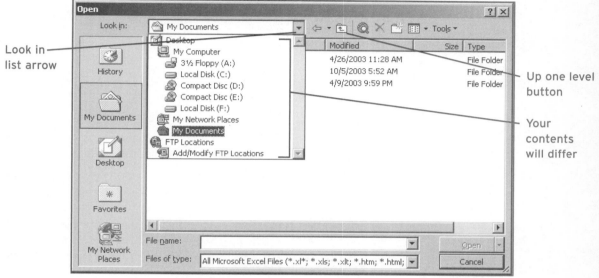

Figure 2-2: Open document

Open workbook's
name in title bar

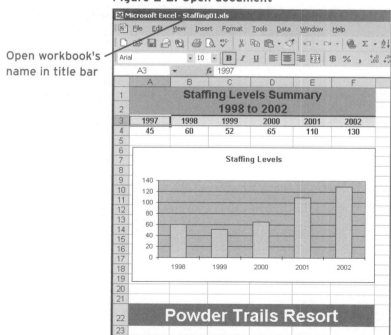

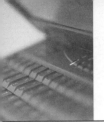

Skill Set 2

Managing Workbooks

Manage Workbook Files and Folders
Create Folders for Saving Workbooks

When you save files, you will often want to create a new folder for storing them. For example, your workbook may be the first file you create for a new project, so you might want to create a folder with that project's name to help you locate it later. You can create a new folder in the Save As dialog box, using the Create New Folder button.

Step 6
You cannot have two files with the same name in one folder. However, you can have files with the same names in different folders.

Activity Steps

 open Guests01.xls

1. Click **File** on the menu bar, then click **Save As**

2. Click the **Save in list arrow**, then navigate to the drive and folder where your Project Files are stored
   See Figure 2-3.

3. Click the **Create New Folder button** in the Save As dialog box toolbar
   The new folder will be created and stored in the open folder where your Project Files are stored.

4. Type **Resort**, click **OK**, then compare your screen to Figure 2-4

5. Select the filename in the File Name box (if it's not already selected), then type **List**

6. Click **Save**
   You have saved a copy of the Guests01 workbook called List in the new folder named Resort. The new folder is in the Project File folder on your Project Disk. The Guests01 file closes automatically, leaving the List workbook open.

 close List.xls

Figure 2-3: Save As dialog box

Your storage location may be different

Create New Folder button

Your view may be different

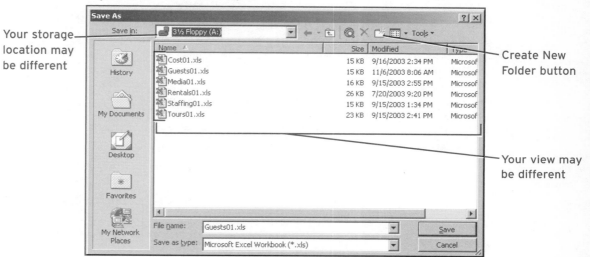

Figure 2-4: Save As dialog box showing new folder

New folder is open

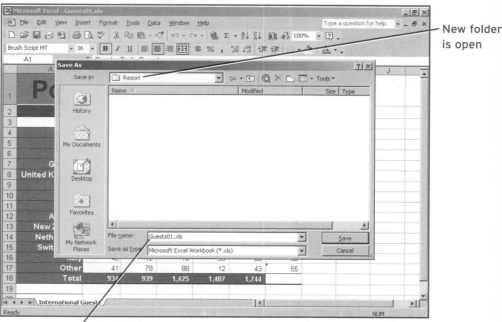

You will save a new version of this file

Skill Set 2
Managing Workbooks

Create Workbooks Using Templates
Create a Workbook from a Template

When you need to create workbooks for everyday use, such as an invoice or a balance sheet, you can save time by using a **template**, a workbook prepared for a specific use that can contain headings, formatting, and formulas. A template is an Excel file saved in a special format that has an .xlt file extension. Several templates are included with Excel; you can open a workbook using any template and customize it. When you use a template, you are not opening the template file itself, but a new workbook with the template's content and format that has an .xls file extension, like any Excel worksheet file. *If you have a standard Excel installation, the program may ask you to insert the Office CD to install the template files.*

Step 2
You can find hundreds more templates for all Office programs in the Template Gallery on the Microsoft Web site (Microsoft.com). In the New Workbook task pane, click Templates on Microsoft.com under New from template, then click any template name to see a preview.

Activity Steps

1. If the New Workbook task pane is not open, click **File** on the menu bar, then click **New**

2. In the New Workbook task pane, click **General Templates** in the New from template section

3. In the Templates dialog box, click the **Spreadsheet Solutions tab** *See Figure 2-5.*

4. Click **Timecard**, then click **OK**
   A workbook based on the Timecard template opens. Excel assigns it the temporary name Timecard1.

5. With cell E10 selected, type your name, press **[Tab]**, then use the horizontal and vertical scroll arrows to view the worksheet
   In this template, the cells in the Total Hours column and row are locked; you cannot place the insertion point in them. If you enter hours in the cells for each day, totals will appear, indicating that there are formulas in the locked cells.

6. Click **cell D19**, type **Bigelow**, press **[Tab]**, type 777, press **[Tab]**, type 8, press **[Tab]**, enter 8 in cells K19, L19, M19, N19, O19, and P19, then observe the total in cell **Q20**

7. Save the workbook as **Weekly** in the drive and folder where your Project Files are stored, then click the **Print Preview button** on the Standard toolbar
   See Figure 2-6.

8. Click **Close** on the Print Preview toolbar

 close Weekly.xls

Figure 2-5: Excel templates available in Office XP

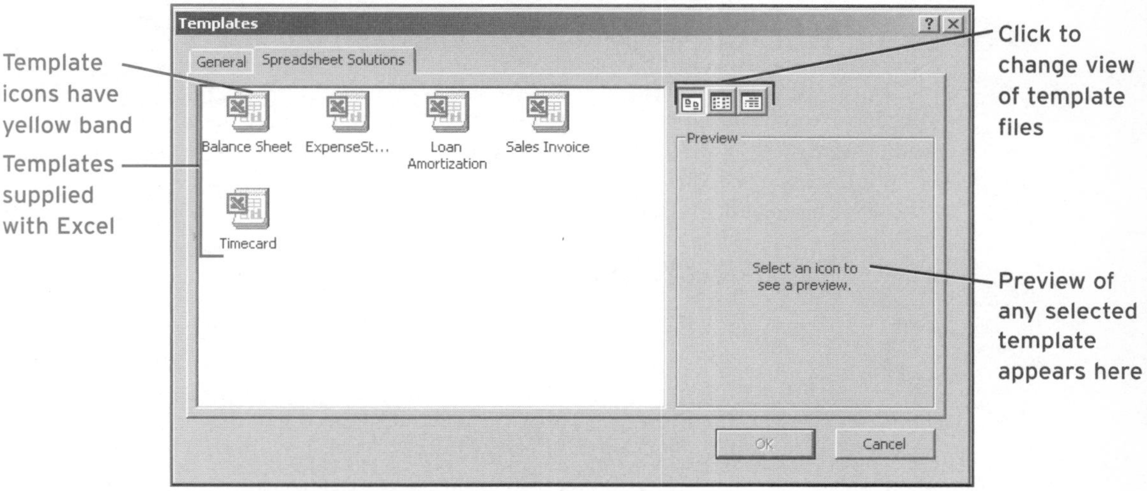

Template icons have yellow band

Templates supplied with Excel

Click to change view of template files

Preview of any selected template appears here

Figure 2-6: Workbook in Print Preview

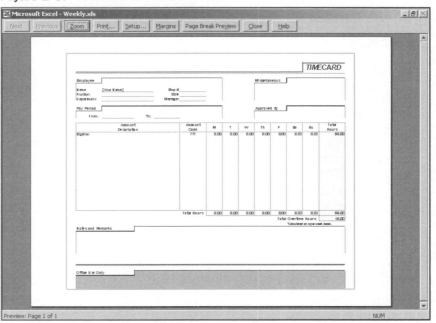

Skill Set 2

Managing Workbooks

Save Workbooks Using Different Names and File Formats

Open a Workbook from a Folder Created for Workbook Storage

As you create workbooks for different purposes using Excel, you will find it convenient to store them in folders. For example, you might want to group all your personal accounting workbooks in a folder named "Personal." You can also "nest" folders inside other folders.

Step 4
To copy a file from one folder to another, open the folder that contains the file you want to copy, right-click the filename, click Copy on the shortcut menu, open the folder where you want to place the file, right-click, then click Paste.

Activity Steps

1. If Excel is open, click the **Minimize button** [■] on the title bar

2. At the Windows desktop, double-click **My Computer**, then navigate to the location where your Project Files are stored
Depending on your computer and operating system, you may need to click Start on the Windows taskbar to find My Computer.

3. Click **File** on the disk window menu bar, point to **New**, then click **Folder**

4. Type **Site**, then press **[Enter]**
See Figure 2-7.

5. Drag the **Cost01** file to the **Site folder**

6. Start Excel (or if Excel is running, click the Microsoft Excel button in the taskbar), then click the **Open button** [🖸] on the Standard toolbar

7. Navigate to the folder where your Project Folders are stored

8. Double-click the **Site folder**, click the **Cost01** file, then click **Open**
See Figure 2-8.

 close Cost01.xls

Figure 2-7: New folder

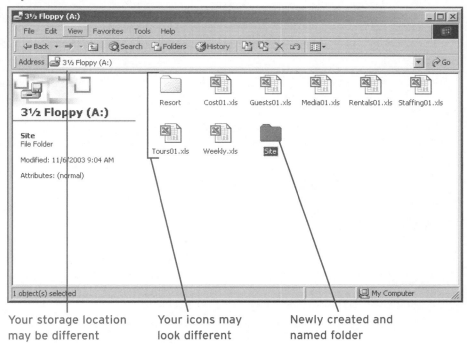

Your storage location may be different

Your icons may look different

Newly created and named folder

Figure 2-8: File opened from newly created folder

Skill Set 2

Managing Workbooks

Save Workbooks Using Different Names and File Formats

Use Save As to Store Workbooks Using Different Names and in Different Locations

After you open a workbook, you have complete control over its name and location. For example, you might want to save an alternative version of a workbook named Address List as Address List2 so you can always return to the original version. Or you might want to save a copy of a workbook on a network drive for others to open and use. You can perform both of these actions in the Save As dialog box.

Step 3
To move up in the file structure, click the Up One Level button in the Save As dialog box.

Activity Steps

 open Tours01.xls

1. Click **File** on the menu bar, then click **Save As**

2. Click the **Save in list arrow**

3. Navigate to the drive and folder where your Project Files are stored, then double-click the **Site folder**
   You have selected the storage location; next you'll change the filename.

4. Select the **File name**, then type **Tours**
   See Figure 2-9.

5. Click **Save**

 close Tours.xls

Figure 2-9: Save As dialog box showing new location and filename

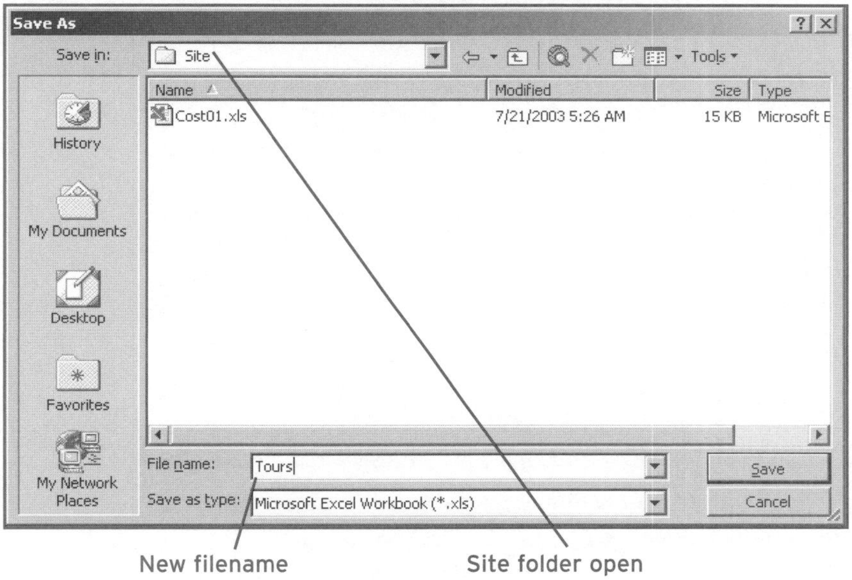

New filename   Site folder open

extra!

Changing views in the Save As dialog box
To change the way files appear using the Save As dialog box, click the **Views list arrow**, then choose the view that displays files the way you want: large icons, small icons, list, or details. List view is very useful for seeing many of your files at once. Details view shows your file dates, file types, and the like.

Skill Set 2

Managing Workbooks

Save Workbooks Using Different Names and File Formats
Use Save As to Store Workbooks in Different File Formats

You will sometimes need to save a workbook in a different file format. For example, a colleague may need a spreadsheet you created, but might be using an earlier version of Excel, such as version 4.0 or 5.0. You can save the workbook in an earlier file format using the Save As dialog box. Keep in mind that workbooks saved in earlier formats may not have all the features that you created in Excel 2002. Table 2-1 lists some common file formats in which you can save Excel 2002 files.

Step 4
Although earlier versions of Excel may not be able to open Excel 2002 files, Excel 2002 can open files created and saved in earlier versions of Excel.

Activity Steps

 open Media01.xls

1. Click **File** on the menu bar, then click **Save As**

2. With the filename selected, type **Media**

3. Click the **Save as type list arrow**, then scroll until you can see Microsoft Excel 5.0/95 Workbook (*.xls)

4. Click **Microsoft Excel 5.0/95 Workbook (*.xls)**
   See Figure 2-10.

5. Click **Save**, then click **Yes** in the dialog box warning that some features may be lost
   The file you created opens in Excel 2002 with the new name and the file extension in the title bar. The original Media01 file closes and remains unchanged on your disk.

 close Media.xls

Figure 2-10: Save As dialog box showing new filename and format

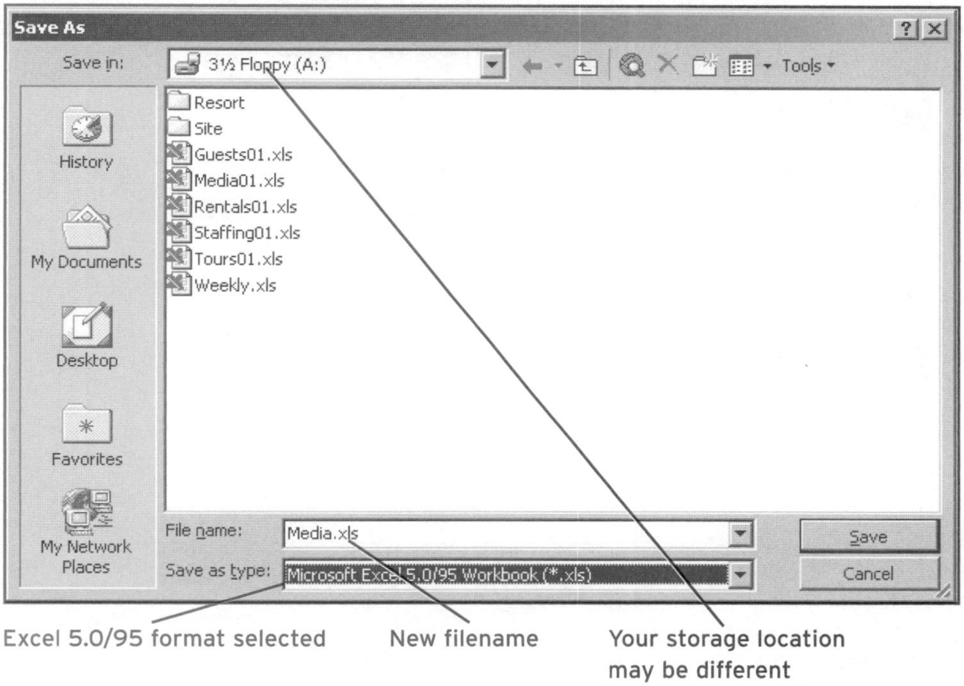

Excel 5.0/95 format selected   New filename   Your storage location may be different

TABLE 2-1: Selected file formats in which you can save Excel files

file format	file extension	what it is
Text (tab delimited)	.txt	Information only with no formatting and with columns separated by tabs; can be opened by many programs
WK3 (1-2-3)	.wk3	Format that can be opened by the Lotus 1-2-3 spreadsheet program
DBF 4	.dbf	Format that can be opened by the dBase IV database program
XML spreadsheet	.xml	XML (Extensible Markup Language) formatted documents can be opened by a variety of programs; program designers can create tags that let people define, transmit, and interpret data between programs

Skill Set 2
Managing Workbooks

Target Your Skills

 open Rentals01.xls

1 Open the file shown in Figure 2-11. At the Windows desktop, create a new folder called Ski in the drive and folder where your Project Files are stored, then save the file as Projection.xls in the Ski folder.

Figure 2-11

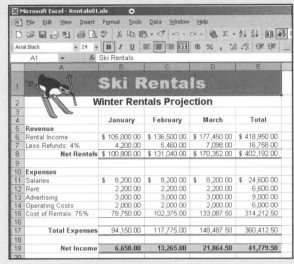

2 Create an Excel file based on the Expense Statement template on the Office XP Spreadsheets Solutions tab. Your screen should look like Figure 2-12. You may need to insert the Office XP CD to install the templates. Save the workbook as Expenses.xls in Excel 97-2002 & 5.0-95 Workbook format, in a new folder named Statements in the drive and folder where your Project Files are stored.

Figure 2-12

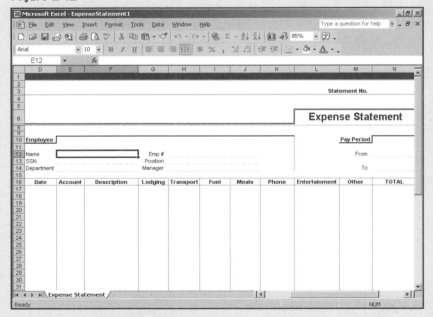

Skill List

1. Apply and modify cell formats
2. Modify row and column settings
3. Modify row and column formats
4. Apply styles
5. Use automated tools to format worksheets
6. Modify Page Setup options for worksheets
7. Preview and print worksheets and workbooks

A good worksheet communicates information clearly. You can format worksheets to add visual impact and to help readers understand your data quickly. Cell **formats** include type styles, sizes, and fonts you can use to make important information more prominent. Cell borders and **fills** (color that fills a cell) can help you visually separate your worksheet sections. For example, you might want to enclose totals in a shaded yellow box or with a heavy black border.

Rows and columns are your worksheet building blocks that you can modify to meet your needs. You can insert and delete rows and columns, as well as hide and redisplay them. In large worksheets, **freezing** rows and columns lets you keep labels visible as you scroll the rest of the worksheet. Changing row heights and column widths also help make your worksheet more readable.

Styles are combinations of number and cell formatting that you can apply to cells and ranges. Excel **AutoFormats** supply combinations of number and cell formats designed for different worksheet types, such as Accounting worksheets or lists.

When your worksheet is ready to print, you can change its layout, including its orientation on the page, its page titles, and which parts of the worksheet print.

Skill Set 3
Formatting and Printing Worksheets

Apply and Modify Cell Formats
Format Cells with Type Styles and Fonts

Readers of your worksheet should be able to distinguish general information from detail at a glance. One way to make this easier is to format column and row labels. To **format** cells, you can use typefaces (such as Arial) and **fonts**, which are the typefaces with formats such as bolding style and type style, to emphasize important text. Font size is measured in units called points; one point is equal to $\frac{1}{72}$ of an inch. You can apply cell formats from the Formatting toolbar or from the Format Cells dialog box.

To change font color, size, and style all at once, click Format on the menu bar, click Cells, then click the Font tab. The Preview box displays a sample of the options you have selected. Select the font, style, size, and color you want, then click OK.

Activity Steps

 open AddressesO1.xls

1. Select the range **A3:F3**
2. Click the **Bold button** B on the Formatting toolbar
3. Select cell **A1**
4. Click the **Font list arrow** `Times New Roman ▾` on the Formatting toolbar, then click **Arial**
5. Click the **Font Size list arrow** `10 ▾` on the Formatting toolbar, then click **24**
6. Click the **Font color list arrow** `A ▾` on the Formatting toolbar, then click the **Red** color (third row, far left column)
   See Figure 3-1.

 close AddressesO1.xls

Figure 3-1: Formatted text

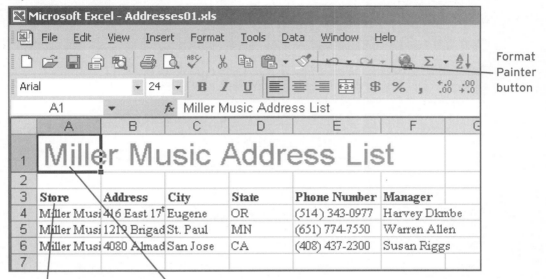

Format Painter button

Bolded text

Text enlarged and with red text color

Skill Set 3

Formatting and Printing Worksheets

Apply and Modify Cell Formats
Format Cells with Borders and Fills

You will often want to place borders around worksheet cells to call attention to their content. You might want to add a bottom border to cells just above a total, place a box around a cell or range containing important information, or place borders around every cell in a range. Borders can have varying lines, styles, and colors. You can also fill cells with a color, called a **fill color**, or pattern to separate worksheet sections. Make sure you preview your worksheets to ensure that fills won't obscure your text when you print.

Activity Steps

 open Projected02.xls

1. Select the range **A7:D7**

Step 2
For more line style and color choices, click Format on the menu bar, click Cells, then click the Border tab or the Patterns tab.

2. Click the **Borders list arrow** on the Formatting toolbar, click the **Bottom Border button** on the Borders palette, then click outside the range

3. Select the range **A10:D10**, click the **Borders list arrow** on the Formatting toolbar, click the **Thick Bottom Border button** on the Borders palette, then click outside the range

4. Select the range **A13:D13**, click the **Borders list arrow** on the Formatting toolbar, then click the **Thick Box Border button** on the Borders palette

5. Select the range **A1:D2**, press and hold **[Ctrl]**, then select the range **A13:D13**

6. Click the **Fill Color list arrow** on the Formatting toolbar, click the **Light Green color** (bottom row, fourth color from the left), then click outside the range
See Figure 3-2.

 close Projected02.xls

Figure 3-2: Worksheet formatted with borders and color

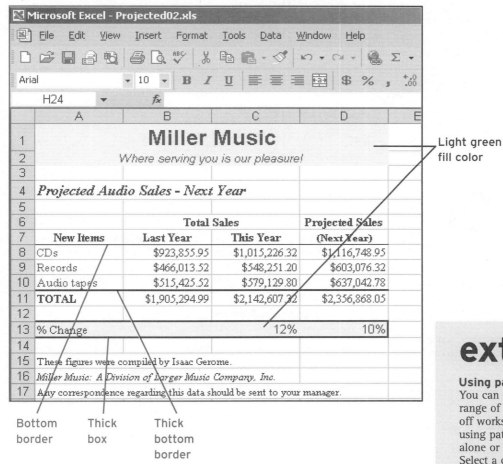

Light green fill color

Bottom border

Thick box

Thick bottom border

extra!

Using patterns
You can obtain a wider range of effects to set off worksheet cells by using patterns, either alone or with colors. Select a cell or range, click **Format** on the menu bar, click Cells, then click the **Patterns tab**. Click the color you want the pattern to be, then click the **Pattern list arrow**. Select a dot, crosshatch, or stripe pattern, then click **OK**. You may have to enlarge or bold the font in a patterned cell to make it visible over the pattern.

Skill Set 3
Formatting and Printing Worksheets

Modify Row and Column Settings
Insert Rows and Columns

After you have created a worksheet with labels, values, and formulas, you may find you need to add more data, often in the middle of existing data. To do this, you can insert one or more rows or columns. The Insert Options list arrow lets you specify whether you want the inserted rows or columns to have the same formatting as the rows or columns on either side.

Activity Steps

 open Instruments01.xls

1. Click cell **C8**
   You can click any cell in the row above which you want to add the new row. If you click a merged cell, the program will insert the same number of columns that the cell spans.

2. Click **Insert** on the menu bar, then click **Rows**
   A smart tag appears near the cell. A **smart tag** is an icon that appears after you modify worksheet cells. In this case the smart tag, an icon with a paintbrush on a white background, presents options for inserting the new row. When you point to the icon, a list arrow appears, along with a screen tip with the smart tag's name.

3. Click the **Insert Options smart tag**
   See Figure 3-3.

4. Click **Format Same As Below**, then click a blank cell

5. In the range A8:E8, enter the following data:
   Accordions [Tab] 3 [Tab] 8 [Tab] 3 [Enter]
   The new row takes on the formatting of the row below it.

6. Right-click cell **B14**, click **Insert**, click the **Entire Column option button**, then click **OK**
   See Figure 3-4.

 close Instruments01.xls

Step 1
To insert more than one row or column, select the number you want to insert. For example, to add four rows, select four rows before you click Insert on the menu bar.

---

extra!

Inserting rows and range references
If you add a row to the bottom or right of a range, Excel automatically includes any values you enter there in formulas directly below the range. However, if you insert a row at the top of a range, any formulas referring to that range will need to be adjusted to include it. In these cases, Excel alerts you by placing a small green triangle in the formula cell. Click the cell, then click the **Smart Tag** that appears, to see the "Formula Omits Adjacent Cells" message, then click **"Update Formula to Include Cells"** to correct the problem.

Figure 3-3: Insert Options list

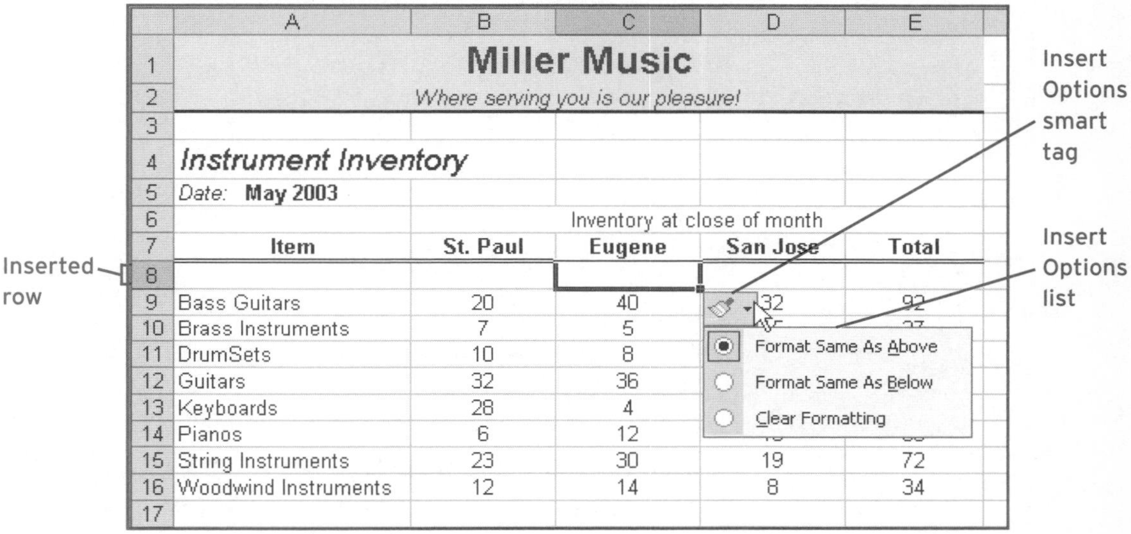

Inserted row

Insert Options smart tag

Insert Options list

Figure 3-4: Worksheet with inserted row and column

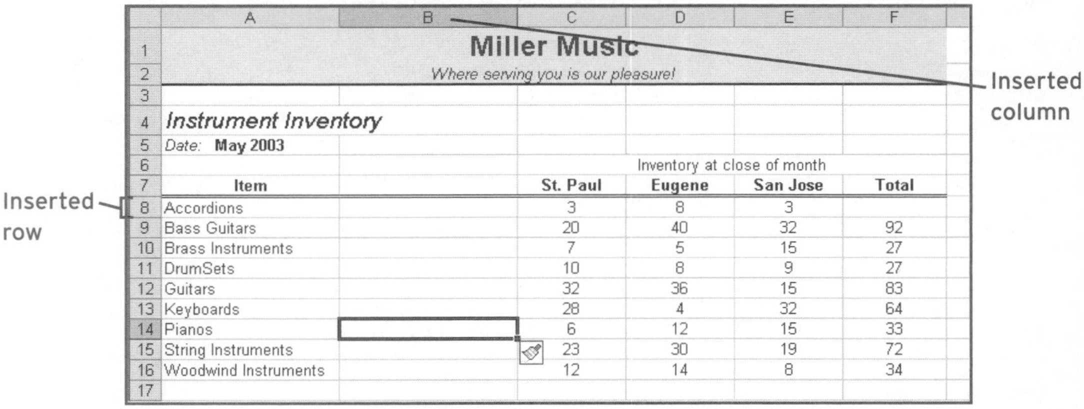

Inserted column

Inserted row

Skill Set 3
Formatting and Printing Worksheets

Modify Row and Column Settings
Delete Rows and Columns

Worksheet data changes over time, and as you use worksheets, you may have to delete entire rows or columns of information. Formulas automatically adjust to reflect the reduced number of rows or columns in a range. If you delete a cell that a formula specifically refers to, however, the cell with the formula displays "#REF!", indicating that you need to modify the formula.

Step 1
To delete a column or row in one step, right click the column or row heading, then click Delete in the shortcut menu.

Activity Steps

 open Instruments02.xls

1. Click cell **B6**

2. Click **Edit** on the menu bar, then click **Delete**
   See Figure 3-5.

3. Click the **Entire row option button**, then click **OK**

4. Click any cell in column E, then observe the totals in column F

5. Click **Edit** on the menu bar, then click **Delete**

6. Click the **Entire column option button**, then click **OK**
   The formulas in the Total column adjust to reflect the deletion.
   See Figure 3-6.

 close Instruments02.xls

Figure 3-5: Delete dialog box

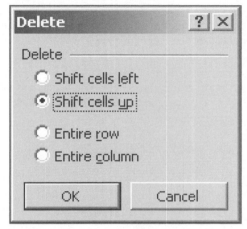

Figure 3-6: Worksheet after deleting row and column

Column
deleted
from
here

Row
deleted
from
here

	A	B	C	D	E
1		**Miller Music**			
2		*Where serving you is our pleasure!*			
3					
4	*Instrument Inventory*				
5	*Date:* **May 2003**				
6	**Item**	**Code**	**St. Paul**	**Eugene**	**Total**
7	Accordions	1000	3	8	11
8	Bass Guitars	2000	20	40	60
9	Brass Instruments	3000	7	5	12
10	DrumSets	4000	10	8	18
11	Guitars	5000	32	36	68
12	Keyboards	6000	28	4	32
13	Pianos	7000	6	12	18
14	String Instruments	8000	23	30	53
15	Woodwind Instruments	9000	12	14	26
16			141	157	298
17					

Adjusted
totals

Skill Set 3
Formatting and Printing Worksheets

Modify Row and Column Settings
Hide and Redisplay Rows and Columns

Your worksheets may contain information that you don't want others to see, such as salaries or other personal data. You can hide these rows or columns. Hidden rows and columns are still in the worksheet, but are not visible; Excel reduces their column width or row height to zero. The row number or column letter of a hidden row or column does not appear; if you hide columns B through D, the column letters will appear as A, E, F, and so on. When you press [Tab], the selected cell skips the hidden column or row.

To hide a row, click any cell in the row, click Format on the menu bar, point to Row, then click Hide. To redisplay, or unhide, a row, select the rows above and below the hidden row, click Format on the menu bar, point to Row, then click Unhide. You can also redisplay rows by dragging the Row Height pointer , and you can redisplay columns by dragging the Column Width pointer .

Activity Steps

open Earnings03.xls

1. Click any cell in column F

2. Click **Format** on the menu bar, point to **Column**, click **Hide**, then click any blank worksheet cell
   Column F no longer appears in the worksheet, and the columns E and G are next to each other.
   See Figure 3-7.
   To redisplay a hidden column, you can select the columns on either side of it, or any two cells on either side of it.

3. Select the range **E12:G12**

4. Click **Format** on the menu bar, point to **Column**, click **Unhide**, then click any blank worksheet cell
   See Figure 3-8.

close Earnings03.xls

Figure 3-7: Worksheet with hidden column

	A	B	C	D	E	G
1				**Miller Music**		
2				*Where serving you is our pleasure!*		
3						
4				**Employee Earnings for July 15-31**		
5						
6				**Gross Profit**		**Employee**
7	**Employee Name**		**Emp #**	**From Sales**	**Commission**	**Earnings**
8	Davis	Jan	233	$4,568.00	$1,370.40	$1,493.74
9	Gibson	Carol	421	$2,321.00	$696.30	$731.12
10	Johnson	Chris	418	$1,588.00	$476.40	$495.46
11	Kniepp	Gordon	403	$2,790.00	$837.00	$887.22
12	Kramer	Joan	390	$1,265.00	$379.50	$390.89
13	McHenry	Bill	378	$2,576.00	$772.80	$819.17
14	Miller	George	347	$3,388.00	$1,016.40	$1,097.71
15	Wallace	Pat	262	$4,224.00	$1,267.20	$1,381.25
16	TOTAL				$6,816.00	$7,296.54
17						

Break in column letter sequence indicates hidden column

Figure 3-8: Worksheet with redisplayed column

Redisplayed column

	A	B	C	D	E	F	G
1				**Miller Music**			
2				*Where serving you is our pleasure!*			
3							
4				**Employee Earnings for July 15-31**			
5							
6				**Gross Profit**			**Employee**
7	**Employee Name**		**Emp #**	**From Sales**	**Commission**	**Bonus**	**Earnings**
8	Davis	Jan	233	$4,568.00	$1,370.40	9%	$1,493.74
9	Gibson	Carol	421	$2,321.00	$696.30	5%	$731.12
10	Johnson	Chris	418	$1,588.00	$476.40	4%	$495.46
11	Kniepp	Gordon	403	$2,790.00	$837.00	6%	$887.22
12	Kramer	Joan	390	$1,265.00	$379.50	3%	$390.89
13	McHenry	Bill	378	$2,576.00	$772.80	6%	$819.17
14	Miller	George	347	$3,388.00	$1,016.40	8%	$1,097.71
15	Wallace	Pat	262	$4,224.00	$1,267.20	9%	$1,381.25
16	TOTAL				$6,816.00		$7,296.54
17							

Skill Set 3
Formatting and Printing Worksheets

Modify Row and Column Settings
Freeze and Unfreeze Rows and Columns

When your worksheet contains so many columns or rows that the entire worksheet is not visible on the screen at one time, you have to scroll to view it. However, when you do this, it can be difficult to remember which column and row labels line up with which values. The Excel Freeze Panes feature lets you **freeze** columns and rows so that the scroll bars display data below and to the right, while the labels stay in place.

Step 2
To freeze only rows, select the entire row below which you want data to scroll. To freeze only columns, select the entire column to the right of the one you want to scroll.

Activity Steps

 open Summary02.xls

1. Click cell **C7**, click **Window** on the menu bar, then click **Freeze Panes**
   Solid lines appear above and to the left of the selected cell, indicating that Excel has frozen the rows and columns above and to the left of the selected cell.
   See Figure 3-9.

2. Click the **Down vertical scroll arrow** twice
   The column labels remain in place as the row contents scroll upward.

3. Click the **Right horizontal scroll arrow** four times
   The row labels remain in place as the column contents scroll left.

4. Click **Window** on the menu bar, then click **Unfreeze panes**
   The solid lines disappear and all the worksheet data reappears.

 close Summary02.xls

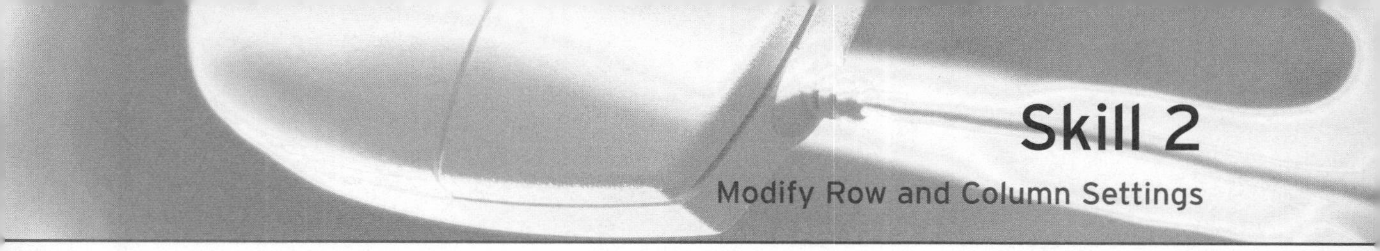

Figure 3-9: Window with frozen panes

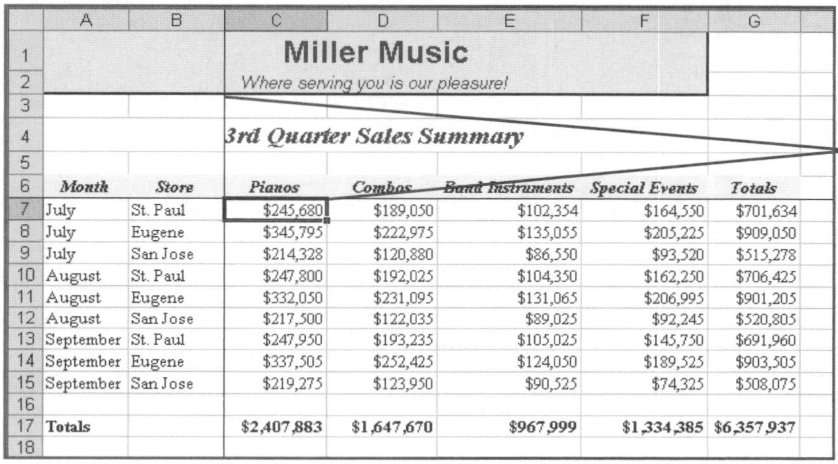

	A	B	C	D	E	F	G
1				**Miller Music**			
2			*Where serving you is our pleasure!*				
3							
4			*3rd Quarter Sales Summary*				
5							
6	*Month*	*Store*	*Pianos*	*Combos*	*Band Instruments*	*Special Events*	*Totals*
7	July	St. Paul	$245,680	$189,050	$102,354	$164,550	$701,634
8	July	Eugene	$345,795	$222,975	$135,055	$205,225	$909,050
9	July	San Jose	$214,328	$120,880	$86,550	$93,520	$515,278
10	August	St. Paul	$247,800	$192,025	$104,350	$162,250	$706,425
11	August	Eugene	$332,050	$231,095	$131,065	$206,995	$901,205
12	August	San Jose	$217,500	$122,035	$89,025	$92,245	$520,805
13	September	St. Paul	$247,950	$193,235	$105,025	$145,750	$691,960
14	September	Eugene	$337,505	$252,425	$124,050	$189,525	$903,505
15	September	San Jose	$219,275	$123,950	$90,525	$74,325	$508,075
16							
17	Totals		$2,407,883	$1,647,670	$967,999	$1,334,385	$6,357,937
18							

Lines indicate frozen columns and rows

extra!

Splitting the worksheet into scrollable panes

To divide the worksheet into two or four scrollable panes, place the pointer over the split box at the top of the vertical scroll bar until it changes to the Window split pointer ⬍, then drag downward. The scroll bar becomes two scroll bars, one for each pane. To remove the split, double-click it. You can split the worksheet horizontally in the same way using the split box to the right of the horizontal scroll bar.

Skill Set 3
Formatting and Printing Worksheets

Modify Row and Column Formats
Modify Row Height

Using fonts and rows of different heights can make your worksheet easier to read. When you change the font size of cell contents, the row height automatically adjusts. In other cases you will want to adjust the row height yourself. You can adjust the height of just one row or several rows; you can resize them to fit cell contents or to set them at a specific height.

Step 4
To adjust the height of several rows, select them, then drag to enlarge one of the selected rows; all of them will adjust to that height. To adjust the height of nonadjacent rows, select the first row, press and hold [Ctrl], select the remaining nonadjacent rows, then drag one to enlarge them all.

Activity Steps

 open Furniture01.xls

1. Position the mouse pointer over the bottom of the **row 4 heading** until the pointer becomes ╪

2. Drag downward to enlarge the row to approximately double its size
   See Figure 3-10.

3. Drag the bottoms of **rows 2** and **19** to approximately double their height

4. Click the **row 6 heading** to select the row

5. Click **Format** on the menu bar, point to **Row**, then click **Height**

6. Type **25**, then click **OK**

7. Click the Row 13 heading to select the row, press [F4], click any blank cell, then press **[PgUp]** or **[PageUp]**
   In Office, the [F4] key repeats the immediately preceding action.
   See Figure 3-11.

 close Furniture01.xls

Figure 3-10: Dragging a row border to change row height

ScreenTip shows height as you drag

Resize pointer

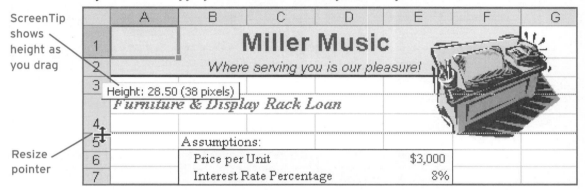

Figure 3-11: Worksheet with modified row height

Heightened rows

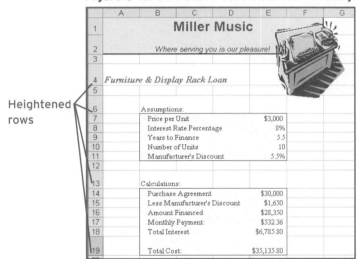

Skill Set 3
Formatting and Printing Worksheets

Modify Row and Column Formats
Modify Column Width

Your worksheets will be easier to read if the data fits well into the worksheet columns. With a good fit, all the data will be visible and as much data as possible will fit on your screen at once, which is useful with large worksheets. Resizing one column in a group of selected columns resizes all the columns in the group.

To make a column the same width as another column in your worksheet, select the column of the desired width, click the Copy button on the Standard toolbar, right-click the destination column's heading, click Paste Special, click Column widths in the Paste Special dialog box, then click OK.

Activity Steps

 open Addresses02.xls

1. Move the mouse pointer over the divider between the **column A and B headings** until the pointer becomes ✛
   See Figure 3-12.

2. Drag the column divider to the right to widen the column to approximately double its size

3. Move the pointer over the divider between **columns B and C headings**, then double-click
   The column automatically resizes to fit its contents; this is called **AutoFit**.

4. Double-click the **divider** between columns D and E

5. Click the **column C heading** then drag to select **columns C through F**

6. Double-click the **right border** of any selected column heading
   AutoFit resizes the selected columns to accommodate their cell contents.
   See Figure 3-13.

 close Addresses02.xls

Figure 3-12: Dragging a column border to change column width

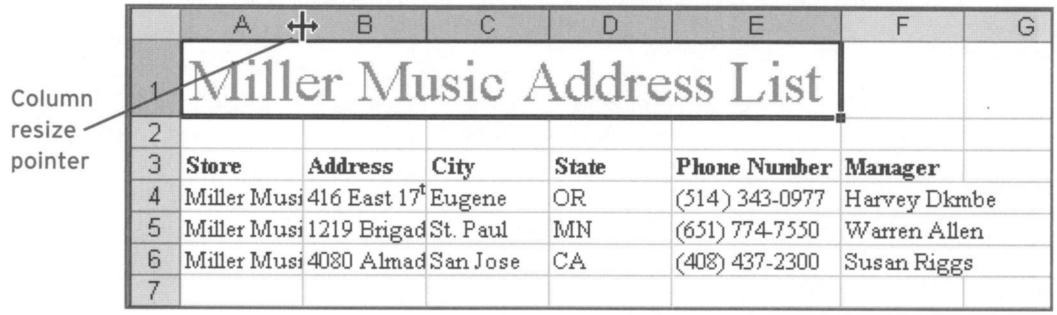

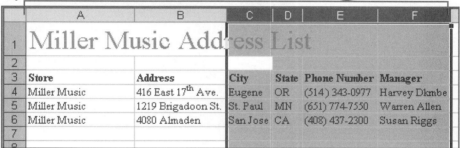

Column resize pointer

Figure 3-13: Worksheet with modified column width

Column widths fit cell contents

Skill Set 3

Formatting and Printing Worksheets

Modify Row and Column Formats
Modify Alignment

When you type data into cells, Excel aligns the data according to its type: text on the left side of the cell and numbers on the right. Both text and numbers are automatically aligned at the bottom of a cell. You can change the horizontal or vertical alignment of any entry using the Formatting toolbar or the Alignment tab in the Format Cells dialog box.

Step 6
You can indent cell contents from the edge of a cell by one character width by clicking the Increase Indent and Decrease Indent buttons on the Formatting toolbar. You can also set a specific number of charac- ter widths on the Alignment tab of the Format Cells dialog box. Cell indents replace other horizontal alignment options.

Activity Steps

open Retire01.xls

1. Select the range A11:A18

2. Click the **Align Left button** on the Formatting toolbar

3. Select the range B11:B18, then click the **Align Right button** on the Formatting toolbar

4. Select the range C11:C18, then click the **Center button** on the Formatting toolbar

5. Click cell **A4**, click **Format** on the menu bar, click **Cells**, click the **Alignment tab**
   See Figure 3-14.

6. Under Text alignment, click the **Vertical list arrow**, click **Center**, then click **OK**

close Retire01.xls

Figure 3-14: Alignment tab in the Format Cells dialog box

Click to change vertical alignment

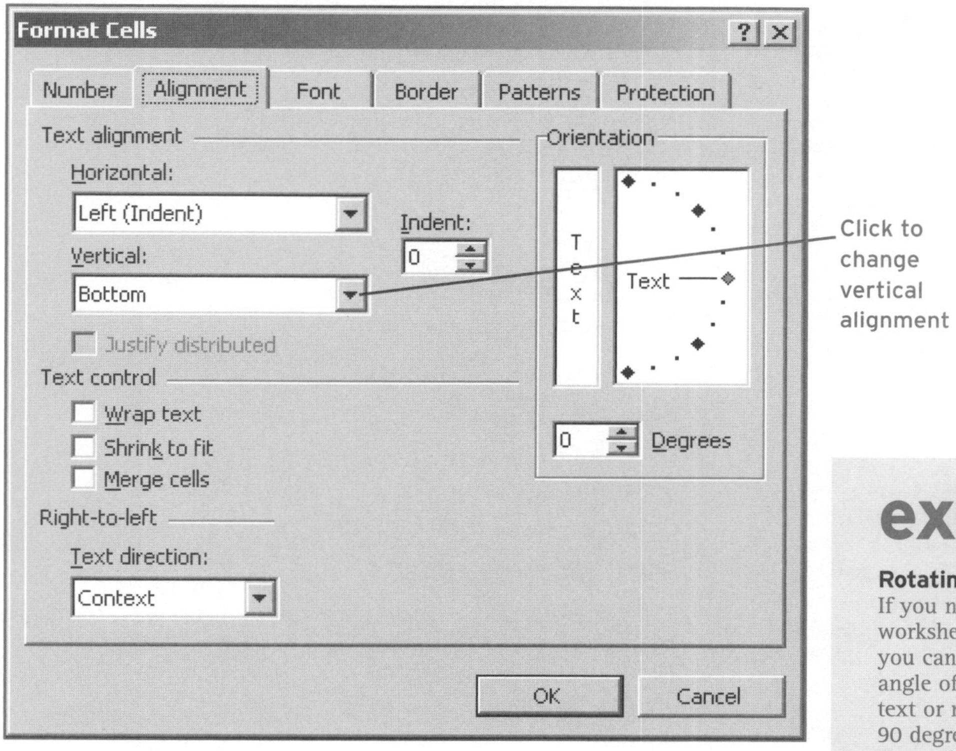

extra!

Rotating cell contents
If you need to compress worksheet data columns, you can change the angle of selected cell text or numbers up to 90 degrees. Click **Format** on the menu bar, click **Cells**, then click the **Alignment tab** in the Format Cells dialog box. Under Orientation, drag the **red diamond** to the desired position, or click the **Degrees list arrow** to enter the number of degrees you want to rotate the contents of the selected cell or range. To have text read from top to bottom in a cell, click the text that is aligned that way under Orientation, then click **OK**.

Skill Set 3

Formatting and Printing Worksheets

Apply Styles

When you need to format a number of cells or ranges the same way, it can be tedious to select and format each one. Instead you can apply a **style** or collection of cell or number formats, such as bold, right-aligned, and red text. Styles help give your worksheets a consistent appearance. The Currency, Percent, and Number buttons on the Formatting toolbar are actually predefined styles that come with Excel. Until you apply another style, the Excel **Normal style** determines the default number format, alignment, and font for text and numbers you enter.

Step 2
To modify an existing style, click Font, click Style; in the Styles dialog box, select a style, then click Modify. Make changes in the Format dialog box. All text and numbers with that style applied will change. Style modifications only apply to the styles in that worksheet.

Activity Steps

 open Drums01.xls

1. Select the range C8 to D13

2. Click **Format** on the menu bar, then click **Style**

3. Click the **Style name list arrow**
   See Figure 3-15.

4. Click **Currency**, then click **OK**

5. Select the range F8:G15

6. Click **Format** on the menu bar, click **Style**, click the **Style name list arrow**, click **Currency [0]**, click **OK**, then click any blank cell
   The Currency [0] and Comma [0] styles display values with no decimal places.
   See Figure 3-16.

 close Drums01.xls

Figure 3-15: Style name list in the Style dialog box

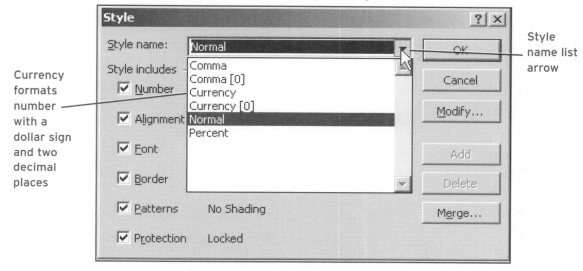

Currency formats number with a dollar sign and two decimal places

Style name list arrow

Figure 3-16: Worksheet formatted with styles

	A	B	C	D	E	F	G	H
1		**Miller Music**						
2		*Where serving you is our pleasure!*						
3								
4	*Drum Inventory*							
5	Date:	7/8/2003						
6					Quantity	Total	Retail	
7		Drum Type	Cost	Price	In Stock	Cost	Value	On Order
8		18" bass drum	$ 155.10	$ 310.20	10	$ 1,551	$ 3,102	21
9		6-1/2" snare drum	$ 115.25	$ 230.50	18	$ 2,075	$ 4,149	28
10		12" x 8" tom-tom	$ 125.95	$ 251.90	15	$ 1,889	$ 3,779	23
11		Small bongos	$ 62.95	$ 125.90	16	$ 1,007	$ 2,014	33
12		Piccolo snare drum	$ 103.45	$ 206.90	10	$ 1,035	$ 2,069	11
13		Timbales	$ 129.99	$ 259.98	15	$ 1,950	$ 3,900	0
14								
15		**Totals**			84	$ 9,506	$ 19,013	116
16								

Numbers formatted with dollar signs and no decimal places

Skill Set 3

Formatting and Printing Worksheets

Use Automated Tools to Format Worksheets

Apply AutoFormats to Worksheets

While Excel provides many formatting options that let you change the font, size, color, shading, and style of your worksheet content, you can also use the automatic formats supplied with Excel. **AutoFormats** contain distinctive combinations of shading, borders, fonts, fills, and alignment. You can apply an AutoFormat to an entire worksheet or to any selected range. If you click only inside a range, Excel will try to detect the correct range.

Step 3
If you don't want to use part of an AutoFomat, such as its alignment or border, click Options in the AutoFormat dialog box, then under "Formats to apply" at the bottom of the dialog box, select or deselect any formatting options.

Activity Steps

 open Drums02.xls

1. Select the range **B6:H15**

2. Click **Format** on the menu bar, then click **AutoFormat**

3. Click the picture of the **Classic 3 AutoFormat** (2nd row, right format)
   See Figure 3-17.

4. Click **OK**, then click any blank cell
   See Figure 3-18.

 close Drums02.xls

Figure 3-17: AutoFormat dialog box

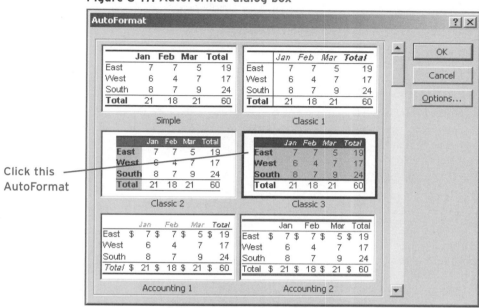

Click this
AutoFormat

Figure 3-18: Worksheet with AutoFormat applied to a range

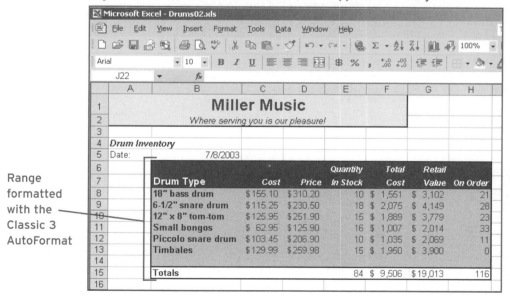

Range
formatted
with the
Classic 3
AutoFormat

Skill Set 3

Formatting and Printing Worksheets

Modify Page Setup Options for Worksheets
Change Worksheet Orientation

Some printed worksheets fit on one 8-1/2" x 11" piece of paper that is taller than it is wide. This is called **portrait orientation**. Any information that does not fit on the page appears on page 2, making it difficult for a reader to see how headings and data line up. To fit data to one page that is wider than it is tall, you use **landscape orientation**. You set page orientation in the Page Setup dialog box, which you can open from the File menu or from the Print Preview window. To save paper and toner, always preview your worksheets before printing to see if you need to change the page orientation.

If your worksheet data does not appear to fit on a single page, you can scale the worksheet to fit the page. In the Page Setup dialog box, under Scaling, click the Fit to option, then enter the number of pages to which you want to fit the worksheet.

Activity Steps

 open Expenses02.xls

1. Click the **Print Preview button** on the Standard toolbar.

2. Click **Next**, then click **Close**
   A dotted line appears between columns G and H. The line is a **page break**, indicating that anything to its right will print on a second page.

3. Click **File** on the menu bar, click **Page Setup**, then click the **Page tab** (if it's not already selected)
   See Figure 3-19.

4. Under **Orientation**, click the **Landscape option button**, then click **Print Preview**
   See Figure 3-20.
   The Next button is dimmed, meaning that all the worksheet data now fits on one page.

5. Click **Close**

 close Expenses02.xls

Figure 3-19: Page Setup dialog box

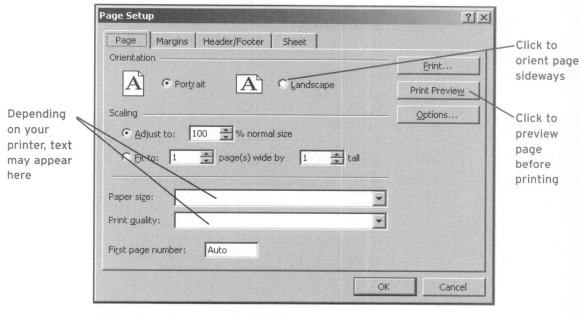

Depending on your printer, text may appear here

Click to orient page sideways

Click to preview page before printing

Figure 3-20: Worksheet in Print Preview

Next button is not active

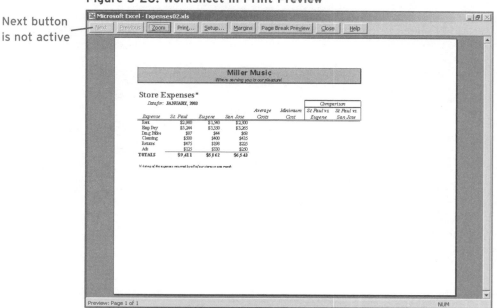

Skill Set 3

Formatting and Printing Worksheets

Modify Page Setup Options for Worksheets

Add Headers and Footers to Worksheets

When you print worksheets, you will frequently want to identify each page of your printout. You can do this easily with **headers**, text that prints at the top of each page, and **footers**, which print at the bottom of each page. A header or footer can contain text, a page number, the date, time, filename, or sheet name; it can also contain a picture you insert, such as a company logo. See Table 3-1 for icons you can use and the corresponding codes they insert.

Activity Steps

Step 1
To add headers or footers to more than one sheet in a workbook simultaneously, first select the sheets while holding down [Ctrl], then add the header or footer just as you would for a single sheet.

 open Markdowns02.xls

1. Click **View** on the menu bar then click **Header and Footer**

2. Click the **Header/Footer tab** (if it's not already selected)
   You could click the Header or Footer list arrow to select predefined headers or footers. To control their content and placement, you need to enter a custom header or footer.

3. Click **Custom Header**
   The word "Page" and the page number code "&[Page]" appear in the Center section.
   See Figure 3-21.

4. Click the **Left section box** (if the insertion point is not already there), click the **Date button** 🗓 in the Header dialog box, click the **Right section box**, then click the **Sheet Name button** 🖵

5. Click **OK** in the Header dialog box, then click **Print Preview** in the Page Setup dialog box

6. Move the pointer across the top of the worksheet until it changes to 🔍, then click once
   See Figure 3-22.

7. Click **Close**

 close Markdowns02.xls

Figure 3-21: The Custom Header dialog box

Date button

Sheet name button

Code for page number

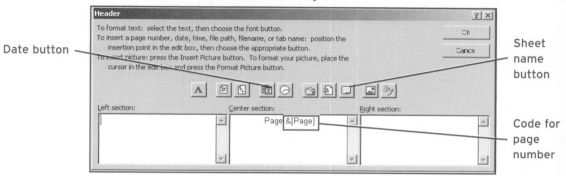

Figure 3-22: Worksheet Header

TABLE 3-1: Icons available in the Custom Header and Footer dialog boxes

click	to	code	click	to	code
A	Format font of selected header or footer text	--		Add path and file	&[Path]&[File]
#	Add page number	&[Page]		Add filename	&[File]
	Add the total number of pages	&[Pages]		Add worksheet	&[Tab] tab name
	Add date	&[Date]		Insert a picture	&[Picture]
	Add time	&[Time]		Format picture	--

Skill Set 3

Formatting and Printing Worksheets

Modify Page Setup Options for Worksheets

Set Page Options for Printing

When printing worksheets, you can control exactly what parts of the worksheet should print, how the sheet should appear (including margins, row, and column headings), and where the worksheet cells should appear on the printed page. You set these features on the Margins and Sheet tabs in the Page Setup dialog box. As you change margins, you can view a worksheet sample with your new settings. When using Page Setup options, it's always a good idea to preview your worksheet to check its appearance before printing.

Step 4
In a multi-page worksheet, you can select any row to appear at the top of every printed page to help readers identify data. Click File on the menu bar, then click Page Setup. On the Sheet tab of the Page Setup dialog box, click the Collapse button next to Rows to Repeat at top, click the row, click the Redisplay button, then click Print Preview or OK.

Activity Steps

 open Budget02.xls

1. Click **File** on the menu bar, then click **Page Setup**

2. Click the **Margins tab**, then click the **Left up arrow** once until 1 appears in the text box

3. Under Center on page, click the **Vertically** check box to select it
   See Figure 3-23.

4. Click the **Sheet tab**, then under Print, click the **Gridlines** and **Row and column headings check boxes** to select them

5. Click **Print Preview**, then click the preview window so you can see the full page
   See Figure 3-24.

6. Click **Close**

 close Budget02.xls

Figure 3-23: Margins tab in the Page Setup dialog box

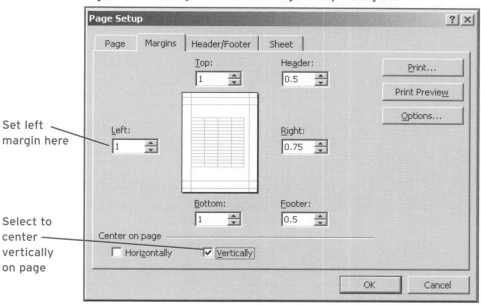

Set left margin here

Select to center vertically on page

Figure 3-24: Page in Print Preview centered vertically and showing row and column headings

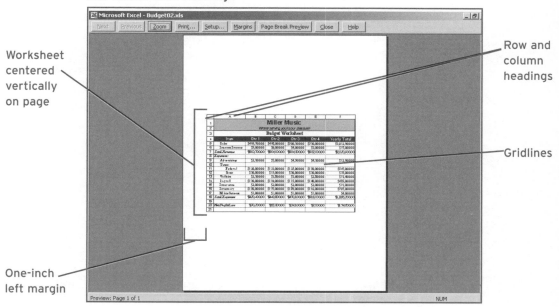

Worksheet centered vertically on page

Row and column headings

Gridlines

One-inch left margin

Skill Set 3

Formatting and Printing Worksheets

Preview and Print Worksheets and Workbooks

Set and Print Print Areas

If you are working on a large worksheet, you might want to print only a portion of it. To print a worksheet section once, you can use the Selection option button in the Print dialog box. To print an area repeatedly, you can set a **print area**, which is an area you designate; that area prints when you click the Print button on the Standard toolbar.

Step 2
You can set different print areas for each worksheet. To clear a print area, click File, point to Print Area, then click Clear Print Area.

Activity Steps

 open Earnings04.xls

1. Select cell A17, enter your name, then select the range A4:G17

2. Click **File** on the menu bar, point to **Print Area**, click **Set Print Area**, then click outside the range
   A dotted line surrounds the print area you set.
   See Figure 3-25.

3. Click the **Print Preview button** on the Standard toolbar
   Only the range you defined as the print area appears.
   See Figure 3-26.

4. Click **Print**, then click **OK** in the Print dialog box

 close Earnings04.xls

Figure 3-25: Print area in worksheet

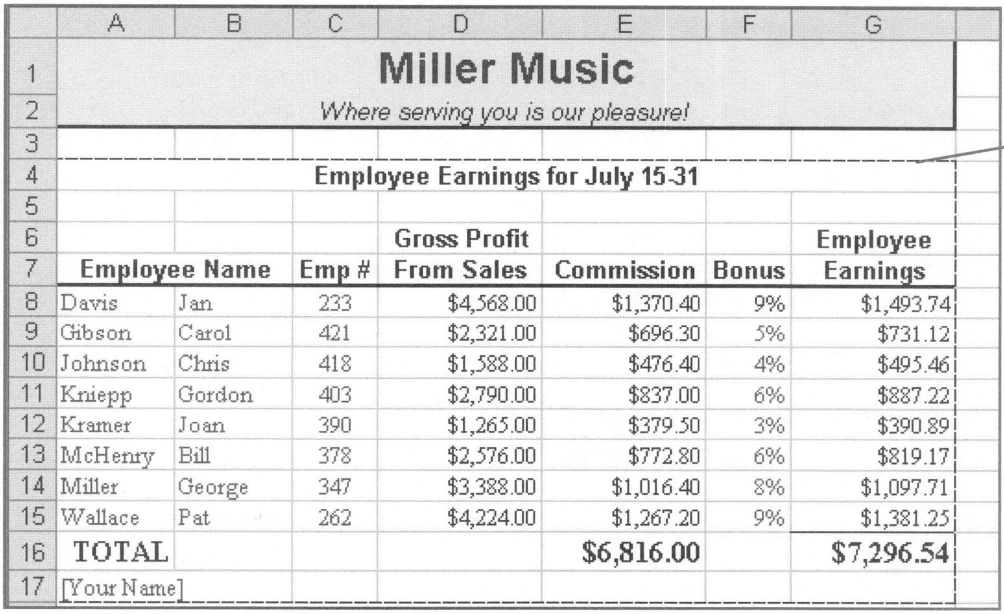

	A	B	C	D	E	F	G
1	Miller Music						
2	*Where serving you is our pleasure!*						
3							
4	Employee Earnings for July 15-31						
5							
6				Gross Profit			Employee
7	Employee Name		Emp #	From Sales	Commission	Bonus	Earnings
8	Davis	Jan	233	$4,568.00	$1,370.40	9%	$1,493.74
9	Gibson	Carol	421	$2,321.00	$696.30	5%	$731.12
10	Johnson	Chris	418	$1,588.00	$476.40	4%	$495.46
11	Kniepp	Gordon	403	$2,790.00	$837.00	6%	$887.22
12	Kramer	Joan	390	$1,265.00	$379.50	3%	$390.89
13	McHenry	Bill	378	$2,576.00	$772.80	6%	$819.17
14	Miller	George	347	$3,388.00	$1,016.40	8%	$1,097.71
15	Wallace	Pat	262	$4,224.00	$1,267.20	9%	$1,381.25
16	TOTAL				$6,816.00		$7,296.54
17	[Your Name]						

Dotted line surrounds print area

Figure 3-26: Print area range in Print Preview

Only contents of Print Area will print

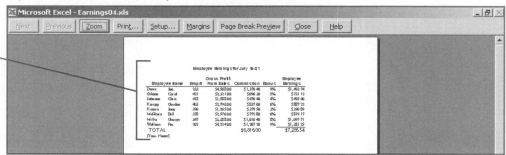

Skill Set 3

Formatting and Printing Worksheets

Preview and Print Worksheets and Workbooks

Preview and Print Non-Adjacent Selections

If you are working on a large worksheet, you may want to preview or print worksheet ranges that are not next to each other (non-adjacent). You can print them at the same time; each range prints on a separate page. In Print preview you can use the Zoom pointer to get a closer look at the worksheet image.

Step 2
The nonadjacent areas must be on the same worksheet.

Activity Steps

 open Summary03.xls

1. Enter your name in cells A5 and A20

2. Select the range **A4:G9**

3. Press and hold down [Ctrl]

4. Select the range **A19:G24**
   See Figure 3-27.

5. Click **File** on the menu bar, then click **Print**

6. Under Print what, click the **Selection option button** to select it, then click **Preview**
   See Figure 3-28.

7. Click **Next** to view the next page, then move the pointer over the top part of the worksheet until the pointer becomes the Zoom pointer ⊗, then click once
   The worksheet view is magnified.

8. Click the worksheet again to reduce the image, then click **Print**

 close Summary03.xls

Figure 3-27: Non-adjacent ranges selected

Selected non-adjacent ranges

	A	B	C	D	E	F	G
4			*3rd Quarter Sales Summary*				
5	[Your Name]						
6	*Month*	*Store*	*Pianos*	*Combos*	*Band Instruments*	*Special Events*	*Totals*
7	July	St. Paul	$245,680	$189,050	$102,354	$164,550	$701,634
8	July	Eugene	$345,795	$222,975	$135,055	$205,225	$909,050
9	July	San Jose	$214,328	$120,880	$86,550	$93,520	$515,278
10	August	St. Paul	$247,800	$192,025	$104,350	$162,250	$706,425
11	August	Eugene	$332,050	$231,095	$131,065	$206,995	$901,205
12	August	San Jose	$217,500	$122,035	$89,025	$92,245	$520,805
13	September	St. Paul	$247,950	$193,235	$105,025	$145,750	$691,960
14	September	Eugene	$337,505	$252,425	$124,050	$189,525	$903,505
15	September	San Jose	$219,275	$123,950	$90,525	$74,325	$508,075
16							
17	Totals		$2,407,883	$1,647,670	$967,999	$1,334,385	$6,357,937
18							
19			*4th Quarter Sales Summary*				
20	[Your Name]						
21	*Month*	*Store*	*Pianos*	*Combos*	*Band Instruments*	*Special Events*	*Totals*
22	October	St. Paul	$328,560	$195,400	$105,425	$172,778	$802,162
23	October	Eugene	$315,680	$220,550	$139,107	$215,486	$890,823
24	October	San Jose	$215,600	$115,880	$89,147	$98,196	$518,823
25	November	St. Paul	$213,452	$180,440	$107,481	$170,363	$671,735
26	November	Eugene	$435,770	$240,994	$134,997	$217,345	$1,029,106
27	November	San Jose	$220,335	$125,690	$91,696	$96,857	$534,578

Figure 3-28: Preview of first selected range

Indicates second range is on next page

First selected range

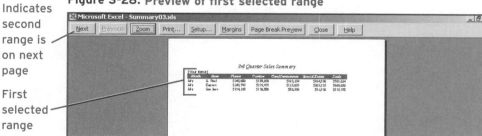

Skill Set 3

Formatting and Printing Worksheets

Target Your Skills

file open Teaching01.xls

1 Format the work-sheet so it looks like Figure 3-29.

Add a custom footer with your name in the left section and the date in the right sec-tion. Print it centered vertically on the sheet, showing gridlines and row and column head-ings. Set a print area that includes only the data in rows 7 through 19, then print only the print area.

Figure 3-29

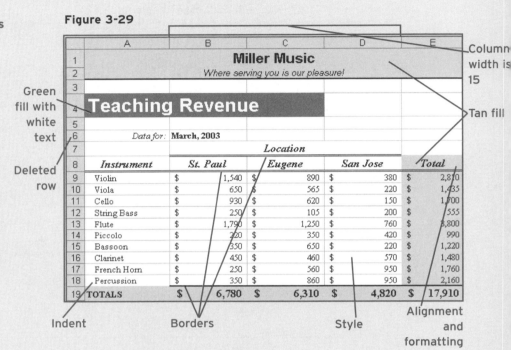

Column width is 15

Green fill with white text

Deleted row

Tan fill

Indent   Borders   Style   Alignment and formatting

file open Bonus01.xls

2 Refer to Figure 3-30. Freeze rows and columns above and to the left of cell B7. Change the work-sheet orientation so the data prints on one page. Then preview and print the two non-adjacent AutoFormatted ranges at the same time, then unfreeze the panes. Hide columns H and I, print the worksheet, then redis-play the hidden columns.

Figure 3-30

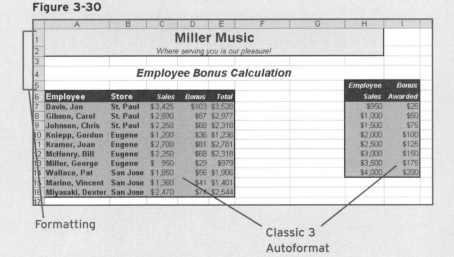

Formatting

Classic 3 Autoformat

Skill Set 4

Modifying Workbooks

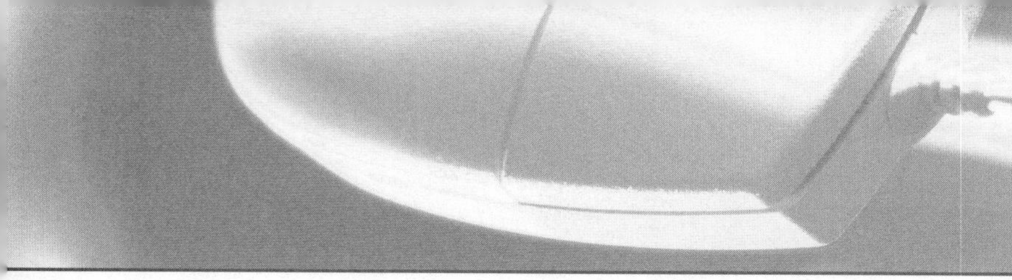

Skill List

1. Insert and delete worksheets
2. Modify worksheet names and positions
3. Use 3-D references

An Excel 2002 **workbook** is a file containing one or more worksheets. A **worksheet** is a grid of rows and columns you use to store and analyze data. On a worksheet, the intersection of every row and column is a **cell** into which you can insert labels, values, and formulas.

In some workbooks, you will only need one worksheet, but in others, you will need two or more. It's important to know how to organize worksheets in workbooks so you can quickly store, view, and use the data they hold. You can easily add, delete, move, and name worksheets. Formatting sheet tabs with color can make it easier to differentiate between sheets. When you have data in multiple worksheets, you can use **3-D references** in formulas to reference data from one or more worksheets.

Skill Set 4

Modifying Workbooks

Insert and Delete Worksheets
Insert a New Worksheet into a Workbook

A new Excel workbook contains three worksheets: Sheet1, Sheet2, and Sheet3. However, you can add as many sheets as you need. Excel inserts a new worksheet to the left of the selected worksheet and assigns it the next number in the sheet numbering sequence. The Insert command on the sheet tab shortcut menu lets you select the type of sheet to add. For example, you might want to add a chart sheet (a sheet that will contain a chart), or a sheet based on a **template**, a presupplied worksheet design. The worksheet command on the Insert menu automatically inserts one standard worksheet. Once you have added the worksheet, you cannot undo the action.

Step 2
Excel adds as many sheets as you have selected. To select more than two adjacent sheets, select the first worksheet tab in the sequence, press and hold [Shift], click the last worksheet tab in the sequence, click Insert on the menu bar, then click Worksheet.

Activity Steps

 open Payroll01.xls

1. **Right-click the June worksheet tab, then click Insert**
   The Insert dialog box lets you insert several different types of sheets, such as a standard worksheet, a chart sheet, or a sheet based on a template.
   See Figure 4-1.

2. **Click the Worksheet icon (if it's not already selected), then click OK**
   A new worksheet named Sheet1 appears to the left of the June worksheet.

3. **Click Insert on the menu bar, then click Worksheet**
   Another new worksheet, named Sheet2, appears to the left of Sheet1.
   See Figure 4-2.

 close Payroll01.xls

Figure 4-1: Insert dialog box

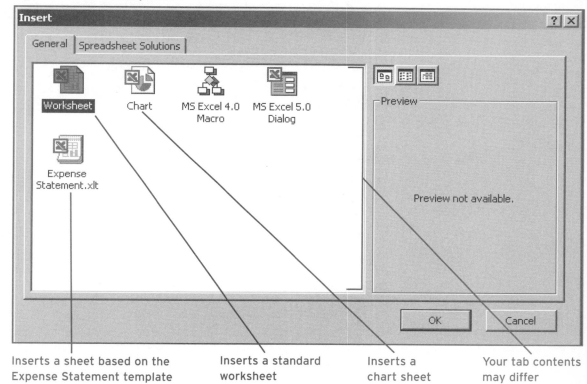

Inserts a sheet based on the
Expense Statement template

Inserts a standard
worksheet

Inserts a
chart sheet

Your tab contents
may differ

Figure 4-2: Workbook with two new worksheets

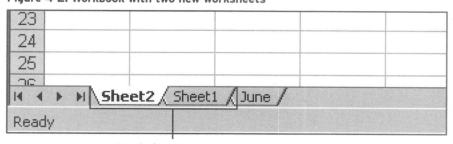

Newly inserted sheets

Skill Set 4

Modifying Workbooks

Insert and Delete Worksheets
Delete Worksheets from a Workbook

If you no longer need a particular worksheet in a workbook, you can delete it. You can also delete multiple selected worksheets. You cannot, however, delete all worksheets; a workbook must have at least one visible (unhidden) worksheet. *In workbooks that contain formulas using cell data from other sheets, recheck your formulas. Deleting a worksheet that has a value used in another sheet's formula can cause inaccurate formula results.*

Step 2
You can also right-click a sheet tab, click Delete, then click Delete again to confirm the deletion.

Activity Steps

 open Helicopters01.xls

1. Click the 2nd Quarter sheet tab

2. Click **Edit** on the menu bar, then click **Delete sheet**
   A message tells you that the sheet contains data and asks you to confirm the deletion.
   See Figure 4-3.

3. Click **Delete**
   One sheet remains in the workbook.
   See Figure 4-4.

 close Helicopters01.xls

Figure 4-3: Confirmation dialog box

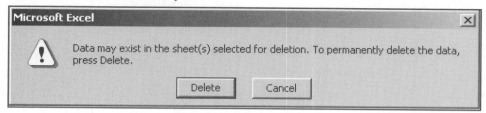

Microsoft Excel ⚠ Data may exist in the sheet(s) selected for deletion. To permanently delete the data, press Delete.

[Delete] [Cancel]

Figure 4-4: Workbook with one remaining sheet

	A	B	C	D	E	F
1	**Powder Trails Resort Helicopter Ski Tours**					
2	*Projected Sales: First Quarter 2004*					
3			Helicopter			
4		Sky Master	Whirlygig	Big Bertha	Totals	
5	REVENUE					
6	Average Cost Per Guest	$ 140	$ 150	$ 220		
7	Total Number of Guests	4800	3000	7200	5672	
8	**Total Helicopter Trip Revenue**	$ 672,000	$ 450,000	$ 1,584,000	$ 2,706,000	
9						
10	EXPENSES					
11	Number of Tours Available	120	150	100		
12	Operating Cost per Helicopter	$ 4,300	$ 3,800	$ 7,400		
13	Total Operating Costs	$ 516,000	$ 570,000	$ 740,000	$ 1,826,000	
14	Advertising Costs	$ 8,500	$ 7,000	$ 8,000	$ 23,500	
15	**Total Expenses**	$ 524,500	$ 577,000	$ 748,000	$ 1,849,500	
16						
17	NET REVENUE	$ 147,500	$ (127,000)	$ 836,000	$ 856,500	
18						
19						
20						
21						
22						
23						
24						

◄ ◄ ► ►◄ \ **1st Quarter** /

Ready

One remaining sheet tab

Skill Set 4
Modifying Workbooks

Modify Worksheet Names and Positions
Moving Worksheets within a Workbook

In a workbook with multiple sheets, you may need to move a worksheet to make the workbook structure clear. You can drag sheets to a new position or use the sheet tab shortcut menu. A word of caution: *In workbooks where formulas contain references to other sheets, always recheck your formulas carefully after moving sheets. Moving sheets can make formula results inaccurate.*

Step 1
You may want to use one worksheet as the basis for another worksheet. To create a copy of a worksheet, click its sheet tab, then press and hold [Ctrl] as you drag the worksheet tab. Excel places a copy called [worksheet-name](2) in the new location.

Activity Steps

 open Commissions01.xls

1. Position the pointer over the **January sheet tab**

2. Press and hold down the mouse button, then drag the pointer left until the pointers 🖑 and ▼ are before the February sheet *See Figure 4-5.*

3. Release the mouse button
   The worksheet is repositioned before the February sheet tab.

 close Commissions01.xls

Skill 2

Modify Worksheet Names and Positions

Figure 4-5: Dragging a sheet to a new location

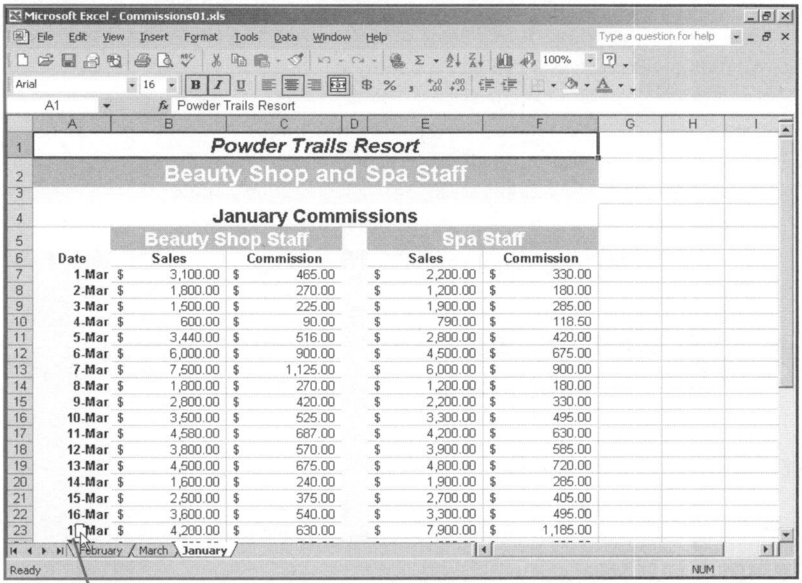

Powder Trails Resort				
Beauty Shop and Spa Staff				
January Commissions				
	Beauty Shop Staff		Spa Staff	
Date	Sales	Commission	Sales	Commission
1-Mar	$ 3,100.00	$ 465.00	$ 2,200.00	$ 330.00
2-Mar	$ 1,800.00	$ 270.00	$ 1,200.00	$ 180.00
3-Mar	$ 1,500.00	$ 225.00	$ 1,900.00	$ 285.00
4-Mar	$ 600.00	$ 90.00	$ 790.00	$ 118.50
5-Mar	$ 3,440.00	$ 516.00	$ 2,800.00	$ 420.00
6-Mar	$ 6,000.00	$ 900.00	$ 4,500.00	$ 675.00
7-Mar	$ 7,500.00	$ 1,125.00	$ 6,000.00	$ 900.00
8-Mar	$ 1,800.00	$ 270.00	$ 1,200.00	$ 180.00
9-Mar	$ 2,800.00	$ 420.00	$ 2,200.00	$ 330.00
10-Mar	$ 3,500.00	$ 525.00	$ 3,300.00	$ 495.00
11-Mar	$ 4,580.00	$ 687.00	$ 4,200.00	$ 630.00
12-Mar	$ 3,800.00	$ 570.00	$ 3,900.00	$ 585.00
13-Mar	$ 4,500.00	$ 675.00	$ 4,800.00	$ 720.00
14-Mar	$ 1,600.00	$ 240.00	$ 1,900.00	$ 285.00
15-Mar	$ 2,500.00	$ 375.00	$ 2,700.00	$ 405.00
16-Mar	$ 3,600.00	$ 540.00	$ 3,300.00	$ 495.00
17-Mar	$ 4,200.00	$ 630.00	$ 7,900.00	$ 1,185.00

Triangle shows new worksheet location

extra!

Moving or copying worksheets from other workbooks

When you want to move or copy a worksheet from another workbook into the current workbook, you can use the Move or Copy dialog box. Open the destination workbook, then open the source workbook containing the sheet you want. Right-click the sheet you want to copy or move, then on the shortcut menu, click **Move or Copy**. Click the **To book list arrow**, click the name of the workbook where you want the sheet, click the sheet name before which you want the new sheet, then click **OK**. *If you have formulas that use values from other sheets, check them carefully after you move or copy sheets; their results may become inaccurate.*

Skill Set 4
Modifying Workbooks

Modify Worksheet Names and Positions
Name Worksheets

Excel worksheets have default names such as Sheet1, Sheet2, and so forth. In a workbook containing multiple worksheets, it is helpful to name sheets so you can easily find the data they contain. The worksheet name should reflect its content; for example, each sheet could have the name of the appropriate month, year, sales rep, or product. A name can contain up to 31 characters and must be unique. As you type the new name, the sheet tab automatically widens to accommodate it. While long sheet names are informative, they can make it necessary to use the sheet scroll buttons to display other sheets. In a workbook with many sheets, it's best to keep sheet names short.

Step 1
You can also click Format on the menu bar, point to Sheet, then click Rename to highlight the existing sheet name.

Activity Steps

 open Payroll02.xls

1. Double-click the **Sheet2 tab**
   See Figure 4-6.

2. Type **July**

3. Press **[Enter]**
   See Figure 4-7.

 close Payroll02.xls

Figure 4-6: Highlighted sheet name

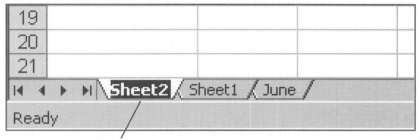

Sheet ready for renaming

Figure 4-7: Renamed sheet

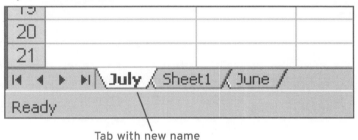

Tab with new name

Skill Set 4
Modifying Workbooks

Modify Worksheet Names and Positions
Shading Worksheet Tabs

In a multi-sheet workbook, you might want to visually differentiate worksheets from one another. Excel lets you do so by adding color to worksheet tabs. You could, for example, shade income sheets one color and expense sheets another. When a sheet is selected, only a strip at the bottom of the tab appears in color. If you assign a dark color, Excel automatically changes the type to white so it is readable.

To remove color from a tab, right-click the tab, click Tab Color, click No Color, then click OK.

Activity Steps

 open Bikes01.xls

1. Right-click the **2003 sheet tab**

2. Click **Tab Color**

3. Click the **turquoise color** (4ᵗʰ row, 5ᵗʰ from the left), then click **OK**

4. Click the **2004 sheet tab** and observe the color of the 2003 tab

5. Right-click the **2004 sheet tab**, click **Tab Color**, then select the **bright red color** (3ʳᵈ row, leftmost color), then click **OK**

6. Click the **Sheet3 tab**
   See Figure 4-8.

 close Bikes01.xls

Figure 4-8: Tabs with color

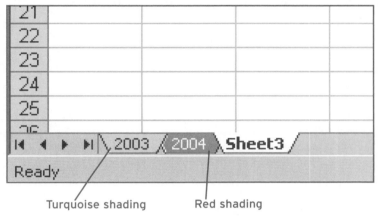

Turquoise shading   Red shading

extra!

Adding a picture as a worksheet background
You can create a sheet background from any graphic you have in electronic form. Click **Format** on the menu bar, point to **Sheet**, then click **Background**. Use the **Look in list arrow** and the **Up One Level arrow** to locate a graphic, select it, then click **Insert**. You may need to shade cells so their contents appear against the background. You can use a variety of picture file formats, including .jpeg, .wmf, and .gif. Background patterns do not print. If your background picture is small, Excel will insert multiple copies on the worksheet background.

Skill Set 4
Modifying Workbooks

Use 3-D References
Create Formulas using 3-D References to the Same Cell

Excel lets you analyze data using information from multiple worksheets in one formula. Because values from other sheets create a third "dimension" in workbooks, they are called **3-D references**; a formula that uses such references is called a **3-D formula**. You can use 3-D formulas to **consolidate**, or gather, data from multiple sheets. For example, a formula that sums the values in cell A6 on several sheets is preceded by a range of worksheet names separated by a colon, followed by the cell reference, as in =SUM(Sheet1:Sheet4!A6). The 3-D reference in parentheses adds the values in cell A6 on Sheets 1 through 4, including Sheets 2 and 3. The exclamation point (!) is called an **external reference indicator**; it separates the sheet name from the cell reference.

Step 2
You can also click the first sheet, type : (a colon), then click the last sheet to enter the range that includes the first, last, and all sheets in between.

Activity Steps

 open Guests02.xls

1. Click cell **B3** then type **=SUM(**

2. Click the **Europe sheet tab**, press and hold [**Shift**], then click the **North America sheet tab**

3. Click cell **B3**
   See Figure 4-9.

4. Type **)** (a closing parenthesis), then click the **Enter** button ☑ on the Formula bar
   The formula in cell B3 of the Summary sheet sums the 1999 figures for the 0-5 years age group in Europe, Asia, and North America.

5. Drag the fill handle from cell **B3** on the Summary sheet through cell **F3**

6. Click cell **F3**, then read its formula
   See Figure 4-10.
   The formulas in the copied cells retain the references to the supporting worksheets.

 close Guests02.xls

Figure 4-9: Formula using a 3-D reference

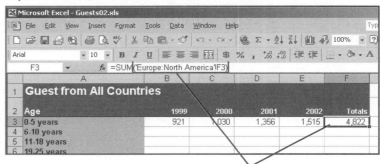

Microsoft Excel - Guests02.xls

File Edit View Insert Format Tools Data Window Help   Type a question for help

Arial   10   B I U

SUM   =SUM('Europe:North America'!B3

1 Guests from Europe

Age	1999	2000	2001	2002	Totals
0-5 years	60	54	62	103	279
6-10 years	SUM(number1, [number2], ...)	96	130	432
11-18 years	120	98	120	130	468
19-25 years	150	120	125	150	545
26-40 years	75	65	96	180	416
41-50 years	62	32	36	65	195
50+ years	63	62	74	96	295
Total	650	517	609	854	2,630

Summary **Europe** Asia North America

Point   NUM

Screen tip shows function structure   3-D reference to cell B3 on three worksheets

Figure 4-10: Copied formula with 3-D references

Microsoft Excel - Guests02.xls

File Edit View Insert Format Tools Data Window Help

Arial   10   B I U $ %

F3   =SUM('Europe:North America'!F3)

1 Guest from All Countries

Age	1999	2000	2001	2002	Totals
0-5 years	921	1,030	1,356	1,515	4,822
6-10 years					
11-18 years					
19-25 years					

Copied formula also contains 3-D reference

Skill Set 4
Modifying Workbooks

Use 3-D References
Create Formulas Using 3-D References to Different Cells

In Excel, **3-D references** are cell references that refer to a sheet other than the current sheet. A 3-D formula uses 3-D references to **consolidate**, or collect, data from other worksheets. A 3-D formula can use data from the same cell in different worksheets, but it can also use data from different cells in other worksheets. An example of such a reference might be =SUM(Sheet1!A5,Sheet2!B6,), which adds the values of cell A5 on Sheet1 and cell B6 on Sheet2. *If you delete sheets in the range you reference, be sure to recheck your formulas; a #REF! Error indicates a missing value in the formula.*

Step 5
To drag more than one sheet, press and hold [Ctrl], select the sheets you want to move, release [Ctrl], then drag the sheets.

Activity Steps

 open Guests03.xls

1. Click cell **B3** then type **=SUM(**
2. Click the **Europe sheet tab**, click cell **B10**, then type **,** (a comma)
   See Figure 4-11.
3. Click the **Asia sheet tab**, click cell **B7**, then type **,**
4. Click the **North America sheet tab**, click cell **B6**, then type **)**
5. Click the **Enter button** on the Formula bar
   See Figure 4-12.
6. With cell B3 selected, drag the fill handle to cell **G3** then click cell **E3**
   The formulas in the copied cells retain the references to the supporting worksheets.

 close Guests03.xls

Figure 4-11: Beginning the 3-D formula

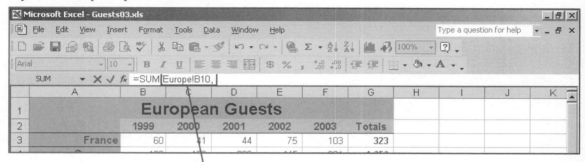

3-D reference to cell B10 on Europe sheet

Figure 4-12: Completed 3-D formula

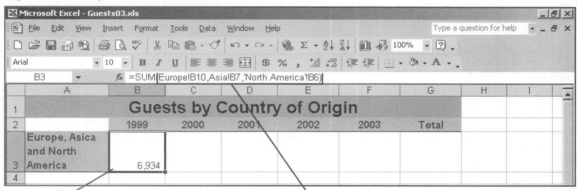

3-D formula result   3-D reference to different cells on different sheets

Skill Set 4

Modifying Workbooks

Target Your Skills

 open Rentals02.xls

1 Follow the instructions of Figure 4-13 to produce the results shown in the figure.

Figure 4-13

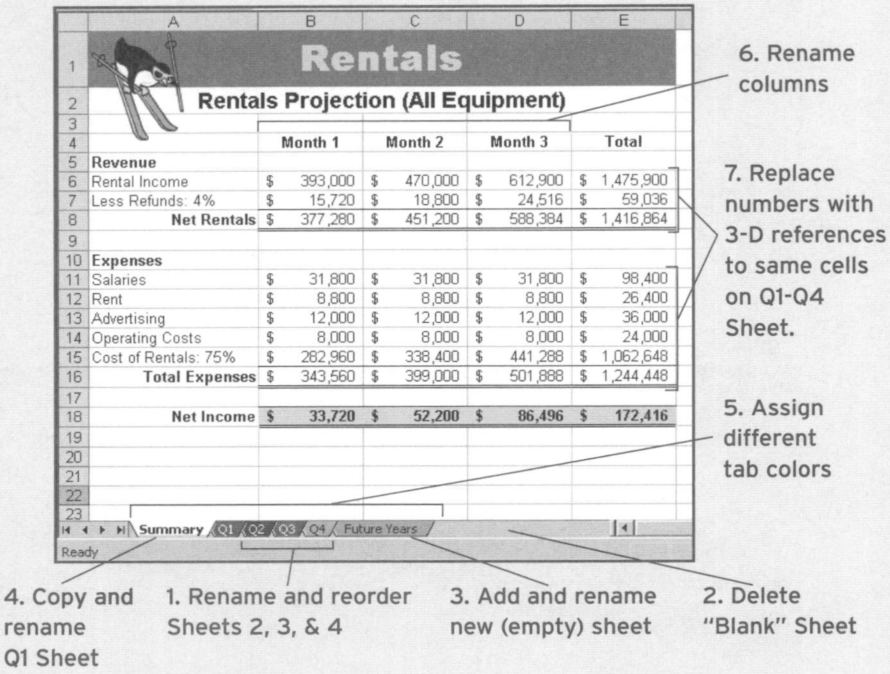

6. Rename columns

7. Replace numbers with 3-D references to same cells on Q1-Q4 Sheet.

5. Assign different tab colors

4. Copy and rename Q1 Sheet

1. Rename and reorder Sheets 2, 3, & 4

3. Add and rename new (empty) sheet

2. Delete "Blank" Sheet

 open Tours02.xls

2 Create formulas in cells B9:C10 that calculate the totals shown in Figure 4-14, using 3-D references to the appropriate figures on the Cross-Country sheet.

Figure 4-14

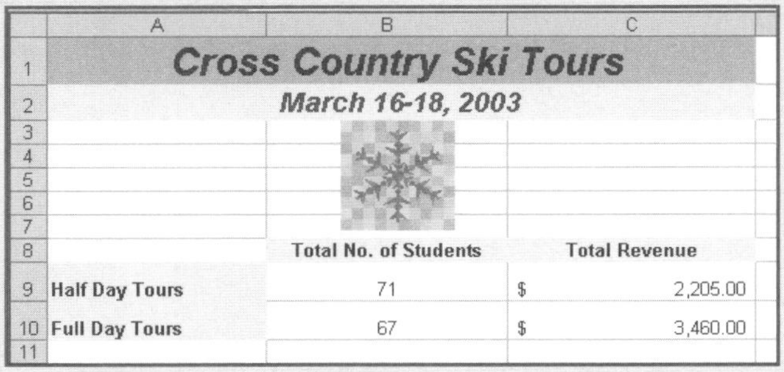

Skill List

1. Create and revise formulas
2. Use statistical, date and time, financial, and logical functions in formulas

The power of Excel lies in its ability to calculate results using the information you enter into a worksheet. You enter **formulas** that tell Excel what type of calculation to perform on which values. Formula results are "tied to" the values they use; when you change the underlying values, Excel instantly recalculates the results. Automatic recalculation saves time and lets you perform basic "what-if" analyses. For example, you can change a price that is used in a profit formula, and immediately see the effect of the new price on profits.

You can enter and edit formulas for any selected cell in the Formula bar. Cell references in formulas tell Excel which values to use; you can type cell references or you can click cells and drag across cell ranges. When you copy formulas to different cells, you can control whether you want the cell references to adjust to their new locations or always refer to the same cells.

You can create your own formulas or use built-in formulas called **functions** that help you perform more complex calculations easily. A series of dialog boxes called the Function Wizard helps you enter each part of the function. Excel contains functions for many common calculations, such as calculating totals, minimum or maximum values, and payments. You can even instruct Excel to enter one result if certain conditions are true and another result if they are not.

Skill Set 5

Creating and Revising Formulas

Create and Revise Formulas

Create Formulas Using the Formula Bar

Excel formulas contain numbers or values, **operators** such as +, -, *, or /, and **cell references**, which are addresses such as A6 or X11. Excel formulas must begin with an equal sign (=). You can enter a formula for a selected cell in the **Formula bar**, the white box above the worksheet column headings. As you enter formulas, you can either type cell references or you can click a worksheet cell to insert a reference. Excel calculates formulas with more than one operator, according to the **order of precedence**, in the following order: 1) calculations inside parentheses; 2) exponents; 3) multiplication and division; then 4) addition and subtraction.

Activity Steps

 open Markdowns03.xls

Step 3
You can also enter a formula or value by pressing [Enter] or [Tab] on the keyboard. Pressing [Enter] moves the active cell down one row, while pressing [Tab] moves it one cell to the right.

1. Click cell **G8**, then click in the Formula bar

2. Type **=**, click cell **E8**, type **-** (a minus sign), type **(**, click cell **F8**, type *****, click cell **E8**, then type **)**
   As you enter each cell reference, the cell becomes surrounded by a moving dotted line, called a **marquee**, so you can easily see the reference.
   See Figure 5-1.
   Your formula multiplies the Original Price by the Markdown percentage to obtain the markdown amount. Then it subtracts the markdown amount from the Original Price to calculate the Sale Price.

3. Click the **Enter button** ☑ on the Formula bar
   The formula result, $716, appears in cell G8.

4. Click cell **E8**, type **900**, then click the **Enter button** ☑ on the Formula bar
   See Figure 5-2.
   Excel automatically recalculates the formula with the new original price and changes the Sale Price from $716 to $720.

 close Markdowns03.xls

Figure 5-1: Markdown formula in Formula bar

Formula appears in Formula bar

Cell reference in formula matches cell outline color

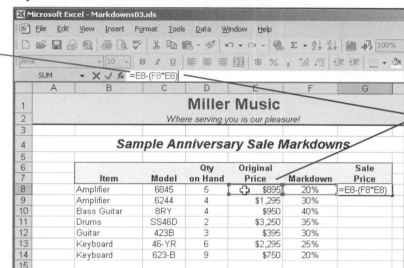

Figure 5-2: Recalculated formula after changing referenced value

Recalculated formula result

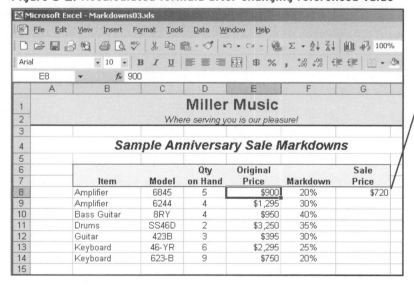

Skill Set 5

Creating and Revising Formulas

Create and Revise Formulas
Edit Formulas Using the Formula Bar

After you enter a formula, you can change it at any time. After selecting the cell containing the formula, you can edit values, cell references, or operators in the Formula bar. You can drag to select values, references, or operators, then type replacements; you can also use [Backspace] and [Delete]. To add to the formula, click the place in the formula where you want to add information, then type or click to enter the new data. In this activity you'll edit a cell to correct an error in a formula.

Step 1
Instead of editing a formula in the Formula bar, you can edit it directly in its cell (called *in-cell editing*) by double-clicking the cell.

Activity Steps

 open Tickets01.xls

1. Click cell **E11**
   The formula in cell E11 has an error. Instead of multiplying the number of concert tickets in cell D11 by the Concert Ticket price in cell C6, the formula multiplies it by the Folk Festival price in cell C5.

2. Move the pointer over the Formula bar until the pointer becomes the **I-beam pointer** Ⅰ

3. On the right side of the formula, drag to select the **5** in the C5 cell reference
   See Figure 5-3.

4. Type **6**

5. Click the **Enter button** ☑ on the Formula bar
   The formula now calculates the total sales of both ticket types for the first employee.
   See Figure 5-4.

 close Tickets01.xls

Figure 5-3: Incorrect cell reference selected in Formula bar

Incorrect
reference
selected in
Formula bar

I-beam
pointer

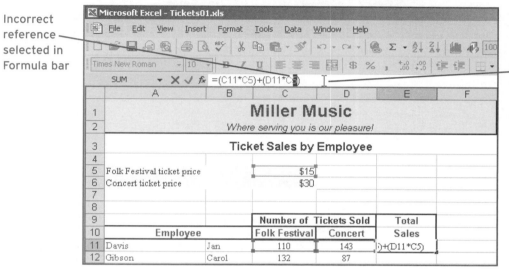

Figure 5-4: Corrected formula

Formula now
contains
correct
references

Formula
result now
correct

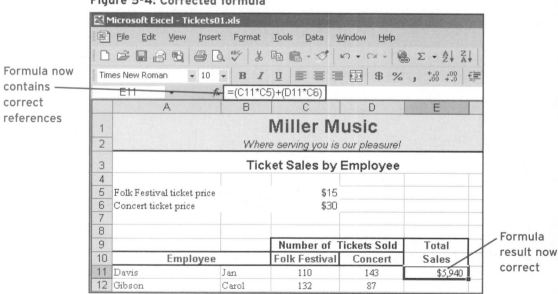

Skill Set 5

Creating and Revising Formulas

Create and Revise Formulas
Enter a Range in a Formula by Dragging

As you enter formulas, you will often enter references to cell ranges. Instead of entering each cell in a formula, such as =A6+A7+A8+A9, you can use a **range reference**, consisting of references to the first and last cell in a range separated by a colon, such as A6:A9. A range reference includes the first and last cells in the reference and all the cells in between them. You can type a range reference, but it is often easier and more accurate to drag across the range. You will start entering the function by typing directly in the cell; you will see the formula in the Formula bar as you type.

Step 4
You don't have to type the closing parenthesis at the end of a formula. After you click the Enter button on the Formula bar, or after you press [Enter] on the keyboard, Excel inserts the closing parenthesis automatically.

Activity Steps

 open Advertising03.xls

1. Click cell **C19**

2. Type **=SUM(**

3. Click cell **B8** and hold the mouse button, then drag to select the range **B8:D10**
   See Figure 5-5.

4. Type **)**

5. Click the **Enter button** ☑ on the Formula bar

6. Use the same techniques to enter the formula **=SUM(B12:D14)** in cell **C21**
   See Figure 5-6.

 close Advertising03.xls

Figure 5-5: Dragging to select the range for the SUM formula

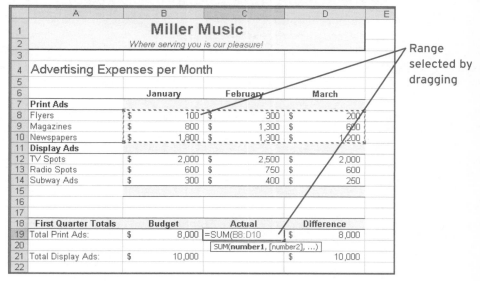

Range selected by dragging

Figure 5-6: Formula showing range reference you entered by dragging

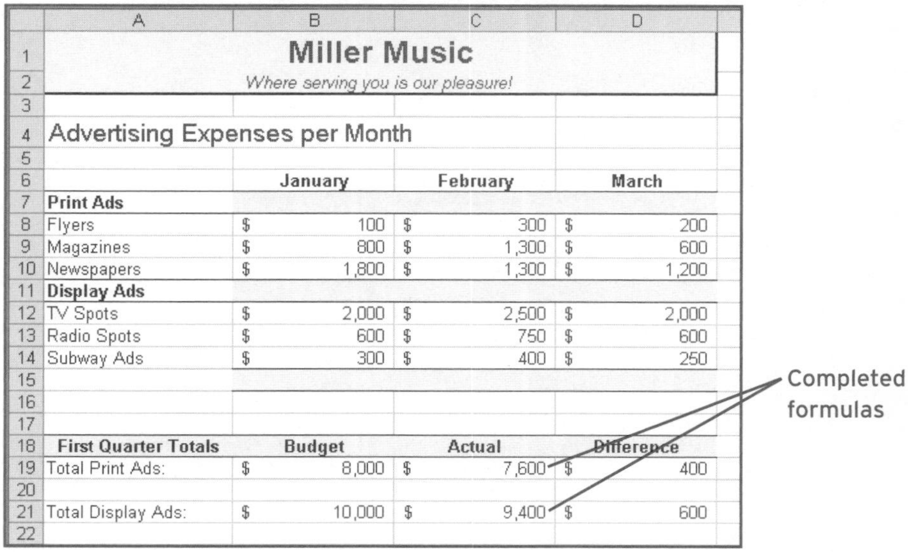

Completed formulas

Skill Set 5
Creating and Revising Formulas

Create and Revise Formulas
Use Relative References in Formulas

When you enter a cell reference in a formula, Excel automatically makes it a relative reference. A **relative reference** adjusts when you copy and paste the formula in a new location. For example, if you enter =A1+B1 in cell C1, then copy the formula to cell C2, the copied formula will automatically read =A2+B2. Excel uses references to cells *relative to* the cell containing the formula.

Step 2
You could also copy the formula by using the Copy and Paste buttons on the Standard toolbar or by pressing [Ctrl][C] on the keyboard, then using the Paste or Paste Special commands on the Edit menu.

Activity Steps

open Tickets02.xls

1. Click cell **C19**
   See Figure 5-7.
   The Formula bar shows that the formula adds the values in the range C11:C18.

2. Drag the **fill handle** on cell **C19** to the right, across cell D19

3. Click cell **D19**
   The Formula bar now reads D11:D18, showing that Excel is using a relative reference to calculate the results of the copied formula.
   See Figure 5-8.

close Tickets02.xls

Figure 5-7: Original formula adds the values in column C

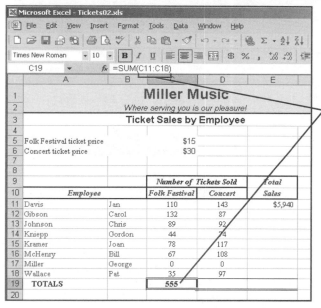

Formula in Formula bar calculates total of range in column C

Figure 5-8: Copied formula automatically adds the values in column D

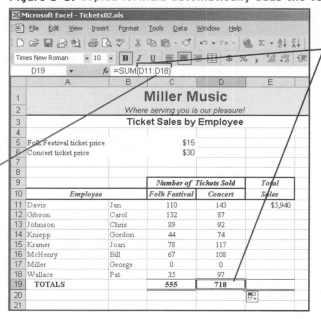

Copied formula totals range in appropriate column because of relative referencing

Column letter automatically adjusted in copied formula

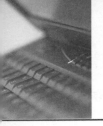

Skill Set 5
Creating and Revising Formulas

Create and Revise Formulas
Use Absolute References in Formulas

When you use cell references in copied formulas, you will sometimes want Excel to refer to a specific cell, regardless of the formula's location. In these cases, you use an **absolute reference**, which uses dollar signs before the row letter and column number. For example, the formula =A2*$A$1 will always multiply the first formula value by the value in cell A1, no matter where the formula is located. The [F4] key changes selected references to absolute references.

Activity Steps

 open Tickets03.xls

1. Click cell **E11**
   In the next step you will intentionally create incorrect formulas.

2. Drag the **fill handle** on cell **E11** down to cell **E18** and observe the formula results
   See Figure 5-9.
   The results are incorrect because Excel automatically made the references to cell C5 and C6 relative references. You want them always to refer to the ticket prices in cells C5 and C6, so you will make them absolute references.

Step 2
Repeatedly pressing [F4] cycles through the cell reference possibilities, from C5, $C$5, C$5, $C5, then back to C5.

3. Click cell **E11**, then double-click the reference to cell **C5** in the Formula bar, then press **[F4]**
   Excel inserts dollar signs before the row and column number, indicating that they are now absolute references.

4. Double-click the reference to cell **C6** in the Formula bar, press **[F4]**, then click the **Enter button** in the Formula bar

5. Drag the **fill handle** on cell **E11** down to copy the corrected formula into the range **E11:E18**, then observe the results

6. Click cell **E16** to deselect the range, then notice that the absolute references remain the same in the copied formulas
   See Figure 5-10.

 close Tickets03.xls

---

extra!

Using mixed references
Sometimes you will need to keep a row reference absolute while making a column reference relative, or vice versa. In these cases, you use a **mixed reference**. A mixed reference contains a dollar sign before either the row or column reference, but not both. The mixed reference $A3 will always refer to column A, but will adjust row references as necessary. A$3 will always refer to row three, but will adjust columns as necessary.

Figure 5-9: Copied formulas are incorrect because ticket price references are relative

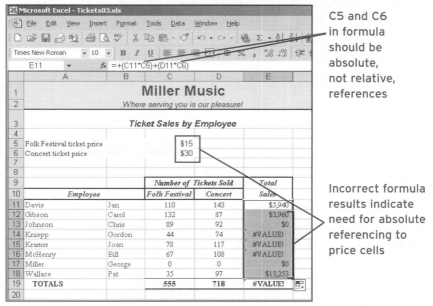

C5 and C6
in formula
should be
absolute,
not relative,
references

Incorrect formula
results indicate
need for absolute
referencing to
price cells

Figure 5-10: Copied formulas now correct with absolute references to ticket prices

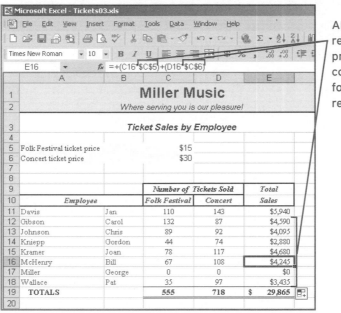

Absolute
references
produce
correct
formula
results

Skill Set 5
Creating and Revising Formulas

Use Statistical, Date and Time, Financial, and Logical Functions in Formulas
Create a Formula Using the SUM Function

A **function** is a predefined formula that comes with Excel. You can use functions alone or in other formulas. A function always has the following form: `=[functionname](argument1,argument2…)`. The function name describes what the function does; it occurs immediately before the arguments in parentheses, with no space after it. The **arguments** are references to the values the function should act on. For example, the SUM function =SUM(A2,A3) totals the values in the cells A2 through A3. You can type a function or use the **Function Wizard**, a series of dialog boxes that lets you search for a function and then prompts you for each function argument. Table 5-1 shows an overview of Excel function categories and some of their related functions.

Step 2
Because the SUM function is so commonly used, Excel supplies an AutoSum button ∑ on the Standard toolbar; click it once to automatically insert the SUM function into the selected cell; drag to select another range, if necessary, then press [Enter].

Activity Steps

 open Update03.xls

1. Click cell B17

2. Click the **Insert Function button** fx on the Formula bar
   In the "Search for a function" box, you can describe the task you want to complete, then Excel will search for an appropriate function.

3. In the Search for a function text box, type **total**, then click **Go**

4. In the Select a function list, click **SUM (if it's not already selected), then click OK**
   Excel "guesses" that you want to sum the range immediately above the function, B8:B16.

5. Click the **Number 1 Collapse dialog box button**, confirm that B8:B16 is entered in the Number 1 text box, then click the **Redisplay dialog box button**
   Excel places a preliminary result at the bottom of the dialog box. *See Figure 5-11.*

6. Click **OK**

7. Drag the **fill handle** on cell B17 to include the range **C17:E17**

 close Update03.xls

Figure 5-11: Function Arguments dialog box

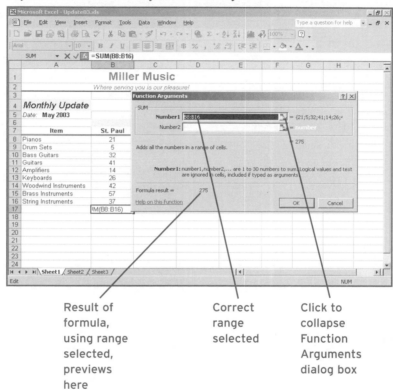

Result of formula, using range selected, previews here

Correct range selected

Click to collapse Function Arguments dialog box

Table 5-1: Excel function overview

function category	examples of functions	use for
Financial	PMT, PV, FV	Analyzing purchases and investments
Date and Time	DATE, TODAY, WEEKDAY	Schedules and calculations based on time
Math and Trig	SUM, TAN, COS	Mathematical calculations
Statistical	AVER, COUNT, MEDIAN, MODE, CHITEST	Summarizing and analyzing numeric data
Logical	IF, AND, FALSE	Testing data against conditions

Skill Set 5
Creating and Revising Formulas

Use Statistical, Date and Time, Financial, and Logical Functions in Formulas
Create Formulas Using the MIN and MAX Functions

MIN and **MAX** are statistical functions. The MIN function finds and displays the lowest, or minimum, value in a range. The MAX function finds and displays the highest, or maximum, value in a range. You might use these functions to determine the highest or lowest price, salary, or grade in a worksheet column, row, or other range. These functions are especially useful in large worksheets, where you would have to scroll repeatedly and scan many numbers to locate such information.

Step 2
As you enter functions, you will sometimes see a Function ScreenTip containing the function name and the correct syntax. Click the function name in the tip to open a Help screen about that function.

Activity Steps

 open Practice01.xls

1. Click cell **H38**

2. Click the **Insert Function button** on the Formula bar
   Instead of searching for a function, you can display a list of function categories, then choose the one you want.

3. Click the **Or select a category list arrow**, then click **Statistical**

4. Scroll down the Select a function list, click **MIN**, then click **OK**

5. Click the **Number 1 Collapse dialog box button**, move the reduced dialog box so you can see the contents of column H, then use the vertical scroll arrow to view rows 38 through 40

6. Compare the range in the Function Arguments dialog box to the worksheet range
   See Figure 5-12.
   You need to adjust the range

7. In the Function Arguments dialog box, edit the reference to cell **H37** to **H36**, then press **[Enter]** twice

8. In cell H40, type **=MAX(H10:H36)**, then click the **Enter button** on the Formula bar
   See Figure 5-13.

 close Practice01.xls

Figure 5-12: Correcting a range in the Function Arguments dialog box

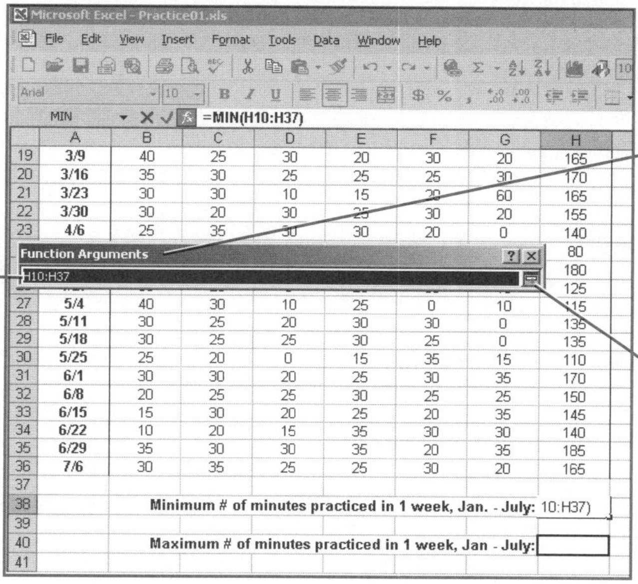
Microsoft Excel - Practice01.xls
=MIN(H10:H37)
Function Arguments
H10:H37
Minimum # of minutes practiced in 1 week, Jan. - July:
Maximum # of minutes practiced in 1 week, Jan - July:
Range Excel inserted by default
Collapsed Function Arguments dialog box lets you see more worksheet area
Click to redisplay Function Arguments dialog box

Figure 5-13: Worksheet with minimum and maximum statistics

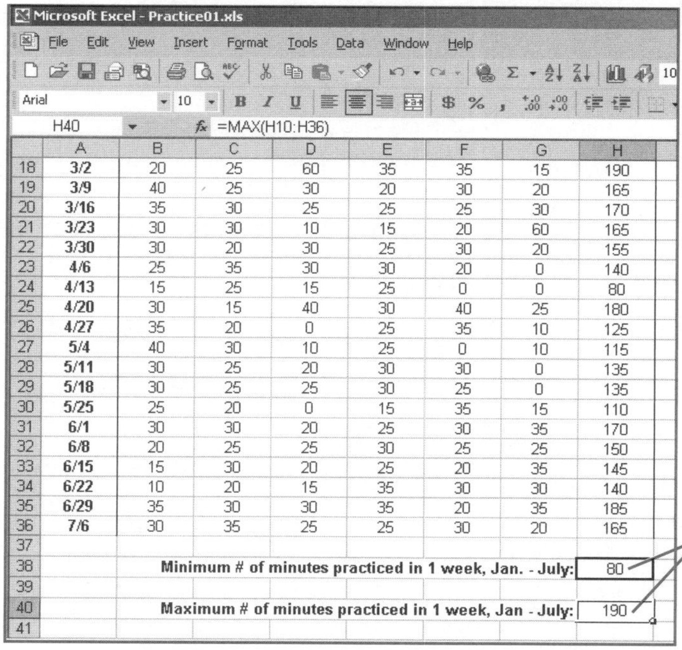
Microsoft Excel - Practice01.xls
H40
=MAX(H10:H36)
Minimum # of minutes practiced in 1 week, Jan. - July: 80
Maximum # of minutes practiced in 1 week, Jan - July: 190
Functions calculate minimum and maximum practice minutes in range H10:H36

Skill Set 5

Creating and Revising Formulas

Use Statistical, Date and Time, Financial, and Logical Functions in Formulas
Use the DATE Function in Formulas

You can use the DATE functions in calculations, for example, to calculate the amount of time worked, days elapsed, and so forth. The DATE function has the syntax DATE(year,month,day). Excel stores dates as serial numbers so they can be used in calculations. The numbers represent the number of days from 1/1/1900. For example, the date 12/15/2003 is stored as 37,970. If you see a serial number instead of a date, you can format it using a Date format to see the date itself.

If you type a date in a cell that has already been formatted using the General format, Excel will automatically format it as a date.

Activity Steps

 open Employment01.xls

1. Click cell **D8**

2. Click the **Insert Function button** [fx] on the Formula bar

3. In the Search for a function box, type **date**, then click **Go**

4. In the Select a function list, click **DATE**, then click **OK**

5. Type the following values in their respective text boxes, in the Function Arguments dialog box, pressing [**Tab**] after typing each value: Year: **2001**, Month: **12**, Day: **5**, then click **OK**

6. Repeat the procedure in cell **E8** but use the following values: Year: **2003**, Month: **10**, Day: **15**, then click **OK**

7. Click cell **F8**, type **=E8-D8**, then click the **Enter button** [✓] on the Formula bar
   The formula result is formatted as a date.

8. Click **Format** on the menu bar, click **Cells**, in the Category list, click **General**, then click **OK**
   See Figure 5-14.

 close Employment01.xls

Figure 5-14: Number of days calculated by subtracting two cells containing the DATE function

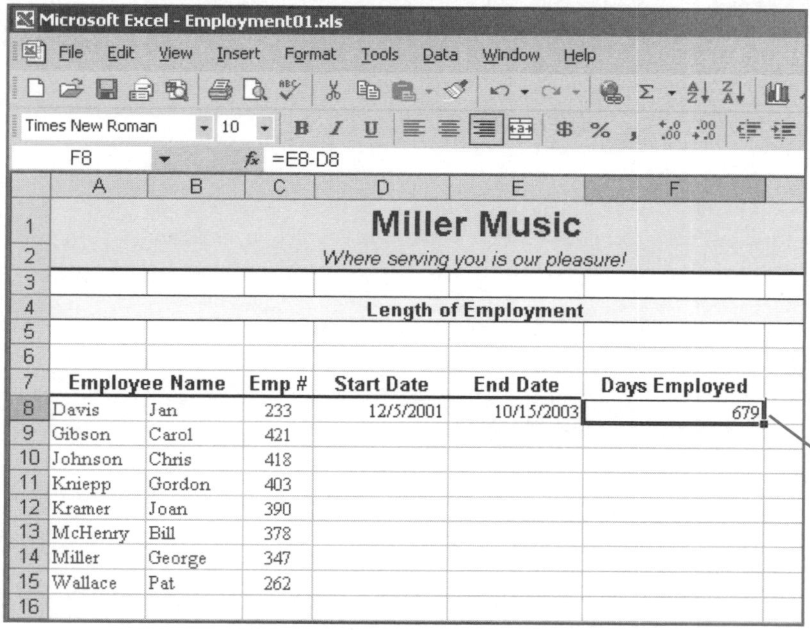

Calculates number of days between Start Date and End Date

extra!

Using the NOW function

The NOW function is an Excel Date and Time function that inserts today's date and time in a worksheet cell. It has no arguments. In the Insert Function dialog box, select the **Date & Time category**, double-click **NOW**, then click **OK**. Excel inserts today's date and time in the selected cell. The NOW function date and time are updated when you reopen the worksheet or any time you press [F9].

Skill Set 5

Creating and Revising Formulas

Use Statistical, Date and Time, Financial, and Logical Functions in Formulas
Use the PMT Function in Formulas

The PMT (payment) function is a financial function that calculates the periodic payment on a loan of a given amount, using a given interest rate and time period. Its syntax is `PMT(rate,nper,pv,fv,type)`, where **rate** is the interest rate per period, **nper** is the number of periods, and **pv** is the present value of the loan. The last two arguments are optional: *fv* (future value) calculates the amount you want the loan to be at the end of the payment periods and *type* indicates whether payments occur at the beginning (1) or end (0) of the payment period. The interest rate, time period, and the number of periods must match. In other words, if you use a monthly interest rate, the number of periods must be months.

Step 5

You can show the payment as a positive amount by typing **-** (a minus sign) before the Pv amount in the function. Click the cell containing the function, then edit the function in the Formula bar or double-click the cell and edit directly in the cell.

Activity Steps

  open Computer01.xls

1. Click cell **C11**

2. Click the **Insert Function button** 🔣 on the Formula bar

3. In the Search for a function box, type **payment**, click **Go**, select **PMT** in the Select a function list, then click **OK**

4. Enter the following information in the Function Arguments dialog box:

Rate	.08/12
Nper	18
Pv	1825

   You leave the Fv (future value) box blank because you assume the future value will be zero—the loan will be completely paid off. You leave Type blank so Excel will assume a value of zero—payment at the end of each period.
   See Figure 5-15.

5. Click **OK**
   See Figure 5-16.
   You divide the yearly interest rate by 12 to make it a monthly rate, to match the 18-month loan term. The loan amount is $1,825. The monthly payment shows as a negative number, indicating an outflow of funds.

     close Computer01.xls

Figure 5-15: Insert Function dialog box for the PMT function

Boldface names indicate required arguments

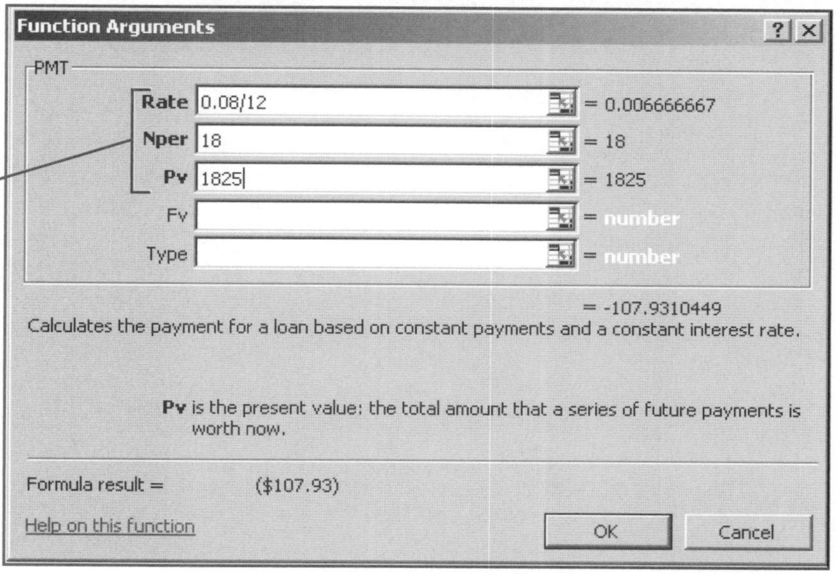

Figure 5-16: Monthly loan payment calculated by the PMT function

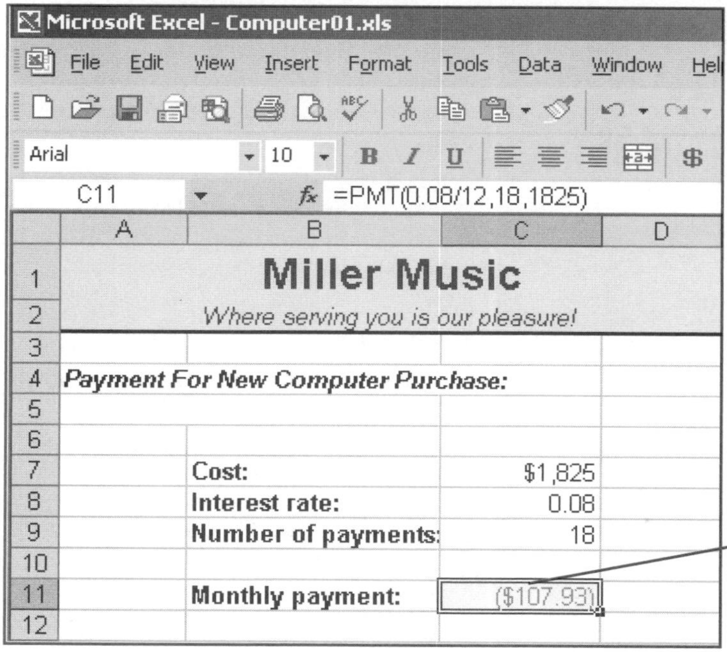

PMT function calculated monthly payment

Skill Set 5
Creating and Revising Formulas

Use Statistical, Date and Time, Financial, and Logical Functions in Formulas
Create Formulas Using the IF Function

The IF function is a logical function that evaluates conditions and calculates a result. Its syntax is `IF(logical_test, value_if_true, value_if_false)`, which you could restate by saying "If condition 1 is true, do X; if it is not, do Y." The **logical text** is the statement Excel uses to determine the function result. To have Excel calculate a 15% bonus if the sales figure in cell A3 exceeds $15,000, the IF function would read: `=IF(A3>15000,(A3*.15),0)`. This function says "If the value in cell A3 is greater than 15,000 (the logical test), multiply that value by .15 and place the calculated amount in this cell (value_if_true); if it does not exceed 15,000, place a zero in this cell (value_if_false)." You can use the comparison operators in Table 5-2 in the logical_test statement.

Step 4
The Function Wizard automatically places quotation marks around the Value_if_true and Value_if_false text, and it places parentheses around the function arguments. If you are typing an IF function directly into a cell, you need to type the quotation marks and opening parenthesis yourself.

Activity Steps

　open Practice02.xls

1. Click cell I10

2. Click the **Insert Function button** 🔣 on the Formula bar

3. Click the **Or select a category list arrow**, click **Logical**, then double-click **IF** in the Select a function list

4. Enter the following information in the Function Arguments dialog box:
Logical_test	H10>120
Value_if_true	OK
Value_if_false	Below average

   You are saying, in effect, "If the student practiced more than 120 minutes during this week, place 'OK' in cell I11; if he practiced less than 120 minutes, place 'Below average' in cell I11."

5. Click **OK**
   See Figure 5-17.

6. Drag the **fill handle** on cell I10 down through cell I36, then click outside the range

7. Double-click the right side of the column I **column heading** to AutoFit the cell contents

　close Practice02.xls

Figure 5-17: Insert Function dialog box for the IF function

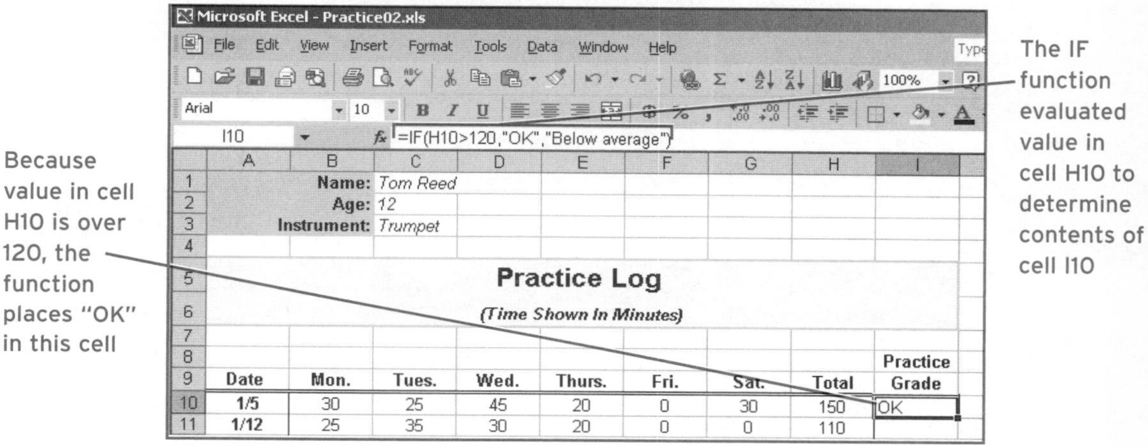

Because value in cell H10 is over 120, the function places "OK" in this cell

The IF function evaluated value in cell H10 to determine contents of cell I10

Table 5-2: Comparison operators for Logical_test statement

operator	meaning
=	Equals
>	Is greater than
<	Is less than
>=	Is greater than or equal to
<=	Is less than or equal to

Skill Set 5

Creating and Revising Formulas

Target Your Skills

 **open Comparison01.xls**

1 Referring to Figure 5-18, use the Formula bar to create the formulas shown. Format values and widen columns as necessary.

Figure 5-18

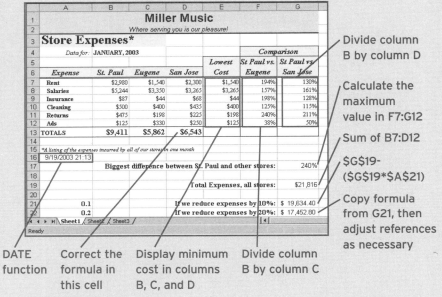

Divide column B by column D

Calculate the maximum value in F7:G12

Sum of B7:D12

$G$19-($G$19*$A$21)

Copy formula from G21, then adjust references as necessary

DATE function

Correct the formula in this cell

Display minimum cost in columns B, C, and D

Divide column B by column C

open Band01.xls

2 Modify the worksheet as shown in Figure 5-19.

Figure 5-19

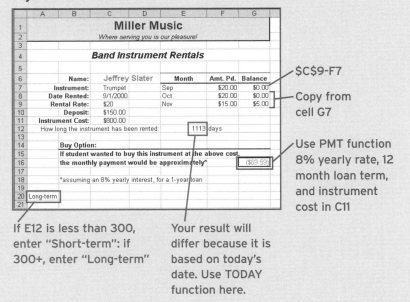

$C$9-F7

Copy from cell G7

Use PMT function 8% yearly rate, 12 month loan term, and instrument cost in C11

If E12 is less than 300, enter "Short-term": if 300+, enter "Long-term"

Your result will differ because it is based on today's date. Use TODAY function here.

Skill List

1. Create, modify, position, and print charts
2. Create, modify, and position graphics

Excel worksheets provide powerful tools to help you analyze your data. To help you see trends and communicate your analyses to others, Excel lets you present your data as 2-dimensional or 3-dimensional charts (sometimes called **graphs**), which summarize your data in the form of a picture. The **Chart Wizard** is a series of dialog boxes that lets you choose from bar, line, pie, scatter, and other types of charts to create the most meaningful picture of your data.

Once you create a chart, you can readily change it to find the chart type that best communicates your information. For example, you might create a bar chart and then, on viewing it, decide that a column chart would be more appropriate. You can change the way your chart looks by adding or deleting labels, legends, or gridlines, or format chart text and graphics for a customized look.

You can place a chart on the worksheet containing the data you used to create it (also called the source data), or on its own worksheet, called a **chart sheet**. A chart is linked to the worksheet you used to create it, so if you change the underlying worksheet data, the chart changes automatically.

You can easily add and modify **graphics**, such as arrows, shapes, text blocks, and drawings to your worksheets and charts to enhance their appearance and draw attention to important trends.

Skill Set 6

Creating and Modifying Graphics

Create, Modify, Position, and Print Charts
Create and Modify a Pie Chart

A **pie chart** displays a data series as pieces of a pie. A **data series** is a group of related data, such as store sales for several departments. Each pie slice is a **data marker** that represents one worksheet cell. As a whole, the pie chart visually compares the contribution of each slice, or portion of data, which is called a **data point**. A pie chart is used only for a single data series.

Activity Steps

 open Sitecost02.xls

1. Drag to select the cell range **A4: B9**

2. Click the **Chart Wizard button** on the Standard toolbar, click the **Standard Types tab**, then under Chart type, click **Pie**

3. Click the middle Chart sub-type in the top row, then click and hold the **"Press and Hold to View Sample" button**
   See Figure 6-1.

4. Release the mouse button, click **Next**, verify that the data range is the range you selected, then click **Next**

5. Click after the text in the Chart title box, press **[Spacebar]**, type **Web Costs**, then Click **Next**

6. Click the **"As object in" option button**, then click **Finish**
   Excel places the chart on the current worksheet. *See Figure 6-2.* The chart toolbar appears at the bottom of the screen when the chart is selected. (If you don't see it there, click **View** on the menu bar, point to **toolbars**, then click **Chart**.) The "Monthly" column label becomes the chart title.

7. Move the pointer around on the chart, until the ScreenTip reads "Chart Area", click and hold the mouse button, drag the **chart** so its top border is under the data in cell B5, then release the mouse button

8. Click cell **B5**, type **200**, observe the "Cable connection" portion of the pie chart, then press **[Enter]**

9. Click cell **B5**, type **55**, then press **[Enter]**

 close Sitecost02.xls

If you don't see the chart toolbar on your screen, click View on the menu bar, point to Toolbars, then click Chart.

Figure 6-1: Chart Type dialog box in the Chart Wizard

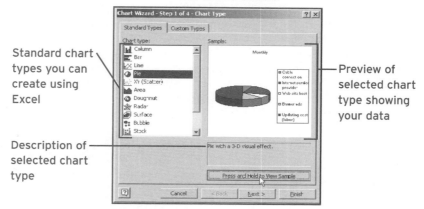

Standard chart types you can create using Excel

Preview of selected chart type showing your data

Description of selected chart type

Figure 6-2: Pie chart

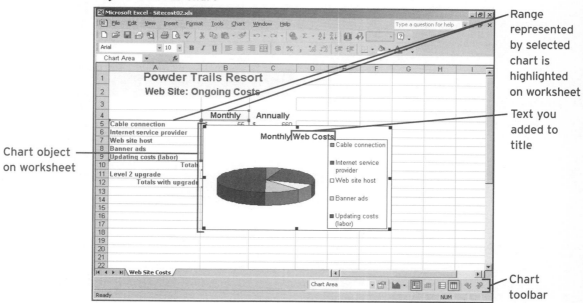

Range represented by selected chart is highlighted on worksheet

Text you added to title

Chart object on worksheet

Chart toolbar

Skill Set 6

Creating and Modifying Graphics

Create, Modify, Position, and Print Charts
Move and Resize a Chart

A chart on a worksheet is an **object**, meaning that you can move and resize it separately from the worksheet. When you resize a chart object, all the chart elements, including text and data markers, automatically adjust to the new chart size. To resize a selected chart, you use its **sizing handles**, the small black squares that surround the selected chart. See Table 6-1 for common chart types.

Step 4
To resize a chart in one direction only, drag the sizing handles on the sides, top, or bottom of the chart area.

Activity Steps

 open Staffing02.xls

1. Move the pointer slowly over different parts of the column chart, reading the ScreenTips that identify each element
   See Table 6-2 for a description of major chart elements.

2. When the ScreenTip reads "Chart Area", click and hold the mouse button, then drag the chart so its top border is under the data, at the top of **row 7**, and its left border is on the left side of **column A**

3. Place the pointer over the chart's **lower right sizing handle** until the pointer becomes ↘

4. Drag down and to the right, until the right side of the chart is at the right side of **column G** and fills row 22
   See Figure 6-3.

   close Staffing02.xls

TABLE 6-1: Common chart types		
type	**looks like**	**used to show**
Column		Data in categories in vertical format
Bar		Data in categories in horizontal format
Line		Data trends over time
Pie		Portions of data in relation to the whole
XY Scatter		Data trends for value pairs
Area		Column changes over time

Figure 6-3: Resizing the chart

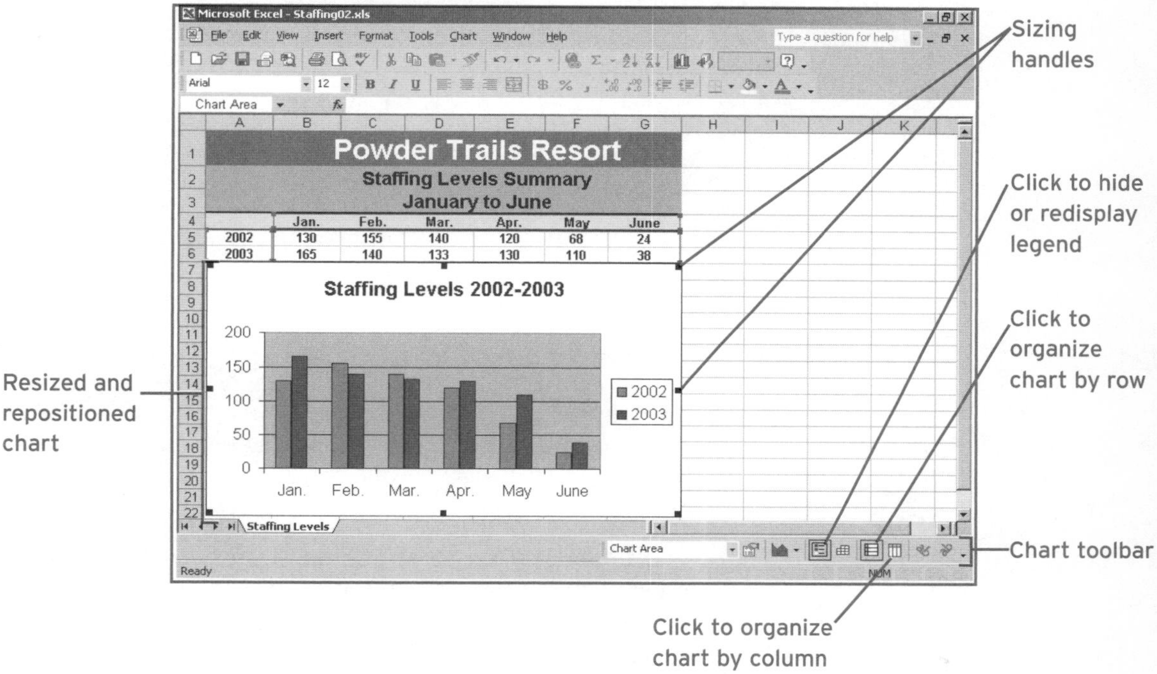

Sizing handles

Click to hide or redisplay legend

Click to organize chart by row

Chart toolbar

Resized and repositioned chart

Click to organize chart by column

TABLE 6-2: Common chart elements

element	what it is
Chart area	The entire chart and its surrounding area; drag this to move a chart
Plot area	The area within the chart axes, where data is plotted
Chart title	The chart name that describes chart content
Legend	Description of the colors assigned to each data point or series
Category axis	Axis that contains the categories being charted
Value axis	Axis that contains the numerical measurements for data points
Major gridlines	The lines behind a chart that help the viewer visually align data points with axis values
Tick marks	Small lines on axes denoting measurement intervals

Skill Set 6

Creating and Modifying Graphics

Create, Modify, Position, and Print Charts
Create a Column Chart

A column chart represents data points as vertical bars. While a pie chart allows you to chart only one series, a column chart lets you plot multiple series, which appear as clusters of vertical bars. The Chart Wizard lets you create the chart, change the data series reference, assign it a title, and specify its location as you create it. When you select worksheet cells to create a chart, you will often need to use [Ctrl] to select **nonadjacent** cells, which are cells located in rows or columns that are not next to each other. You will place this chart on the same sheet as the data.

Activity Steps

 open Resorts01.xls

1. Drag to select the range **A3:A12**

2. Press and hold **[Ctrl]**, then drag to select the range **G3:H12**

3. Click the **Chart Wizard button** on the Standard toolbar

4. Click **Column** (if it is not already selected), click the upper-left Chart sub-type, **Clustered Column**, verify that Clustered Column appears in the lower-right description box, then click **Next**

5. Verify that the ranges in the Data Range box are correct, then click **Next**
   With two columns of data, Excel does not add a default chart title.

6. Click the **Chart title box**, type **Resort Cost Comparison**, then click **Next**

7. Click the **As new sheet option button**, then type **Costs Chart** to name the chart sheet

8. Click **Finish**
   See Figure 6-4.

 close Resorts01.xls

Step 1
When you use [Ctrl] to select nonadjacent rows or columns, the ranges you select must be the same size.

Figure 6-4: Completed column chart created from nonadjacent rows

Chart title

Newly-created chart sheet

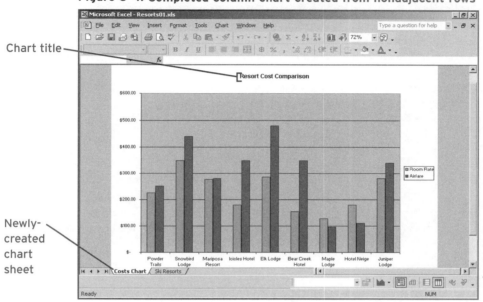

Skill Set 6

Creating and Modifying Graphics

Create, Modify, Position, and Print Charts
Change a Chart Type

After you create a chart, you may find that a different chart type would be more appropriate for your data. You can select from the many Excel standard chart types, or use Excel preformatted custom chart types. You can also create and save your own customized chart types. Make sure that the type of chart you select suits your data. Refer to Table 6-1 and the Chart Wizard dialog box for reminders on the best uses for each chart type.

Activity Steps

 open Guests04.xls

1. Click **Chart** on the menu bar, then click **Chart Type**

2. Click **Bar**, then under Chart sub-type, click the top-left subtype, **Clustered Bar** (if it's not already selected)
   The name and description appear in the lower-right box after you select a sub-type.
   See Figure 6-5.

3. Click **OK**

4. Click **Chart** on the menu bar, then click **Chart Type**

5. Click **Line**, then under Chart sub-type, click the bottom-left sub-type, **3-D Line**, then click **OK**

6. Click **Chart** on the menu bar, then click **Chart Type**

7. Click **Area**, under Chart sub-type, click the middle sub-type in the top row, **Stacked Area**, then click **OK**
   See Figure 6-6.

 close Guests04.xls

Step 2
To use preformatted custom chart types, click the Custom Types tab in the Chart Type dialog box.

Figure 6-5: Selecting a clustered bar chart

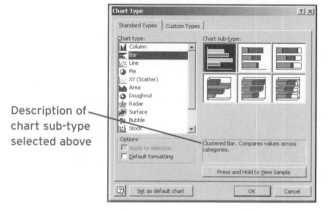

Description of chart sub-type selected above

Figure 6-6: Stacked area chart

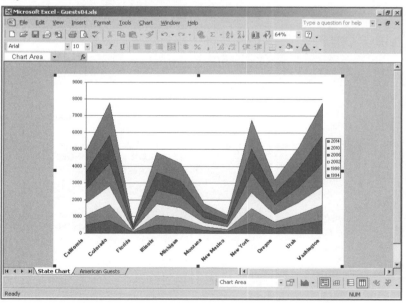

Skill Set 6

Creating and Modifying Graphics

Create, Modify, Position, and Print Charts
Modify Chart Options

Once you have created a chart, you will often want to change its appearance, such as adding or deleting a chart title, axis labels, a legend, or gridlines. You might also want to add **data labels**, which are text that appear next to each data point, such as its category or series name or its value. For certain charts, it is helpful to display a **data table**, a grid that appears under a chart and that contains the values on which the chart is based. A data table is most effective when a chart is on a chart sheet. You can set all of these options in the Chart Options dialog box. To delete any options you add, just click the title, label, legend or gridlines, then press [Delete].

Step 2
You can add labels to any or all data series. Double-click any data point. Click the Data Labels tab in the Format Data Series dialog box, select the label contents you want, then click OK. To change a label's position on the chart, double-click any data label, then use the Label Position scroll box on the Alignment tab in the Format Data Labels dialog box.

Activity Steps

 open Bikes02.xls

1. Click **Chart** on the menu bar, then click **Chart Options**

2. Click the **Titles tab** if it's not already selected, click the **Chart title box**, then type **Projected Income Q3 & Q4, 2003**
   After a moment, the preview displays the new title.

3. Click the **Value (Y) axis box**, then type **Projected U.S. $**

4. Click the **Legend tab**, then click the check mark next to **Show legend**, to remove it

5. Click the **Data Table tab**, then click **Show data table** to select it
   See Figure 6-7.

6. Click the **Gridlines tab**, then under Category (X) axis, click **Major gridlines** to select it

7. Click **OK**

8. Drag the **Y axis label** closer to the chart as shown in Figure 6-8, then click the gray area outside the chart
   The data table contains a color key for each data series, so there is no need for a legend.

 close Bikes02.xls

Figure 6-7: Data Table tab in Chart Options dialog box

Value (Y) axis label

Data table contains data and color key

New title in preview

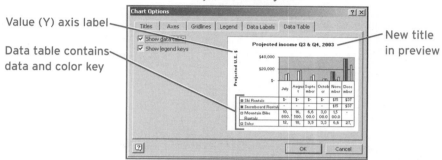

Figure 6-8: Modified chart

Major gridlines on X axis

Repositioned Y axis label

Data points

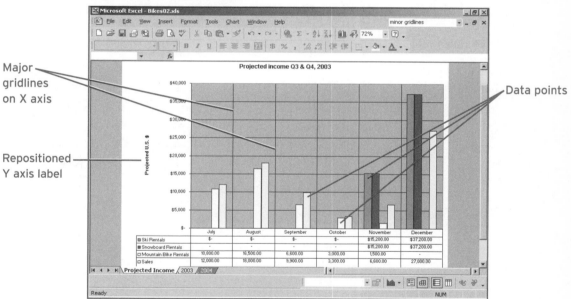

Skill Set 6
Creating and Modifying Graphics

Create, Modify, Position, and Print Charts
Print Charts

You can print a chart, whether it is on a worksheet with data or on its own chart sheet. If it's on a chart sheet, you print it as you would any worksheet. If the chart is on a worksheet, you can print it with the sheet data, or print it separately by selecting it first. The Page Setup dialog box lets you scale the chart on the page.

Activity Steps

 open Winter01.xls

1. Click the **chart title**, click after Helicopter, press **[Spacebar]-[Spacebar]**, type your name, then click any blank cell

2. Click the chart on the worksheet to select it, then click the **Print Preview button** on the Standard toolbar

3. Click **Setup**, then click the **Chart tab**

4. Click the **Scale to fit page option button**, then click **OK**
   See Figure 6-9.

5. Click **Print**, then click **OK** in the Print dialog box

6. Click the **Rev vs Exps Chart sheet tab**, then add your name to the chart title as you did in step 1 above

7. Click the **Print Preview button** on the Standard toolbar

8. Click **Print**, then click **OK** in the Print dialog box

 close Winter01.xls

Step 2
You can click the Margins tab in the Print Preview window, then drag margins to new locations.

Figure 6-9: Chart in Print Preview

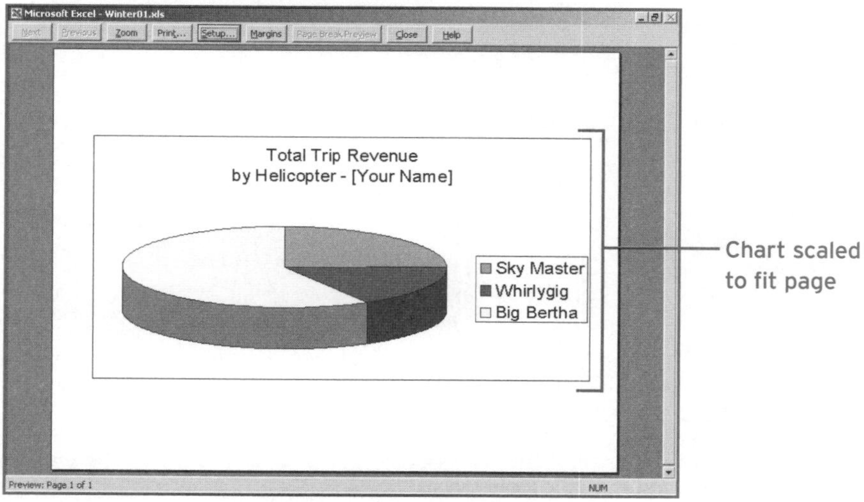

— Chart scaled to fit page

extra!

Using Page Break Preview

You can use Page Break Preview to change the chart location. In the Print Preview window of a multi-page worksheet, click Page Break Preview. The Welcome to Page Break Preview dialog box may open with a brief explanation about how to adjust page breaks; if this appears, click OK. Page breaks appear as blue dotted lines. Drag **page breaks** or the **chart** to achieve the layout you want. To return to Normal view, click the Print Preview button on the Standard toolbar, then click Normal View.

Skill Set 6

Creating and Modifying Graphics

Create, Modify, Position, and Print Charts
Format Chart Text

Once you create a chart, you can format any chart element. You can change the font, font size, style, alignment, or color of any text.

Activity Steps

 open Party01.xls

1. Click the chart title, **Winter Party Budget**, to select it
2. Click the **Format button** on the Chart toolbar
   The ScreenTip name of the Format button on the Chart toolbar reflects the selected object, in this case, the chart title.
3. Click the **Font tab**, under Size select **18**, click the **Patterns tab**, then click the **Shadow check box** to select it
   See Figure 6-10.
4. Click **OK**, then click in the Chart Area to deselect the title
5. Double-click any value on the Value (vertical, or Y) axis, click the **Number tab**, click the **Decimal places down arrow** twice, to display **O** (zero) decimal places, then click **OK**
   Double-clicking a chart object is often the fastest way to display the Format dialog box. The dialog box tabs present options appropriate to the object you select.
6. Double-click the **legend**, click the **Placement tab** in the Format Legend dialog box, click the **Bottom option button** to select it, then click **OK**
7. Drag the right sizing handle on the legend to the right about a half inch, then click in the Chart Area to deselect the legend
8. Double-click **Cost** (the vertical, or Y, axis title), click the **Alignment tab** in the Format Axis Title dialog box, drag the **red diamond** to the 12:00 mark (90 degrees) on the dial, then click **OK**
9. Click the gray area outside the Chart Area to deselect the axis and the chart
   See Figure 6-11.

 close Party01.xls

Step 2
You can also use the buttons on the Formatting toolbar to format a selected text object.

Figure 6-10: Patterns tab in Format Chart Title dialog box

Select to add shadow to chart title box

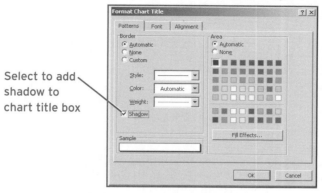

Figure 6-11: Formatted chart text

Font now 18 point with shadowed box

Value axis no longer shows decimals

Y axis title vertically aligned

Legend appears below chart

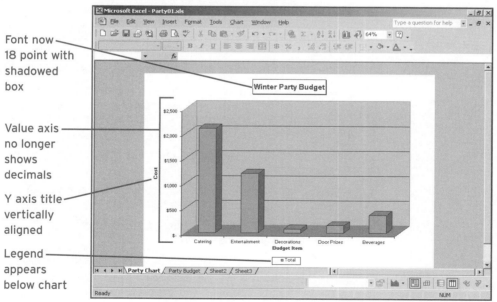

Skill Set 6

Creating and Modifying Graphics

Create, Modify, Position, and Print Charts
Format Chart Graphics

You can format any filled object, area, or line of a chart, including the fill color, pattern, style, or border. You can customize the data points, the chart background, or the plot area. The colors you choose should go well together, be appropriate for your audience, and should not detract from the message you want the chart to communicate. You can also add a picture to the chart area, the plot area, or a data point.

Activity Steps

 open Holiday01.xls

1. Double-click the **legend**, click the **Patterns tab** (if it's not already selected), then click the **pale yellow fill color** (fifth row down, third color from the left)
   See Figure 6-12.

2. Click **OK**

3. Click anywhere on the pie chart to select it, click the largest slice, then double-click the slice

4. In the Format Data Point dialog box, under Area, click **Fill Effects**

5. In the Fill Effects dialog box, click the **Two colors option button** to select it; click the **Color 1 list arrow**, select the **light green color** (fifth row, fourth from the left), verify that Color 2 is white, then click **OK** twice

6. Double-click the **Chart Area**, click **Fill Effects**, then click the **Picture tab**

7. Click **Select Picture**, select **Ski** from the location where your Project Files are stored, then click **Insert**

8. Click **OK** in the Fill Effects dialog box, then click **OK** in the Format Chart Area dialog box
   See Figure 6-13.

 close Holiday01.xls

Step 2
If you add data labels to a chart and if your chart background is dark, click the Font color list arrow, then select a light color for the text.

Figure 6-12: Format Legend dialog box

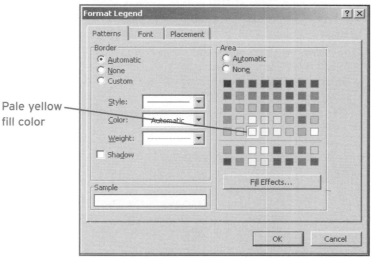

Pale yellow fill color

Figure 6-13: Chart with modified graphic elements

Chart area with picture

Guest Budget for Holiday Ski Weekend

Exploded pie slice with two-color shading

Legend with yellow fill

Skill Set 6

Creating and Modifying Graphics

Create, Modify, and Position Graphics
Create Graphics

A **graphic** is a shape, line, or block of text that you can add to any chart or worksheet. Add graphics by using tools on the Drawing toolbar. In addition to creating shapes such as squares, circles, lines and arrows, you can add predrawn shapes called **AutoShapes**, such as brackets, stars, banners, or arrows. You can also create **callouts**, which are text boxes with attached lines. When you drag callouts, their boxes and lines move together, making it easy to annotate screen items quickly. Use AutoShapes or callouts to create text annotations that call attention to worksheet features.

Use the Draw menu on the Drawing toolbar to change the alignment, grouping, or stacking order of any selected drawing objects.

Activity Steps

 open Rentals03.xls

1. If the Drawing toolbar does not appear below the worksheet tabs (or elsewhere on your screen if a previous user has moved it), click the **Drawing button** on the Standard toolbar to display it

2. Click the **Oval button** on the Drawing toolbar

3. Position the + pointer in the Chart Area above the value axis, press and hold down the mouse button, drag down and to the right to create an oval about an inch and a half wide, then release the mouse button

4. Type **Annotated by**, type your name, then click in the gray area outside the chart to deselect the object

5. Click **AutoShapes** on the Drawing toolbar, point to **Callouts**, then click **Line Callout 2** (second row, second callout from the left)

6. Click and hold the mouse button on the red Net Income bar portion for March, drag up and right into the chart area, then release the mouse button

7. Type **Net income is 16% of sales**, then click in the gray area to deselect the callout

8. Click the callout, press and hold [Shift], click the oval, then click the **Fill Color list arrow** on the Drawing toolbar

9. Click the **Light Yellow color** (fifth row, third from left), then click the gray area
   See Figure 6-14.

 close Rentals03.xls

Figure 6-14: Callout annotating chart data point and Oval AutoShape

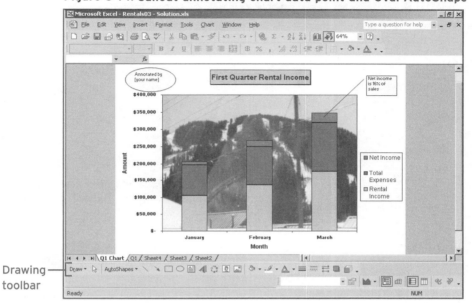

Drawing toolbar

extra!

Adding graphics to charts

You can enhance your chart's visual appeal by adding presupplied pictures called **clip art**, or shaped words called **WordArt**. To insert clip art, open the task pane, then display the **Clip Art pane**. Type a subject, then click **Go**. Click any graphic to insert it in the worksheet. To create WordArt, click the **Insert WordArt button** on the Drawing toolbar. Select a style, click **OK**, type the text you want to style, then click **OK**. You can drag any graphic object to a new location or resize it by dragging one of its round white sizing handles. If you have a dial-up Internet connection on your computer, your clip art collection will be smaller; if you are continually on line, Excel goes to the Web and makes a large collection available.

Skill Set 6

Creating and Modifying Graphics

Create, Modify, and Position Graphics
Modify and Position Graphics

Any graphic you create using the Drawing toolbar is an object that you can select, move, and resize separately from a worksheet or chart. You can format a graphic with fill colors, patterns, or shaded fill effects; you can modify the borders or add 3D or shadow styling. Before you modify or position a shape or an AutoShape, you must select it.

Step 3

If you select an AutoShape with the Move Cell Pointer ⁺ᵗ↗, it highlights with a dotted outline, meaning that any change will apply to the entire graphic; if you select an AutoShape using the I-Beam pointer Ⅰ, it highlights with a striped outline, meaning that you can only add or edit text. You can rotate any selected shape by dragging the green circle attached to it.

Activity Steps

  open Quarters01.xls

1. Click the **large star shape** to select it

2. Position the pointer over the **lower-right sizing handle**, then drag the ↖ pointer up and left until the shape is about one inch across
   The sizing handles on AutoShapes are white circles, not black squares like those on a selected chart.

3. Position ⁺ᵗ↗ over the **dotted border** of the shape, then drag it left until it overlaps the Helicopter Skiing chart line
   See Figure 6-15.

4. Click ⁺ᵗ↗ on the edge of the callout AutoShape under the legend

5. Drag the **dotted border** up and to the left so it's just underneath the $800,000 gridline

6. Drag the **yellow diamond** on the AutoShape until it is at the **QTR 3 data point** for the Mountain Biking series

7. Click the **Fill Color list arrow** on the Drawing toolbar, then click the **Light Yellow color** (fifth row, third from left)

8. Click the **3-D Style button** on the Drawing toolbar, click the **3-D Style 1 button** in the upper left, then click in the gray area outside the chart
   See Figure 6-16.

  close Quarters01.xls

Figure 6-15: Resizing a graphic

Repositioned AutoShape

Title created in WordArt

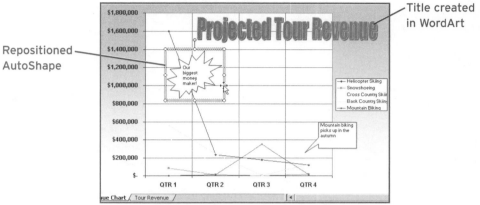

Figure 6-16: Callout AutoShape with fill color and 3-D effect

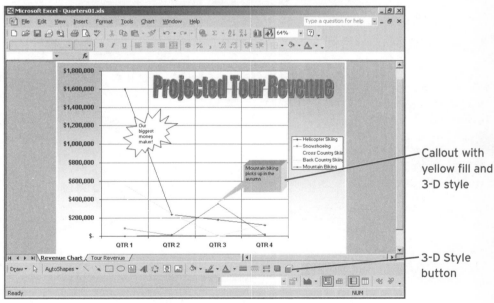

Callout with yellow fill and 3-D style

3-D Style button

Skill Set 6

Creating and Modifying Graphics

Target Your Skills

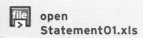
open Statement01.xls

1 Use Figure 6-17 as a guide to chart the data in rows 3, 8, and 14 of the Income Statement (not including the totals in column N) as a line chart. Print the chart, using the Scale to Fit Page option.

Figure 6-17

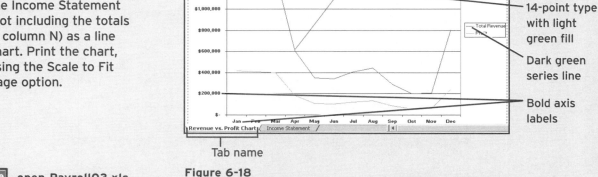

Your name

No decimal places

Light yellow background

14-point type with light green fill

Dark green series line

Bold axis labels

Tab name

open Payroll03.xls

2 Create the chart shown in Figure 6-18, using the data in F6:I6, and F13:I13. Use a Pie chart with a 3-D visual effect, place it on the worksheet, and size and position it as shown.

Figure 6-18

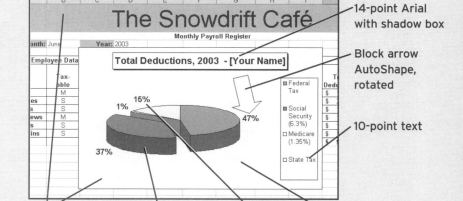

14-point Arial with shadow box

Block arrow AutoShape, rotated

10-point text

Light yellow background

Print worksheet with chart; print chart only scaled to fit page

Bright red; select and drag away from pie

Bold data labels

Skill List

1. Convert Worksheets into Web Pages
2. Create Hyperlinks
3. View and Edit Comments

Computer users can now share information easily using the **Internet**, a world-wide network of computers and smaller networks, and company **intranets**, or networks within organizations. Users communicate over these networks using the **World Wide Web**, an interconnected collection of electronic documents called **Web pages**. **Workgroups**, people in an organization who exchange information, can now collaborate, or work together, on documents to make their work more efficient.

You can share your Excel worksheets or workbooks with others by saving them as specially-formatted files that you can place on the Web or an intranet. Before you save them, you can **preview** them in Excel to see how they will look as Web pages. Any worksheet can also have hyperlinks to other worksheets, other workbooks or documents, or locations on the World Wide Web. **Hyperlinks** consist of text or graphics that users click to display other documents. Hyperlinks are available to users of your worksheets in both Excel and Web versions.

As you communicate with others using Excel documents, perhaps by placing them on a centralized company computer, you can attach **comments** to worksheet cells that others can read and then respond to with their own comments.

You can also use **discussion comments** to communicate about an Excel document. This powerful feature lets you conduct continuous discussions with others about a workbook. Unlike workbook comments, discussion comments are not attached to a particular cell. You need to have access to an **Office-Extended discussion server** to use this feature. *This is a MOUS requirement; be sure you learn the steps covered in the box on page 167 on how to insert and answer discussion comments.*

Skill Set 7
Workgroup Collaboration

Convert Worksheets into Web Pages
Preview and Create Web Pages

You can place a worksheet or workbook on the Internet or on a company intranet for others to use. To do this, you need to save it in a special file format that other users can open in their **Web browsers**, which are programs that let you view documents on the Web; **Internet Explorer** is a commonly used Web browser. Before you resave the file and place it on the Web, you should preview it. When saving your file as a Web page, Excel saves it in a special file format called **Hypertext Markup Language**, or **HTML**. When saving your worksheet in HTML format, Excel creates a document with the file extension htm as well as a folder of supporting files in a folder called [filename]_files.

Activity Steps

 open Sales02.xls

1. Click **File** on the menu bar, click **Web Page Preview**, maximize the preview window

2. Close the preview window, make sure no worksheet objects are selected, click **File** on the menu bar, then click **Save as Web Page**

3. Click the **Save in list arrow**, navigate to the location where your Project Files are stored, then click the **Selection: Sheet option button** (If you have saved this sheet previously, the button will read "Republish: Sheet")

4. Highlight the existing filename, then type **newitems**

5. Click **Change Title**, type **Price vs. Cost for New Items at Miller Music**, then click **OK**
   The text you typed will appear in the Web page title bar.
   See Figure 7-1.

6. Click **Save**
   The Excel Workbook remains open.

7. Open your Web browser program, click **File** on the menu bar, then click **Open**

8. Click **Browse**, navigate to the location where your Project Files are stored, select **newitems.htm**, click **Open**, then click **OK**
   See Figure 7-2.

9. Click the **Close button** ☒ on the Browser window

 close Sales02.xls

The newitems.htm file is saved in your Project File location, along with a folder called newitems_files that contains supporting graphics and other file infomation.

Figure 7-1: Completed Save As dialog box

Only current worksheet will be saved

Text will appear in Web page title bar

Some computer systems prefer 8-character htm filenames

Location where HTML file will be saved (your location may be different)

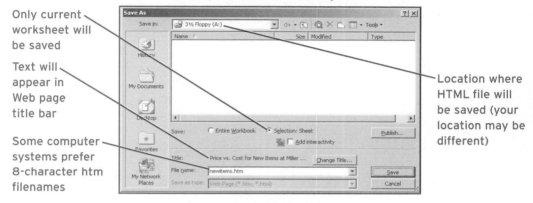

Figure 7-2: Web page opened in Internet Explorer browser

Your location may be different

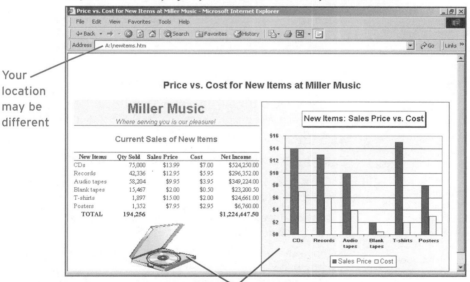

Depending on your browser and operating system, graphics may not be visible

Skill Set 7

Workgroup Collaboration

Create Hyperlinks
Create Hyperlinks

A **hyperlink** is a word or graphic that you click to display (or "jump to") another location in the document, another document, or a location on the Web, known as the **target** or **destination**. In an Excel workbook, a hyperlink might take you to another sheet in the same workbook, it might open another workbook containing more detailed information, or it might take you to a Web site that has additional information of interest. You can also use hyperlinks to display photos or other graphics that might not fit well in a worksheet cell. After you click a hyperlink, use the **Back button** on the Web toolbar to return to the original document.

Step 9
To remove a hyperlink, right-click it, then click Remove Hyperlink. To select a cell with a hyperlink (instead of going to the hyperlink target), click the link and hold down the mouse button until you see the white cross pointer ✛ .

Activity Steps

 open Checkbook01.xls

1. On the February worksheet, notice the beginning balance is in cell F8; click the March sheet tab, then notice the beginning balance is also in cell F8

2. Click the Summary sheet, click cell C7, then click the **Insert Hyperlink button** 🔗 on the Standard toolbar

3. Under Link to, click **Place in This Document**
   See Table 7-1 for other options in the Insert Hyperlink dialog box.

4. In the Type the cell reference box, select any text, then type **F8**

5. In the Text to Display box, select any text, then type **Click here**

6. Click **Screen Tip**, type **Click here to see beginning monthly balance**, then click **OK**

7. In the Or select a place in this document list, click **February**, compare your screen to Figure 7-3, then click **OK**

8. Move the pointer over the hyperlink in cell **C7**, read the ScreenTip, shown in Figure 7-4, then click once with the 🖑 pointer; observe how the destination worksheet appears with the destination cell, F8, selected

9. If the Web toolbar does not appear on your screen, click **View** on the menu bar, point to **Toolbars**, click **Web**, then click the **Back button** ⬅ on the Web toolbar
   When you return to the Summary worksheet, you will notice that the hyperlink has become purple, indicating that it has been used. It will remain purple until you close and reopen the workbook.

 close Checkbook01.xls

Figure 7-3: Insert Hyperlink dialog box

Indicates hyperlink will jump to a location in the current document

Place in This Document

The worksheet the hyperlink will jump to

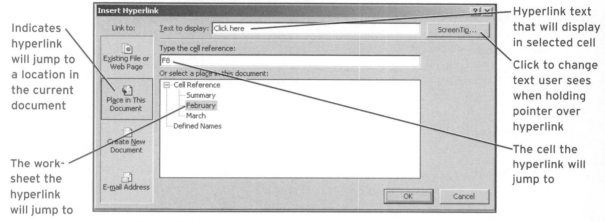

Hyperlink text that will display in selected cell

Click to change text user sees when holding pointer over hyperlink

The cell the hyperlink will jump to

Figure 7-4: ScreenTip

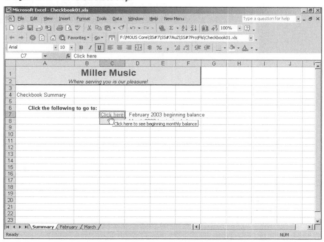

TABLE 7-1: Specifying other hyperlink destinations

to create a hyperlink that will display	click in Insert Hyperlink dialog box	then
Another file	Existing file or Web page	Navigate to file location
A Web page	Existing file or Web page	Click Browse the Web button, go to site
A new Excel document	Create New Document	Type name of document and specify storage location
A blank e-mail to a particular address	E-mail address	Type address and subject, or select address from list

Skill Set 7

Workgroup Collaboration

Create Hyperlinks
Modify Hyperlinks

After you create a hyperlink, you might want to edit it to change its destination, its ScreenTip, or the text that users click to display the hyperlink. If the destination is a Web site, you may want to change the site to a more current one; if it's a location in the current document, you might want to change it to another cell or worksheet. You make these changes using the same dialog box you used to create the hyperlink itself.

Step 2
To remove a hyperlink, right-click it, then click Remove Hyperlink.

Activity Steps

 open Drums03.xls

1. Click the **drum graphic**, then notice that it displays the Brass Suppliers sheet, not the Drum Suppliers sheet

2. Click the **Back button** ⬅ on the Web toolbar

3. Point to the **drum graphic** until the pointer becomes 🖑

4. Right-click the graphic (the Picture toolbar also opens), then click **Edit Hyperlink**

5. Under Or select a place in this document, click **Drum Suppliers**
   See Figure 7-5.

6. Click **OK**

7. Click cell **A1** to deselect the graphic, then click the **drum graphic**
   The Drum Suppliers worksheet appears.
   See Figure 7-6.

8. Click the **Back button** ⬅ on the Web toolbar

 close Drums03.xls

Figure 7-5: Hyperlink destination selected

Correct worksheet name for hyperlink

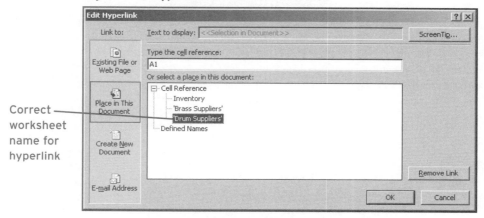

Figure 7-6: Hyperlink destination displayed

Skill Set 7

Workgroup Collaboration

View and Edit Comments
Attach and Edit Cell Comments

As part of collaborating with members of a workgroup, you will want to share your reactions to documents and have others respond to your ideas. Excel lets you attach notes called **comments** to any worksheet cell. Others who use a shared document can read your comments and insert their own. Each comment is preceded by the computer user's name, making it easy to identify who said what. You can also edit any worksheet comment.

Step 4
If you click a blank cell and the comment still appears, click Tools, click Options, click the View tab, then under Comment, click the Comment indicator only option button.

Activity Steps

 open Loan01.xls

1. Right-click cell **C6**

2. Click **Insert Comment** on the shortcut menu
   See Figure 7-7.

3. Type **Is this the quantity price we got from Groveland?**

4. Click a blank worksheet area
   Cell C6 displays a small red triangle called a **comment indicator**, indicating that it has an attached comment.

5. Move the pointer over cell **C6**, then read the comment in the comment balloon

6. Right-click, then click **Edit Comment** from the shortcut menu

7. Press ←, press **[Spacebar]**, type in **January**, then click on a blank worksheet area

8. Point to cell **C6** to review the edited comment
   See Figure 7-8.

 close Loan01.xls

Figure 7-7: New comment

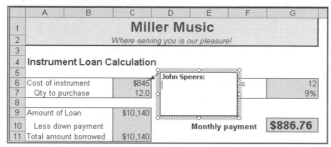

Figure 7-8: Edited comment

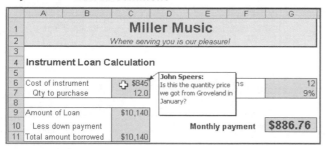

Responding to a Discussion

In any Excel document that will be saved in HTML format and placed on the Web, you can insert and respond to discussion comments relating to the document. All comments are **threaded**, or placed one after another, so you can follow the "thread" of the discussion. *You must have access to a discussion server to use this feature.* All comments are stored on the discussion server. Click Tools on the menu bar, point to **Online Collaboration**, then click **Web Discussions**. To insert a discussion comment, click the **Insert Discussion about the Workbook button** on the Web Discussions toolbar. Other users can reply by clicking the Discuss button on the Standard Buttons toolbar in Internet Explorer to display the Discussion toolbar. Then they click the Insert Discussion in the Document button and enter comments.

Skill Set 7
Workgroup Collaboration

Target Your Skills

 open Instruments03.xls

1 Make the changes shown on Figure 7-9, then preview the file as a Web page.

Figure 7-9

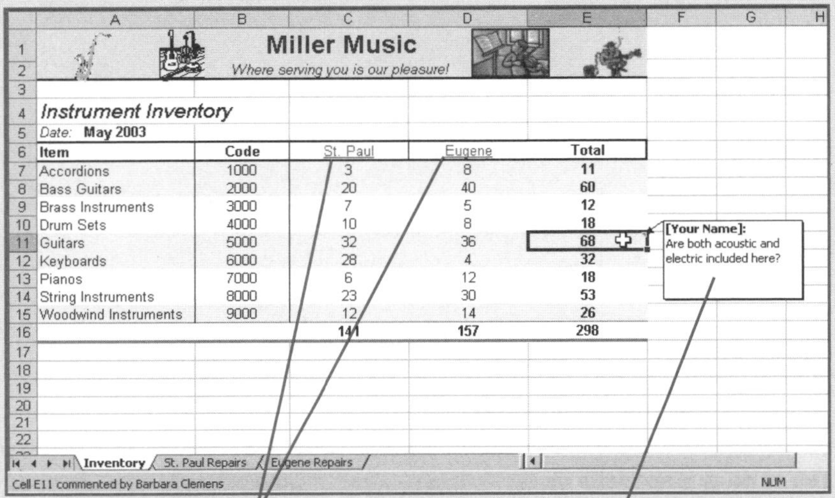

	A	B	C	D	E	F	G	H
1			**Miller Music**					
2			*Where serving you is our pleasure!*					
3								
4	*Instrument Inventory*							
5	*Date:* **May 2003**							
6	**Item**	**Code**	St. Paul	Eugene	**Total**			
7	Accordions	1000	3	8	11			
8	Bass Guitars	2000	20	40	60			
9	Brass Instruments	3000	7	5	12			
10	Drum Sets	4000	10	8	18			
11	Guitars	5000	32	36	68			
12	Keyboards	6000	28	4	32			
13	Pianos	7000	6	12	18			
14	String Instruments	8000	23	30	53			
15	Woodwind Instruments	9000	12	14	26			
16			141	157	298			

[Your Name]: Are both acoustic and electric included here?

Inventory / St. Paul Repairs / Eugene Repairs /

Cell E11 commented by Barbara Clemens   NUM

Create links to the appropriate worksheets

Insert comment shown, then insert "guitars" after "electric"

 open Markdowns04.xls

2 Make the changes shown in Figure 7-10. Preview the worksheet as a Web page. Save the worksheet as a Web page named specials.htm using the title "Special Instrument Markdowns," then open it in your browser.

Figure 7-10

	A	B	C	D	E	F	G
1			**Miller Music**				
2			*Where serving you is our pleasure!*				
3							
4			*Sample Anniversary Sale Markdowns*				
5							
6				Qty	Original		Sale
7		**Item**	**Model**	**on Hand**	**Price**	**Markdown**	**Price**
8		Amplifier	6845	5	$895	20%	$716
9		Amplifier	6244	4	$1,295	30%	$907
10		Bass Guitar	8RY	4	$950	40%	$570
11		Drums	SS46D	2	$3,250	35%	$2,113
12		Guitar	423B	3	$395	30%	$277
13		Keyboard	46-YR	6	$2,295	25%	$1,721
14		Keyboard	623		$750	20%	$600
15							
16							
17		Description:					
18		Full-range keyboard, 21 synthesized sounds					
19		With effects pedals					

Click here for model details

Sale Markdowns / Sheet2 / Sheet3 /

Add a hyperlink here to any amplifier manufacturer's site

Add a comment that reads "You won't find a price like this anywhere else!"

Skill Set 8

Skill List

1. Import data to Excel
2. Export data from Excel
3. Publish worksheets and workbooks to the Web

If you have data that was created in another program, you don't have to retype it to use it in Microsoft Excel 2002. Excel lets you bring in, or **import**, a variety of information, including unformatted data files and data from the World Wide Web. The commands you use vary depending on the type of information you want to import. Similarly, you can **export** Excel workbook information to other programs. Exporting can include placing copies of entire worksheets or worksheet ranges in other documents, such as Microsoft PowerPoint presentation slides or Microsoft Word word processing documents.

You can export Excel workbooks and worksheets to the Web for users to view or to interact with using their Web browsers. You can also publish a Web page directly to a Web site, and have Excel automatically update and republish the page every time you save the workbook.

Skill Set 8
Importing and Exporting Data

Import Data to Excel
Import a Text File

You may have data created in another program that you want to analyze in Excel. Because that data is in the **source program's** file format, you cannot always open the file in Excel using the Open command on the File menu. Instead, many source programs let you save files as **text files** (also called **ASCII** files), which contain only data without formatting, formulas, or other information. Then you **import**, or bring in, the text file to an Excel worksheet for analysis using the Text Import Wizard. In a text file, data columns are separated by a character such as a tab, with a return character at the end of each line. Such a file is called a **tab-delimited text file**; a **delimiter** is a separator. Commas and spaces can also act as delimiters. The Text Import Wizard lets you specify how you want Excel to interpret the file.

Activity Steps

1. With Excel running and a blank worksheet open, select cell **A1** (if it's not already selected), click **Data** on the menu bar, point to **Import External Data**, then click **Import Data**

2. In the Select Data Source dialog box, navigate to the location where your Project Files are stored

3. Click the **Files of type list arrow**, then select **Text files (*.txt, *.prn, *.csv, *.tab, *.asc)**
   Now that you have selected the file type, only the text files appear.

4. Click **Rooms01.txt**, then click **Open**

5. In the Step 1 of 3 dialog box of the Text Import Wizard, make sure the **Delimited option** is selected, then examine the file preview at the bottom of the box

Step 7
You don't have to import all the text file columns. Select any column in the Step 3 of 3 dialog box, then click to select "Do not import (Skip)". Excel will not import that column.

6. Click **Next**; in the Step 2 of 3 box, make sure the **Tab option** is selected, observe how the columns are divided by lines in the preview box, then click **Next**
   See Figure 8-1.

7. In the Step 3 of 3 box, make sure **General** is selected under Column data format, then click **Finish**

8. With the **Existing worksheet option** selected, then click **OK**
   The text file opens in the existing worksheet. The Total Revenue column and the Totals row display as values. The External Data toolbar opens.

9. Click **File** on the menu bar, click **Save As**; notice that in the **Save as type list, Microsoft Excel workbook (*.xls)** is already selected, type **Rooms02**, then click **Save**
   See Figure 8-2.

 close Rooms02.xls

Figure 8-1: Step 3 of 3 of the Text Import Wizard

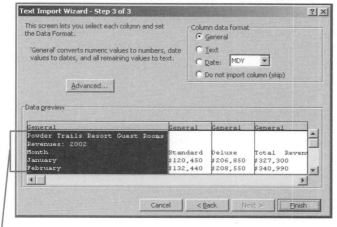

Preview of
imported file

Figure 8-2: Imported text data in Excel

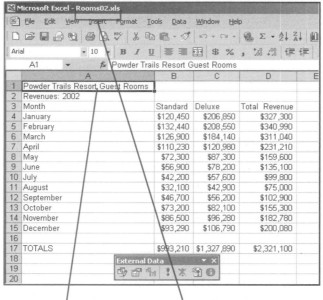

Make sure there is no data below
and to the right of the selected
cell; imported data will replace it

Text file
saved in
Excel format

extra!

Opening files created in other programs

Excel lets you open
files created in many
programs, including
earlier versions of
Excel, Web pages, and
spreadsheets created in
several other spread-
sheet programs, such as
Lotus 1-2-3. In the
Open dialog box, click
the **Files of type list
arrow**, then select the
file type you want to
view. Double-click the
filename to open it in
Excel. Formatting and
formulas created in the
source program may be
lost, but the data values
will be intact.

Skill Set 8

Importing and Exporting Data

Import Data to Excel
Import Access Database Tables

Often you will want to import data that was created in a **database program**, a program that lets you organize and analyze large amounts of information. **Microsoft Access 2002** is the database program that is part of the Microsoft Office XP suite. A **database file** is similar to an Excel list in that it contains **records**, or rows of information for each item in the database. A record is information divided into **fields**, or columns of information; each field represents one piece of information about an item, such as Last Name or Age. Access files are organized into one or more **tables**, which contain all the information for a particular part of a database, such as a company's customers or suppliers. A database program like Access allows you to perform complex data manipulations not available in Excel. Yet sometimes you want to import Access information into Excel to perform statistical or graphical analyses not available in Access.

Activity Steps

 open Staff01.xls

1. Click **Data** on the menu bar, point to **Import External Data**, then click **Import Data**

2. In the Select Data Source dialog box, click the **Look in list arrow**, then navigate to your Project Files location

3. Click the **Files of type list arrow**, then select **All Data Sources (*.odc;*.mdb;*.mde...)** (if it is not already selected)

4. Click **Access01.mdb**, then click **Open**
   Because the database contains two tables, the Select Table dialog box opens, allowing you to choose the table you want to import.
   See Figure 8-3.

5. Click **Staff List**, then click **OK**

6. With the Import Data dialog box open, click the worksheet cell **A4**
   See Figure 8-4.

7. Click **OK**

8. Click the **Housekeeping Staff sheet tab**, repeat steps 1-4, click **Housekeeping**, then click **OK**

9. On the worksheet, click cell **A4**, then click **OK**
   You have imported the two Access tables in the Access01.mdb database to separate Excel worksheets. Each range is now an **external data range**, a range of worksheet data that originated outside of Excel, that you can analyze, format, and update.

 close Staff01.xls

Step 6
The Import Data dialog box also lets you import a table to a blank worksheet.

Figure 8-3: Select Table dialog box

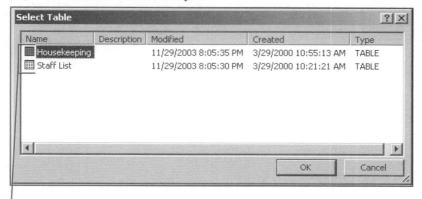

Tables in
Access01.mdb
database

Figure 8-4: Import Data dialog box with destination cell selected

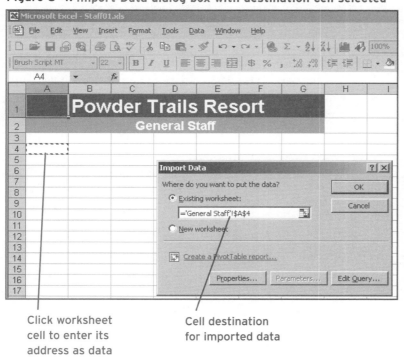

Click worksheet
cell to enter its
address as data
destination

Cell destination
for imported data

extra!

Refreshing an external data range
An external data range in Excel retains a connection to the location of its source file, which means that you can **refresh**, or update, the data in Excel at any time, so your range will reflect any changes to the source file since you imported it. To refresh an external data range, first display the External Data toolbar (if it is not already displayed): Click **View** on the menu bar, point to **Toolbars**, click **Customize**, select **External Data** on the Toolbars tab, then click **Close**. Click in the external data range, click the **Refresh Data button** on the toolbar.

Skill Set 8

Importing and Exporting Data

Import Data to Excel
Import Data Using a Query

When you import a database you may want to import only part of the data in a table; for example, only sales transactions above a certain amount. In these cases, you use a **query**, which is a specific request you make about the data. A query is a file with the .dqy file extension that you can save and use again. The external data can be an Access database, other databases, or another Excel file. To query an external data source, you use **Microsoft Query**, a program that comes with Excel. *Microsoft Query is not installed as part of a standard Excel installation, so you may need access to the Microsoft Office CD the first time you use it, or see your system administrator.*

Step 5
In the Filter dialog box, you can specify another filter and have Query apply it along with the first filter (an AND condition), or as an alternative to the first filter (an OR condition), such as Last Name >g AND Last name <p, which would choose people whose last names begin with G through O in the alphabet.

Activity Steps

1. With Excel running and a blank worksheet open, click **Data** on the menu bar, point to **Import External Data**, then click **New Database Query**

2. In the Choose Data Source dialog box, click **MS Access Database**, then click **OK** (a Connecting to data source message appears)

3. In the Select Database dialog box, display your Project Files location

4. Under Database Name, click **Access01.mdb**, then click **OK** The **Query Wizard** opens.

5. Click **Staff List**, then click **>** to select this table's fields *See Figure 8-5.*

6. In the columns in your query box, click **Status**, then click **<** to eliminate it from the query, then click **Next** Microsoft Query lets you **filter**, or screen out, data to include only the data you specify for any fields; you can also **sort**, or reorder, the data.

7. In the Query Wizard - Filter Data dialog box, click **Last Name** in the Column to filter list, click the **Last name list arrow**, then click **is greater than** See Figure 8-6.

8. Click the **top right text box**, type **g**, then click **Next**

9. Click the **Sort by list arrow**, click **Last Name**, click **Next**, click **Finish**, then click **OK**

10. Save the file as **Housekeeping01.xls**

 close Housekeeping01.xls

Figure 8-5: Selecting fields to import

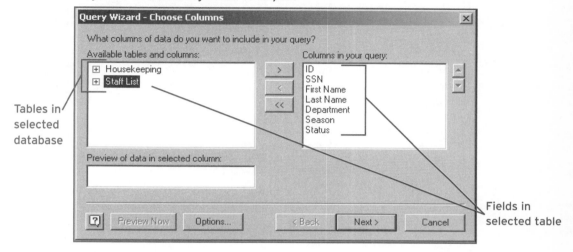

Tables in selected database

Fields in selected table

Figure 8-6: Filtering imported data

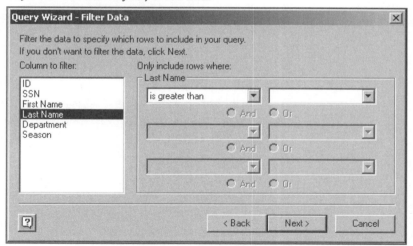

Skill Set 8
Importing and Exporting Data

Import Data to Excel
Import Graphics

You can import a variety of graphics to enhance your worksheets. A **graphic** is a picture or photograph file stored on disk. You can insert many common types of graphics (shown in Table 8-1) using the Picture/From File commands on the Insert menu. A picture you import from a file becomes a worksheet **object** that you can move or resize as you would a drawn shape you create using the Drawing toolbar. You can also **crop**, or clip off, any part of a selected picture using the cropping tool on the Picture toolbar.

Activity Steps

 open Resorts02.xls

1. Right-click any toolbar; if Picture does not have a check mark next to it, click **Picture** to display the Picture toolbar
   Your Picture toolbar may appear at the bottom of the screen or elsewhere if a previous user has moved it.

2. Click the **Insert Picture From File button** 🖼 on the Picture toolbar

3. In the Insert Picture dialog box, click the **Look in list arrow**, then navigate to the location where your Project Files are stored
   See Figure 8-7.

4. Click the **Ski.jpg** picture, then click **Insert**

5. With the picture selected, drag the lower right **sizing handle** so the right side of the picture aligns with the right side of **column J**

6. Click the **Crop button** 📐 on the Picture toolbar, then drag the **lower left corner** of the picture to the right about an inch

7. Drag the picture to the right side of the data

8. Click the **Line Style button** ☰ on the Picture toolbar, click the bottom line style, then click any blank cell
   See Figure 8-8.

 close Resorts02.xls

Step 6
You can also use the buttons on the Picture toolbar to adjust a selected picture's brightness, contrast, or rotation. Click the Format Picture button 🖌 for finer control of picture features.

Figure 8-7: Insert Picture dialog box

Depending on your operating system, your view may differ

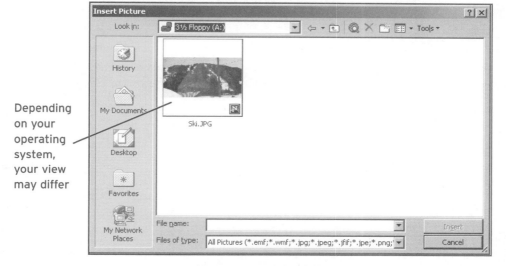

Figure 8-8: Repositioned picture with border

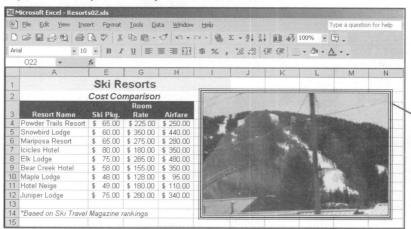

Cropped, resized, and repositioned picture with border

TABLE 8-1 Selected graphic formats you can import to Excel 2002

file format	name	file format	name
.emf	Enhanced Metafile	.bmp	Microsoft Windows Bitmap
.jpg	Joint Photographic Experts Group	.gif	Graphics Interchange Format
.png	Portable Network Graphics	.wmf	Windows Metafile

Skill Set 8
Importing and Exporting Data

Import Data to Excel
Import Data from the World Wide Web

While you can easily import information from text, database, and graphics files into Excel, you are not limited to these. You may find information on the World Wide Web that you want to analyze in an Excel worksheet. Excel makes it easy to import data from Web pages. You can use the drag-and-drop or the cut-and-paste method to import data, text, and graphics. If the information you import contains **hyperlinks** ("live" areas you click to display other locations on the Web), they will still work when the data is in a worksheet. *In order to perform all the steps in this lesson, your computer needs to have access to the World Wide Web, and you must have Internet Explorer version 4.1 or later.*

Activity Steps

1. With Excel running and a blank workbook open, click **Start** on the taskbar, point to **Programs**, then click **Internet Explorer**

2. Click the **Address box**, type **www.goski.com**, then press **[Enter]**

3. Locate and click the link for **Canada**, click the link for **Alberta**, then click the **Lake Louise link**
   If the Web site has changed and you cannot locate the site or the links, use the site and links of your choice.

4. Scroll down until you see **Profile** information in a table format

5. Click the **Restore Down button** 🗗 in the title bar, make the window half the size of the screen, then drag it to the right side of your screen

6. Click **Microsoft Excel - Book 1 button** in the taskbar, click the program window's **Restore Down button** 🗗 in the title bar, then resize and drag it to the left side of your screen; scroll as necessary until your screen looks like Figure 8-9

7. In the Internet Explorer window, drag to select the **Profile information** from Vertical Drop down through the Web Site address

8. Position the **arrow pointer** ⥼ over the selected text, drag it over the Excel worksheet until the upper left corner of the outline is in cell A1, release the mouse button, then click a blank worksheet cell
   See Figure 8-10.

9. Save the file in Excel workbook format as **Profile01.xls** in the location where your Project Files are stored, then click the Browser window **Close button**

 close Profile01.xls

Step 8
You can also use the Copy and Paste commands from the Edit menu instead of dragging.

Figure 8-9: Worksheets positioned for importing data

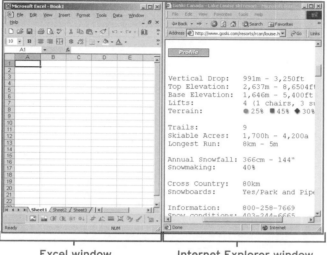

Excel window   Internet Explorer window

Figure 8-10: Data in worksheet after dragging from Web page

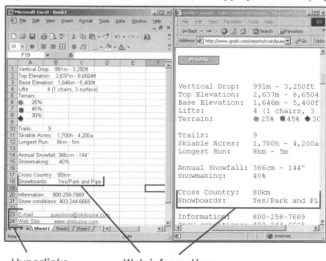

Hyperlinks   Web information
work in Excel   in Excel worksheet

extra!

Importing Web data
When you import Web
data, check the Web
page's legal statement,
usually at the bottom
of the page, to ensure
that you are not vio-
lating any copyright
or usage restrictions.

Skill Set 8

Importing and Exporting Data

Export Data from Excel
Embed an Excel Chart in a Word Document

To export Excel information to Microsoft Word documents, you don't need to save or convert the Excel file in a different format. Instead, you can place any chart or worksheet as an **object** that you can move and resize in the Word document using a process called **object linking and embedding (OLE)**. When you **embed** an Excel object (the **source object**) in a Word document (the **destination file**), you actually place a copy of the source object, which you can double-click to edit using source program tools. Although you can edit the object in Word using Excel tools, an embedded spreadsheet or graphic is not connected to the source workbook. Any changes you make to the copy in Word will not be made to the Excel source workbook.

Activity Steps

1. Click the **Start menu** on the Windows taskbar, point to **Programs**, then click **Microsoft Word**

2. In the New Document task pane, click **More documents**; click the **Look in list arrow**, then navigate to the location where your Project Files are stored

3. Double-click **Memo01.doc**; click in the blank area below the text line that reads "See the following:" to indicate where you want to place the embedded chart

4. Click **Insert** on the menu bar, click **Object**; in the Object dialog box, click the **Create from File tab**

5. Click **Browse**, double-click **Helicopters02.xls**
   See Figure 8-11.

6. Click **OK**
   The Excel chart appears at the location of the insertion point.

7. Click the **embedded chart** to select it, then, scrolling as necessary, drag the chart's **lower right sizing handle** until it is about as wide as the memo text

8. Double-click the **embedded chart**, click the **1st Quarter sheet tab**, then click the **Q1 Revenue per Guest sheet tab**
   See Figure 8-12.

9. Click in the memo outside the chart
   With the object deselected, the Word toolbars now appear.

 close Memo01.doc

Step 8
When you double-click an embedded object, the menu bar and toolbars above the memo change to Excel tools that you can use to modify the embedded copy of the chart or worksheet.

Figure 8-11: Locating the file to embed

Path to file you want to embed

Your path may be different

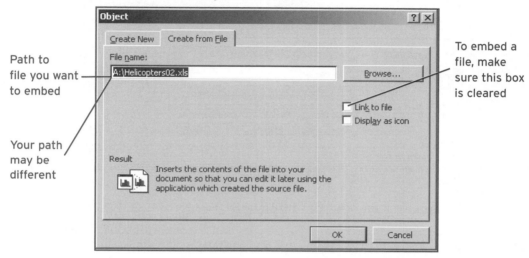

To embed a file, make sure this box is cleared

Figure 8-12: Excel chart embedded in a Word document

Word title bar

Excel menu bar and toolbars

Embedded chart in Word memo

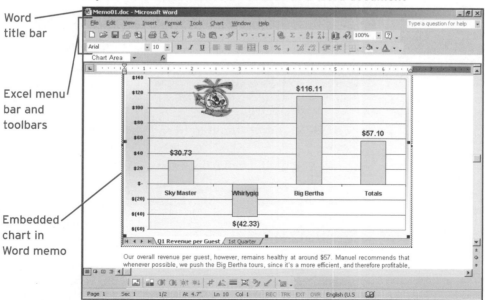

Skill Set 8

Importing and Exporting Data

Export Data from Excel
Link Excel Data to a PowerPoint Presentation

Using Microsoft Office programs—Word, Excel, Access, and PowerPoint—you can easily **integrate**, or combine, information created in one program in any of the other programs. For example, you can place an Excel chart in any Word document, or display any Word document in a PowerPoint slide. Sometimes, however, you want to paste information that will change over time, such as a sales report, and you want to make sure that the information in the **destination document** (the document that receives the data) contains the most recent information that you put in the source document. In these cases, you **link** the information using the Paste Link command on the Edit menu. Any changes to the source, or linked, information are automatically reflected in the destination document. You can link all or part of an Excel worksheet.

Step 7
To display the linked object as an icon, click the Display as icon check box in the Paste Special dialog box. Presentation users can double-click the icon to display the worksheet.

Activity Steps

1. With Excel open and a blank workbook displayed, click the **Start menu** on the Windows taskbar, point to **Programs**, then click **Microsoft PowerPoint**

2. In the New Presentation task pane, click **More presentations**, click the **Look in list arrow**, navigate to the location where your Project Files are stored, then double-click **Packages01.ppt**

3. Press **[Page Down]** three times to display slide #4, **Free Transportation**

4. Click the **Microsoft Excel - Book 1 button** on the taskbar, then open the file **Shuttle02.xls** from your Project File location

5. Drag to select the range **A1:C14**, click the **Copy button** on the Standard toolbar, then click the Microsoft PowerPoint - **Packages01.ppt button** on the taskbar

6. Click **Edit** on the menu bar, then click **Paste Special**
   See Figure 8-13.

7. Click the **Paste link option button**, then click **OK**

8. Drag the **linked object** up and left, then drag its **lower right resizing handle** so it fills the area under the text

9. Click the **Microsoft Excel - Shuttle02.xls button** on the taskbar, change the time in cell **B3** to **7:10**, then press **[Enter]**; click the Microsoft PowerPoint - **Packages01.ppt button** on the taskbar, then observe that the departure time in the slide has been automatically updated
   See Figure 8-14.

 close Packages01.ppt
   Shuttle02.xls

Figure 8-13: Linking a file in the Paste Special dialog box

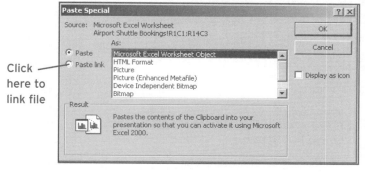

Click here to link file

Figure 8-14: Linked worksheet range on PowerPoint Slide

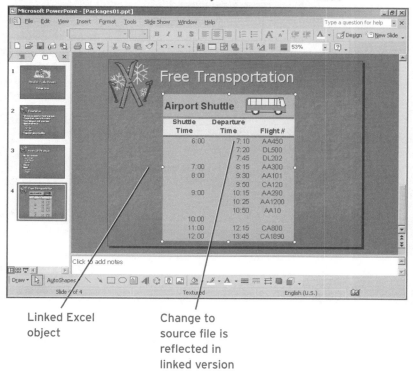

Linked Excel object

Change to source file is reflected in linked version

extra!

Updating linked information

You can have the destination program update your linked information automatically, or you can have it update only when you specify. In the destination program, click **Edit** on the menu bar, then click **Links**. In the Links dialog box, click the **Manual button**. To update a link, click to select the **link** in the list, then click **Update Now**. You can also use this dialog box to open the source document or to break the link.

Skill Set 8

Importing and Exporting Data

Export Data from Excel
Convert a List to an Access Table

To import Excel data into Microsoft Access to perform more sophisticated database tasks, you need to use the Import Spreadsheet Wizard in Access. An Excel list becomes an Access **table**, a collection of data about one subject, such as customers or suppliers. The Wizard asks you to indicate the sheet, the heading row, the sheet where you want to place the data, which columns you want, the **primary key** (the field that contains unique information for each record, or row), and the name of the new table.

Activity Steps

Step 1

Be sure your list does not contain any extra characters or formats in surrounding columns or rows. Your Excel list field names cannot contain any spaces or any characters such as periods, exclamation points, or brackets. If Access sees that your field names do not meet its field name requirements, it offers to convert them to acceptable names.

1. Click the **Start menu** on the Windows taskbar, point to **Programs**, then click **Microsoft Access**

2. Under New in the New File task pane, click **Blank Database**, then navigate to the location where your Project Files are stored

3. Select the **db1.mdb** in the File name box (if it's not already selected), type **Employees** to name the database, then click **Create**; click **File** on the menu bar, point to **Get External Data**, then click **Import**

4. Make sure your Project File storage location appears in the Look in box, click the **Files of type list arrow**, click **Microsoft Excel (*.xls)**, click **Rooms02.xls**, then click **Import**
See Figure 8-15.

5. In the Import Spreadsheet Wizard dialog box, make sure the **Show Worksheets option button** is selected, view the sample data, then click **Next**

6. Click the **First Row Contains Column Headings check box** to select it, then click **Next**; make sure the **In a New Table option** is selected, then click **Next**

7. You want to import all the fields, so click **Next**; make sure **Let Access add primary key** is selected, click **Next**, type **Employees**, click **Finish**, then click **OK**
Access has created a table named Employees.
See Figure 8-16.

8. Double-click **Employees** to open the table
See Figure 8-17.

9. Click the **Close button** 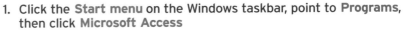 on the Access program menu bar

Figure 8-15: Import Spreadsheet Wizard

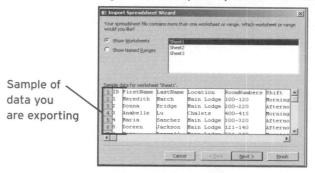

Sample of
data you
are exporting

Figure 8-16: Table name in Access window

New Access
table created
from exported
Excel data

Figure 8-17: Exported Excel data in Access table

Access
assigned an ID
number field

Exported
Excel data in
Access table

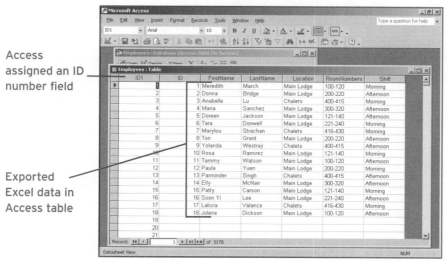

Skill Set 8

Importing and Exporting Data

Publish Worksheets and Workbooks to the Web
Publish a Worksheet Range to the Web

You can publish Excel worksheets and workbooks in HTML format for use on the Internet, World Wide Web, or an intranet. To save an entire workbook, you use the Save As command on the File menu. To publish a worksheet or worksheet range, you use the Publish option in the Save As Web Page dialog box. You can publish a worksheet or a workbook to a disk or directly to a Web or network server. When Excel publishes your data, it saves the data as an HTML file with the file extension .htm. It also creates a folder of supporting files in a folder called [filename]_files.

Activity Steps

 open Providers02.xls

1. Click **File** on the menu bar, click **Save As Web Page**, then click **Publish**

2. In the Publish as Web Page dialog box, click the **Choose list arrow**, then click **Range of cells**

3. Click the **Collapse dialog box button** , drag to select the range **A1:H16**, then click the **Expand dialog box button**

4. Click **Browse**, navigate to the location where your Project Files are stored, select the existing file name, type **analysis**, then click **OK**
   If you were publishing directly to a Web or network server, you would navigate to its online location. Also, it's best to name HTML files a maximum of eight characters, with no capital letters. Some networks do not handle long filenames well.

5. Click **Change**, type **Vail Internet Providers**, click **OK**, then click to select the check box next to **Open published web page in browser** if it's not already selected
   See Figure 8-18.

6. Click **Publish**
   After a moment, the file opens in your browser.

7. If your browser window is not already maximized, click its **Maximize button** on the title bar
   See Figure 8-19.

8. Close the Web browser window.

 close Providers02.xls

Step 6
Once you have saved a workbook, you can open the HTML file in Excel to modify it. You do not have to modify the original .xls file and republish it.

Figure 8-18: Saving a worksheet

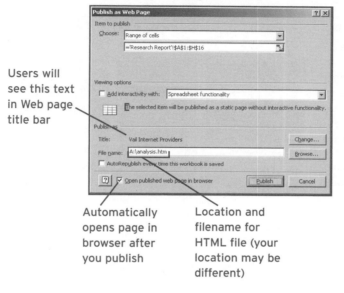

Users will see this text in Web page title bar

Automatically opens page in browser after you publish

Location and filename for HTML file (your location may be different)

Figure 8-19: Worksheet in HTML format in browser window

Your storage location may be different

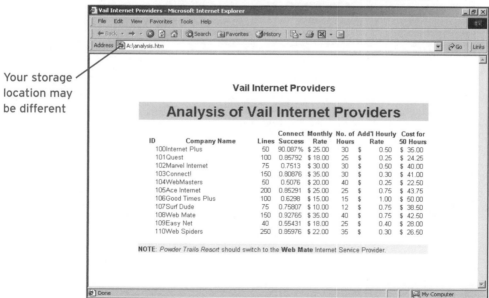

Skill Set 8

Importing and Exporting Data

Publish Worksheets and Workbooks to the Web

Publish an Interactive Workbook to the Web

When a workbook or worksheet is saved as an **interactive** HTML file, users can not only view it in their browsers, but they can also manipulate the information in it (provided they are using Microsoft Internet Explorer version 4.1 or later). They can switch among worksheets, manipulate data, and change formulas. For example, you could publish a worksheet that calculates net profit, and users could enter various sales numbers to see how the profit figure changes. Any changes users make, however, are not saved in the HTML document; the changes are lost when the user closes the browser. To retain modifications to an interactive worksheet you have already published, you have to modify the original Excel worksheet, then republish it.

Step 6
When you save a workbook with interactivity, it appears in a smaller window within your browser window, and wrapped text will no longer be wrapped. Be sure to test your files to make sure they look the way you want.

Activity Steps

 open Calculators01.xls

1. Click **File** on the menu bar, click **Save As Web Page**

2. Click to select the **Entire Workbook option button** (if it's not already selected), then click to select the **Add interactivity check box**
   See Figure 8-20.

3. Click **Publish**

4. Click **Browse**, navigate to the location where your Project Files are saved; in the File name box, select the existing file name if it's not already selected, type **mortgage**, then click **OK**

5. Deselect the **Open published page in Web browser** check box (if it's not already deselected); click to select the **AutoRepublish every time this workbook is saved check box**
   See Figure 8-21.

6. Click **Publish**
   The HTML file is saved as mortgage.htm. You could have previewed the file in your Web browser, but you will get a better view of the workbook if you open your browser first, then open the file, which you will do in the next lesson.

 close Calculators01.xls

Figure 8-20: Saving an interactive workbook

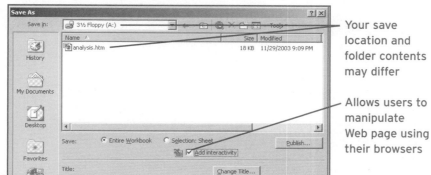

Your save location and folder contents may differ

Allows users to manipulate Web page using their browsers

Figure 8-21: Publish dialog box

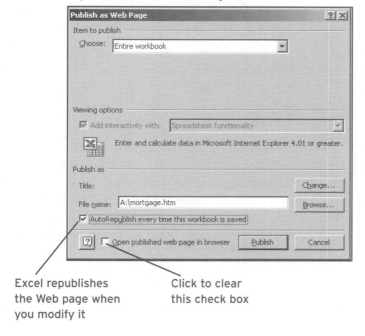

Excel republishes the Web page when you modify it

Click to clear this check box

extra!

Publishing worksheets with spreadsheet functionality

You can save worksheets with **spreadsheet functionality**, meaning that users can enter, format, calculate, analyze, and sort and filter all kinds of data. You can save the following with spreadsheet functionality: worksheets, external data ranges, PivotTable reports, cell ranges, filtered lists, and print areas. In the Publish as Web page dialog box, under Viewing options, select **Add interactivity with**, then make sure the box reads **Spreadsheet functionality**.

Skill Set 8

Importing and Exporting Data

Publish Worksheets and Workbooks to the Web

Use Interactive Workbooks

After you save a workbook or worksheet in HTML format, Excel saves the file with an .htm file extension and creates a folder containing any supporting files. Some objects will not appear in the htm file, such as embedded objects. You can view the HTML file in your browser at any time to see how it will look on the Web. To use an interactive workbook, you must use Internet Explorer version 4.1 or later. *Keep in mind that other users who do not have this software will not be able to view your worksheet at all; instead, they will see an error message, so you might not want to place an interactive worksheet on a public Web site.* Any changes you make to an interactive workbook using the browser are not saved to the HTML file or the original Excel file. After you close your browser, the file returns to its original state.

Step 7
To change the appearance of the selected cell or range, click the Commands and Options button on the Interactive workbook toolbar, then use the options on the Formatting tab. The changes remain in effect until you close Internet Explorer.

Activity Steps

1. Click **Start** on the Windows taskbar, point to **Programs**, then click **Internet Explorer**; if necessary, maximize the browser window

2. Click **File** on the menu bar, then click **Open**

3. Click **Browse**, click the **Look in list arrow**, then navigate to the location where your Project Files are stored

4. Click **calcs.htm**, then click **Open**
   See Figure 8-22.

5. Click **OK**

6. Click the **Condos sheet tab**, then click **Time Shares**

7. Click the **6.00%** figure after Interest Rate, type **5.00**, then watch the monthly payments as you press **[Enter]**
   See Figure 8-23.

8. Click **10** after # years, type **20**, then watch the monthly payments as you press **[Enter]**

9. Click the **Time Shares sheet tab**, click **Condos**, change the interest rate and loan term as you wish, then click the **Close button** ⊠ on the Internet Explorer title bar

Figure 8-22: Internet Explorer Open dialog box

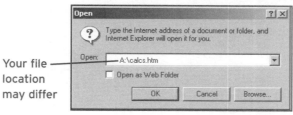

Your file location may differ

Figure 8-23: Monthly payments change after input cell is changed

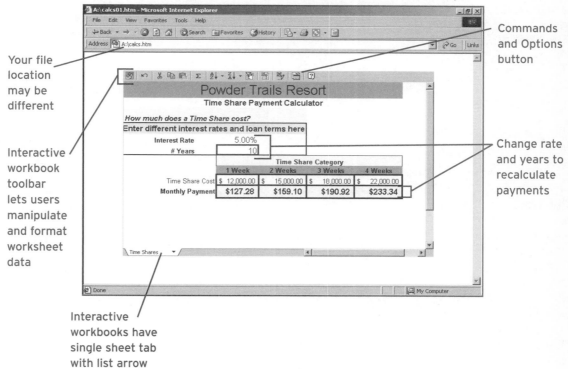

Your file location may be different

Commands and Options button

Interactive workbook toolbar lets users manipulate and format worksheet data

Change rate and years to recalculate payments

Interactive workbooks have single sheet tab with list arrow

Skill Set 8

Importing and Exporting Data

Target Your Skills

1 Import the text file School01.txt to Excel, accepting default settings, then save the file as School02.xls. Then import and format the data shown in Figure 8-24. Save the worksheet as revenue.htm without automatic republishing, then preview it in your browser.

Figure 8-24

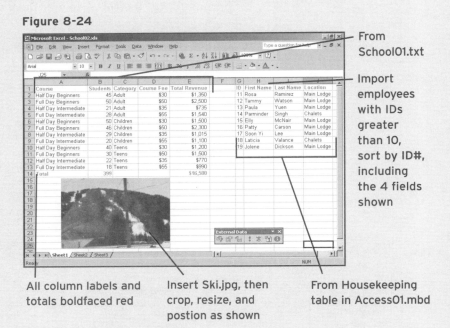

From School01.txt

Import employees with IDs greater than 10, sort by ID#, including the 4 fields shown

All column labels and totals boldfaced red

Insert Ski.jpg, then crop, resize, and postion as shown

From Housekeeping table in Access01.mbd

2 Import the text file Weather01.txt to a blank worksheet, accepting defaults, then save it as Weather02.xls. Make the changes shown in Figure 8-25. Save the file as an interactive workbook named "weather.htm". Open it in Internet Explorer. Add one formula, then format the cells using the Commands and Options button ▣.

Figure 8-25

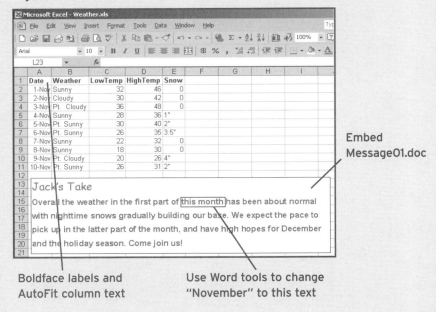

Embed Message01.doc

Boldface labels and AutoFit column text

Use Word tools to change "November" to this text

Skill Set 9

Managing Workbooks

Skill List

1. Create, edit, and apply templates
2. Create workspaces
3. Use data consolidation

As you use Excel, you will find there are particular workbook types you use repeatedly. Instead of recreating the same workbook with the same column headings, formatting, and formulas, you can create an Excel **template** to duplicate workbooks with the same design.

You may also find that you often work with more than one workbook open at the same time, such as a customer list and a customer report. Instead of opening each one separately, you can create a **workspace** to open both at the same time, in an arrangement that suits the way you work.

Often, you will have data in multiple worksheets (or workbooks), such as sheets detailing individual sales rep sales totals, that you want to combine into one sales sheet detailing all sales reps' totals. Excel lets you do this quickly using **data consolidation**.

Workbook icon

Template icon

Workspace icon

Skill Set 9
Managing Workbooks

Create, Edit, and Apply Templates
Create a Workbook Template

As you use Excel, you will create workbooks that you want to use repeatedly, such as budgets, expense or sales reports, and invoices. You could open a previously created workbook and resave it, but you would need to delete the existing data and resave the workbook using a new name. You can save time by creating a **template**, a workbook file with an .xlt file extension, that you use as a basis for new workbooks with the same design. A template can contain text, formatting, formulas, macros, charts, or data. You usually store templates in the Templates folder created when you installed Excel, in C:\Documents and Settings\[your user name]\Application Data\Microsoft. Templates stored in the Templates folder appear on the General Templates tab in the Templates dialog box, which appears when you click New from template in the New Workbook task pane. *Because readers of this book might be using a shared computer and might not have access to the Templates folder, you will save the template to the location where you store Project Files.*

Activity Steps

 open Budget03.xls

1. Select the data in the range **B5:D6**, press and hold **[Ctrl]**, select **B9:D17**, press **[Delete]**, then click cell **A1**
   Although the data is no longer in the worksheet, the formulas and formatting remain.

2. Click **File** on the menu bar, then click **Save As**

3. Click the **Save as type list arrow**, then click **Template (*.xlt)**
   The Template folder opens automatically.

4. Navigate to the location where your Project Files are stored

5. Edit the file name so it reads **Budget Template01**
   See Figure 9-1.

6. Click **Save**
   See Figure 9-2.

7. Click **File** on the menu bar, click **Properties**, click the **Summary tab** (if it's not already selected), click the **Save Preview Picture check box** to select it, click **OK**, then click the **Save button** 🖫 on the Standard toolbar
   An image of the first worksheet will now appear in the Preview section of the Templates dialog box when you create a workbook based on this template.

 close Budget Template01.xlt

Step 2
A template you create also contains a workbook's print areas, the number and type of sheets, hidden sheets, data validation settings, and any custom calculation options.

Figure 9-1: Saving a workbook as a template

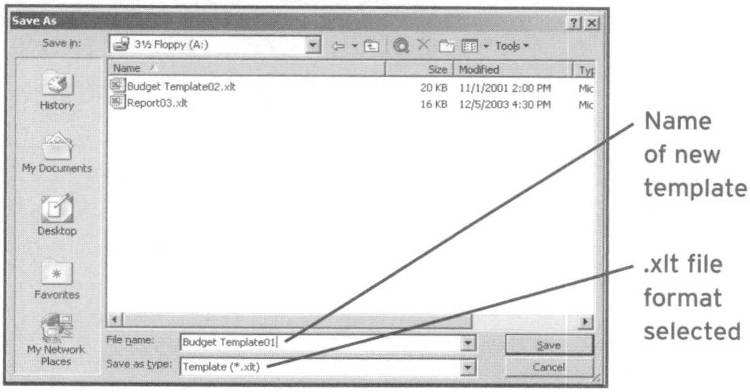

Name of new template

.xlt file format selected

Figure 9-2: Template file

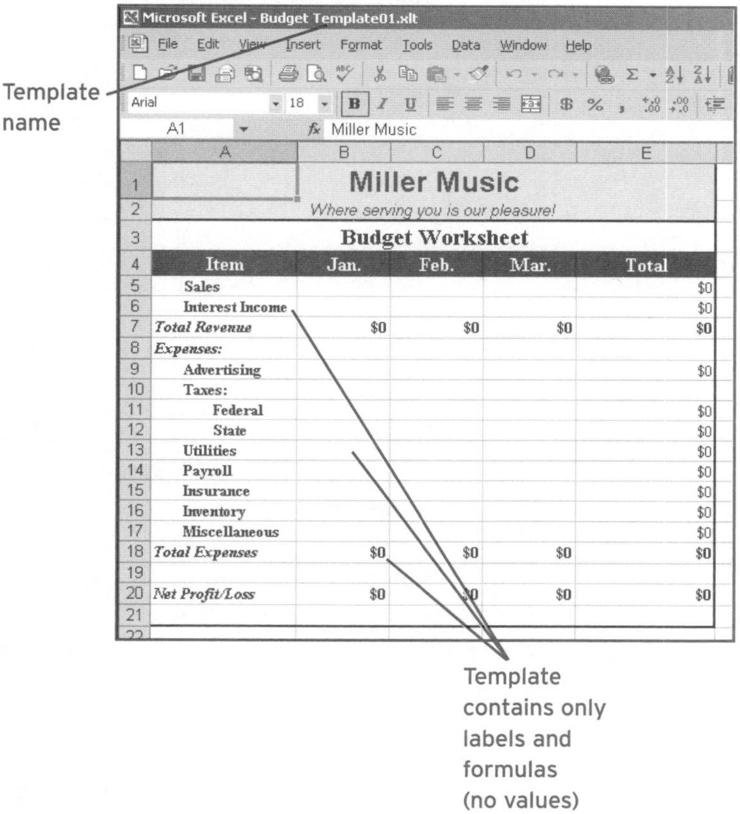

Template name

Template contains only labels and formulas (no values)

extra!

Creating worksheet templates

You can also create templates for the new worksheets you add to workbooks. For example, you might want all new worksheets to contain your company name, colors, font style, or logo in the footer. Create a workbook with one worksheet, then format it as you want all new worksheets to appear. Save it in the XLStart folder using the filename "sheet." The XLStart folder contains any items you want to open automatically every time you start Excel. Every new Excel worksheet will then have the features you added.

Skill Set 9

Managing Workbooks

Create, Edit, and Apply Templates
Create a New Workbook Based on a Template You Created

A workbook template is the basis for your future workbooks. Using a template is safer than resaving an older workbook because you are creating a fresh copy without the possibility of overwriting an older workbook. A workbook created from your template contains all the worksheets, formulas, formatting, styles, and macros in the template. You usually save your templates in the Templates folder created when you installed Excel, located at C:\Documents and Settings\[your user name]\Application Data\Microsoft. Templates stored in the Templates folder appear when you click General Templates in the New Workbook task pane. *Since you may be using a networked computer and may not have access to the Templates folder, you saved your template in the previous lesson in your Project File location. Therefore, this lesson has you open a workbook based on your template using the Choose workbook command in the New Workbook task pane. On the exam, however, the template you open and modify may be in the Templates folder. In this case, you should use the General Templates command under New from template in the New Workbook task pane to create the new workbook.*

Activity Steps

Step 2
You can use the New from existing workbook command in the New Workbook task pane to open a workbook based on any Excel workbook, not just templates.

1. If the New Workbook task pane is not displayed, click **File** on the menu bar, then click **New**

2. Under New from existing workbook, click **Choose workbook**

3. Navigate to the location where your Project Files are stored

4. Click **Budget Template02.xlt**
   See Figure 9-3.

5. Click **Create New**
   A new workbook opens based on the Budget Template02 workbook.

6. Enter the following information in the range B5:D5: **50,000, 40,000, 30,000**; enter the following information in the range B9:D9: **10,000, 8,000, 6,000**

7. Click each **chart tab**, then click the **Budget tab**
   The charts are based on the worksheet information you entered.

8. Click **File** on the menu bar, click **Save As**, change the filename to **Q1 Budget**

9. Click **Save**
   See Figure 9-4.

 close Q1 Budget.xls

Figure 9-3: Choosing a template

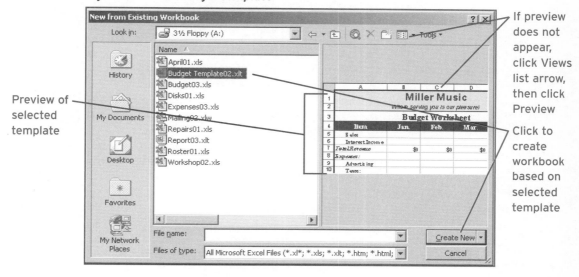

Preview of selected template

If preview does not appear, click Views list arrow, then click Preview

Click to create workbook based on selected template

Figure 9-4: Workbook based on a template

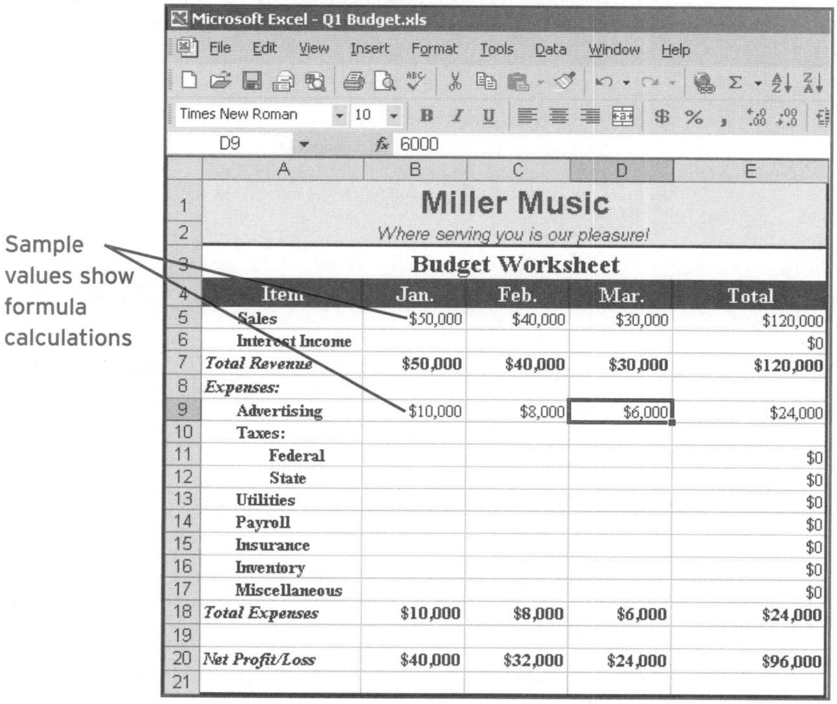

Sample values show formula calculations

Skill Set 9
Managing Workbooks

Create, Edit, and Apply Templates
Modify a Workbook Template

To modify a workbook template, you open the .xlt file from the Open dialog box. After modifying the file, you save the changes. All future workbooks you create based on the template will reflect your changes. Workbooks you created using the unrevised template, however, retain the original design. *Normally, templates are stored in the Templates directory folder created when you installed Excel, usually located at C:\Documents and Settings\[your user name]\Application Data\Microsoft. Templates stored in the Templates folder appear when you click General Templates in the New Workbook task pane. If you are using a networked computer you may not have access to the Templates folder in this activity you will open and save the template in your Project File location. On the exam, however, keep in mind that the template you open and modify may be in the templates folder.*

Activity Steps

Step 4
If you want to display only templates, you can select Templates (*.xlt) in the Files of type list.

1. If the New Workbook task pane is not visible, click **File** on the menu bar, then click **New**

2. Click **More workbooks** in the New Workbook task pane

3. In the Open dialog box, navigate to the location where your Project Files are stored

4. Make sure the Files of type box reads **All Microsoft Excel Files** to display workbooks and templates

5. If your files are not displayed in Preview view, click the **Views list arrow**, then click **Preview**

6. Click **Report03.xlt**, compare your screen to Figure 9-5, then click **Open**

7. Click the **column B heading** to select the column, click **Format** on the menu bar, point to **Column**, then click **Width**

8. Type **20**, then click **OK**

9. Click cell **A22**, then type **Original receipts must be submitted for all expenses**

10. Press **[Ctrl][Enter]**, then click the **Save button** on the Standard toolbar
    The next time you or another user creates a document based on the template, it will have the wider column and the added text.
    See Figure 9-6.

    close Report03.xlt

Figure 9-5: Opening the template

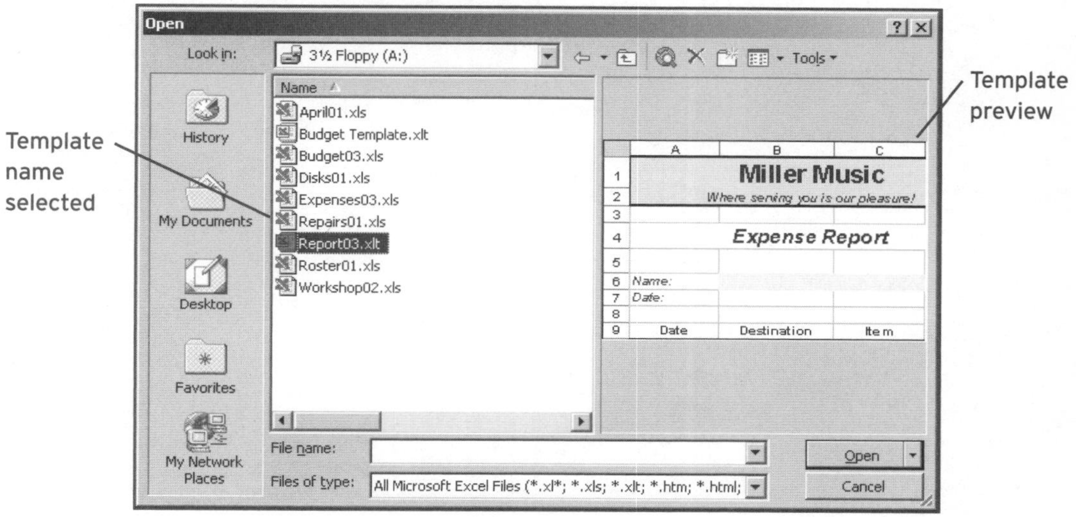

Template name selected

Template preview

Figure 9-6: Modified template

Column widened

Text added

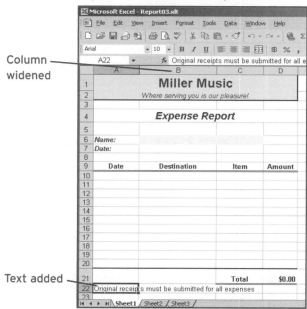

Skill Set 9

Managing Workbooks

Create Workspaces
Create a Workspace File

If you frequently work with a particular set of workbooks that you need to have open at the same time, it can be time-consuming to open and reposition each one at the start of every work session. Using an Excel workspace file can help. A **workspace** is an Excel file with an .xlw file extension that contains the location, window sizes, and display settings of selected workbooks. Then, instead of opening each individual file, you open the workspace file, which automatically opens the workbooks in the arrangment and settings you specified. You can include two or more Excel workbooks in a workspace. The workspace file does not contain the workbooks themselves, so when you back up the files by copying them to another disk, be sure to copy the workbooks, not just the .xlw file.

Activity Steps

 open Roster01.xls
Workshop02.xls

1. With Roster01 and Workshop02 open, click **Window** on the menu bar, then click **Arrange**

2. Click **Vertical**, then click **OK**

3. Click the **Roster01.xls** title bar, click the **Zoom list arrow** on the Standard toolbar, then click **75%**

4. Click **Tools** on the menu bar, click **Options**, click the **View tab** (if it's not already selected), under Window options click to deselect the **Row & column headers** check box, then click **OK**
   A workspace preserves most, but not all, of the settings you choose in the tabs of the Options dialog box.
   See Figure 9-7.

5. Click **File** on the menu bar, then click **Save Workspace**

6. Navigate to the location where your Project Files are stored, double-click **resume** (the default file name in the File Name box), then type **Mailing01**
   See Figure 9-8.

7. Click **Save**

8. Click **No** to close the Roster01 project file without saving your changes, then close both files without saving

 close Roster01.xls
Workshop02.xls

Step 6
If you want to open the workbooks every time you start Excel, place the workspace file in your XLStart folder. The XLStart folder location can vary, depending on the way Excel was installed. Use the Search/For Files or Folders command on the Start menu to locate it.

Figure 9-7: Workbook arrangement

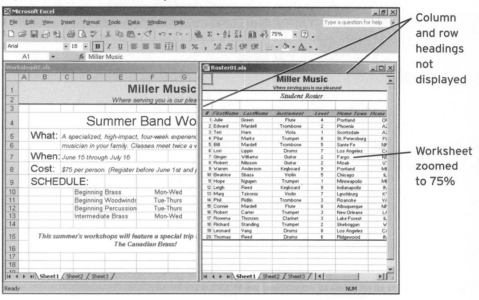

Column and row headings not displayed

Worksheet zoomed to 75%

Figure 9-8: Saving a workspace file

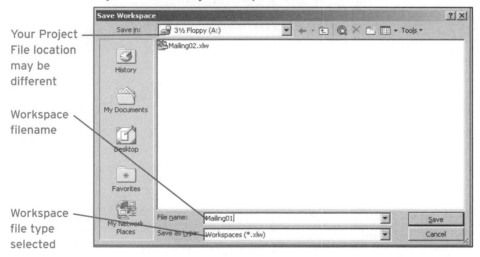

Your Project File location may be different

Workspace filename

Workspace file type selected

Skill Set 9

Managing Workbooks

Create Workspaces
Open a Workspace

Once you have created a workspace file, the file itself, named [filename].xlw, is stored in the location you specified. When you open the workspace file, Excel automatically opens the files that were open at the time you created the workspace, using the window arrangement, magnification settings, and options you specified.

Step 4
You can also select All Files (*.*) to display files of all types, including those created in other programs, or All Excel files to display all files created using Excel, including workbooks, templates, and workspaces.

Activity Steps

1. If the New Workbook task pane is not open, click **File** on the menu bar, then click **New**

2. Click **More workbooks** in the New Workbook task pane

3. In the Open dialog box, navigate to the location where your Project Files are stored (if it's not already displayed)

4. Click **Mailing02.xlw**, then compare your screen to Figure 9-9

5. Click **Open**
   The two workbooks referred to in the Mailing02.xlw workspace file open with the window arrangement and zoom settings that were saved at the time the Mailing02.xlw file was created.
   See Figure 9-10.

 close Roster01.xls
   Workshop02.xls

Figure 9-9: Opening a workspace file

All Microsoft
Excel files
displayed

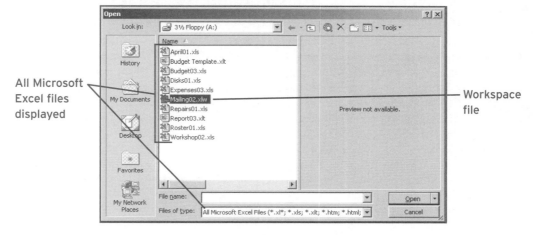

Workspace
file

Figure 9-10: Workbooks open in workspace

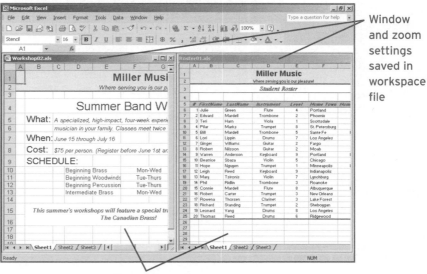

Window
and zoom
settings
saved in
workspace
file

Depending on your
monitor, your screen may
look slightly different

Skill Set 9
Managing Workbooks

Use Data Consolidation
Consolidate Data from Multiple Worksheets with the Same Layout

As you use Excel, you may want to **consolidate**, or combine, information from multiple worksheets in one summary worksheet. For example, you might have monthly sales data on separate worksheets that you want to consolidate as quarterly sales figures on one summary sheet. You can use 3-D formula references, but Excel also features a Consolidate command that offers more options for combining data. If the worksheets you want to combine have an identical layout, you can consolidate **by position**, which combines data from the exact same cell locations. In the example you will use below, each store has CDs in the same categories, so you can consolidate the data by position. You can consolidate data using many standard functions, including SUM, AVERAGE, MIN, and MAX.

Step 4
If the range on the supporting worksheet has a name, you can enter it in the formula instead of selecting the range each time. Range names can save time and ensure accuracy when you are working with large worksheets.

Activity Steps

 open Disks01.xls

1. Maximize the Excel window if necessary; on the All Stores worksheet, select the range **C8:C16**, click **Data** on the menu bar, then click **Consolidate**

2. If necessary, move the dialog box right so you can see column C

3. Under Function, make sure **Sum** is selected

4. Click the **Eugene sheet tab**, (if the Consolidate dialog box is obscuring column C, drag the dialog box **title bar** so you can see the column contents), select the range **C8:C16**, then click **Add** *See Figure 9-11.*

5. Click the **St. Paul sheet tab** Because the worksheets have the same categories, the correct range is already selected.

6. Click **Add**

7. Click the **San Jose sheet tab**, then click **Add**

8. Click **OK**, then click any blank worksheet cell *See Figure 9-12.*

 close Disks01.xls

Figure 9-11: First consolidation range

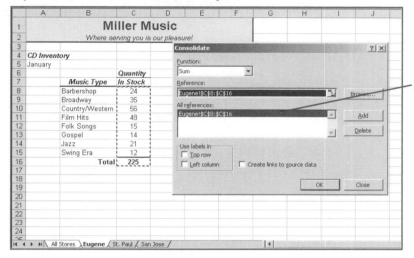

Figure 9-12: Consolidated data for three stores

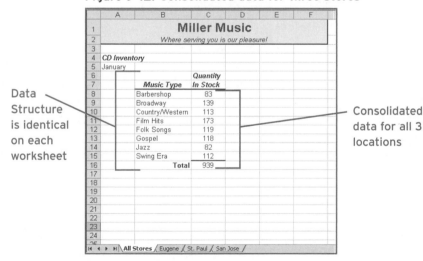

Data Structure is identical on each worksheet

Consolidated data for all 3 locations

extra!

Consolidating data from different workbooks

You can consolidate data from other workbooks as well as other worksheets. Make sure the supporting workbooks are open. References to cells in other workbooks have the filename in brackets before the sheet name, such as [Filename]Sheetname! Reference. You can also use range names in supporting workbooks.

Skill Set 9

Managing Workbooks

Use Data Consolidation

Consolidate Data from Multiple Worksheets with Different Layouts

You can consolidate by position when all sheets have an identical layout, but when sheets have different layouts, you must consolidate **by category**. To do this you use the Consolidation command, but you let Excel create the category listings from the supporting sheets. In the example you will use below, each store has identical expense categories in rows 10 to 15, but the San Jose and Eugene stores have additional distinct categories in rows 16 and 17.

Activity Steps

 open Expenses03.xls

1. Maximize the Excel window if necessary

2. Click cell **B10**, click **Data** on the menu bar, click **Consolidate**, then move the dialog box to the right so you can see column C
   When you consolidate by category, you only select the upper left corner of the consolidation range.

3. Under Function, make sure **Sum** is selected; if there are references listed under All references, click each one, then click **Delete**

4. Click the **San Jose sheet tab**, select the range **A10:B18**, then click **Add**

5. Click the **Eugene sheet tab**, select the range **A10:B17**, then click **Add**

6. Click the **St. Paul sheet tab**, select the range **A10:B16**, then click **Add**

7. Under Use labels in, click the **Left column check box** to select it (if it's not already selected)

8. Click the **Create links to source data check box** to select it
   See Figure 9-13.

9. Click **OK**, then click any blank cell on the Consolidation sheet
   See Figure 9-14.

 close Expenses03.xls

Step 7
After you perform a consolidation, Excel saves the consolidation references in the All references list; you can repeat the consolidation by choosing Data/Consolidate, then clicking OK.

Figure 9-13: Completed Consolidation dialog box

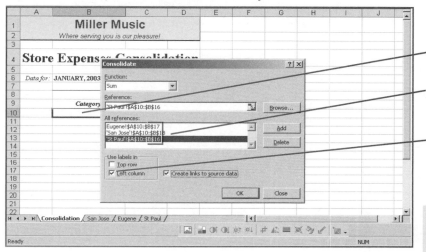

Select upper left corner of consolidation range

Ranges are different on each sheet

Tells Excel to use labels from left column in each range

Figure 9-14: Consolidated data

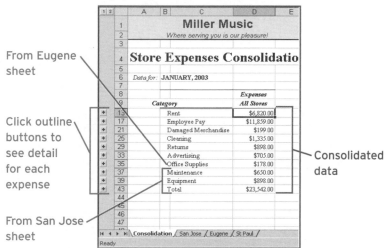

From Eugene sheet

Click outline buttons to see detail for each expense

From San Jose sheet

Consolidated data

extra!

Learning more about consolidation links

Unlike 3-D formulas, consolidation ranges are not automatically linked to the supporting data. This means that if you change data on the supporting sheets, you must repeat the consolidation. When you select the Create links to source data check box in the Consolidation dialog box, you link the source ranges to the consolidation sheet. When this option is selected, Excel creates an outline that links each source reference to the consolidation, along with a summary entry. Excel creates additional rows and columns for each unique entry and links formulas for each one.

Skill Set 9

Managing Workbooks

Target Your Skills

file Repairs01.xls

1 Create a template named Repairs.xlt containing only text and formulas from Repairs01.xls, then close the template. Create a workbook, enter data in the Accordions line, then save it as January.xls. Open both the template and the January workbook, tile the windows as shown in Figure 9-15, then save the workspace as Both.xlw. Close the workbooks, open the workspace, then close it. Reopen the template, then modify it as shown in Figure 9-15, saving your changes.

Figure 9-15

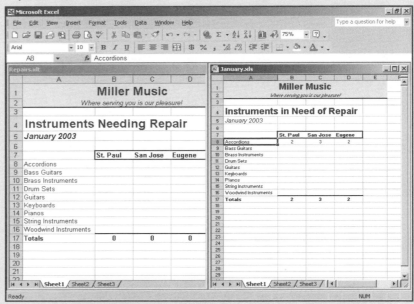

file April01.xls

2 Create the consolidation sheet shown in Figure 9-16, consolidating by category and linking the consolidation to the source.

Figure 9-16

1 2		A	B	C	D	E	F
	1			**Miller Music**			
	2			*Where serving you is our pleasure!*			
	3						
	4		**Sales**				
	5		*April 2003*				
	6						
	7		**Category**	**Total Sales**			
+	11		CDs	$ 160,490			
+	15		Audio Tapes	$ 54,950			
+	17		Scores	$ 1,650			
+	19		Videos	$ 25,860			
+	21		DVDs	$ 15,810			
+	24		Song Books	$ 8,570			

Skill List

1. Create and apply custom number formats
2. Use conditional formats

You can apply many standard number formats (such as Currency and Percent) and cell formats (such as bolding and colors) to cell contents. As you become more proficient at using Excel and create more complex worksheets, you might want to format numbers in special ways. **Custom number formats** are formats that you create, usually by modifying existing formats. You can create a format that contains a specific number of decimal places not found in the standard formats, or a format that displays negative values in a particular color. You create custom formats in the Format Cells dialog box; they are then available for future use.

In other situations, you may want worksheet values to display with a specific format only if a particular condition is true. For example, if you want all the dates after January 1st to display in red, or all the values over 1,000,000 to display in bold, Arial type, you can specify these conditions using the Excel **conditional formatting** feature.

Skill Set 10

Formatting Numbers

Create and Apply Custom Number Formats
Create and Apply a Custom Number Format

You are not limited to the number formats Excel supplies. You can define your own formats to display text and values using the Custom category in the Format Cells dialog box. Excel supplies over 30 custom formats, but you can customize any of them to meet your needs. You use formatting codes to set custom formats: # represents any digit, and 0 represents a digit that will always be displayed, even if the digit is 0. The code #,### will display 3456 as 3,456. The code 0.000 will display .123 as 0.123. A number format can have four parts, each one separated by semicolons: [positive numbers];[negative numbers];[zeroes];[text]. You don't need to specify all four parts. If you specify only one part, your format will apply to anything you type in that cell. If you specify two parts, they will apply to positive and negative numbers. Always begin by selecting a cell with values in it before opening the Format Cells dialog box so that Excel will display a sample of the selected value using the format you have selected or created.

Activity Steps

 open Bikes03.xls

1. Click cell **B21**
   The formula calculates net profit or loss, and is currently in Accounting format with two decimal places, which displays negative values in parentheses.

2. Click **Format** on the menu bar, click **Cells**, click the **Number tab** (if it's not already selected), then under Category, click **Custom**

3. Scroll the Type list until you see the last format that begins with a dollar sign (the 13th format): **$#,##0.00_);[Red]($#,##0.00)**, then click it once
   This custom format displays numbers with dollar signs and two decimal places. The _) inserts a space the width of a closing parenthesis after the number so that negative numbers in parentheses will align with positive numbers. The [Red] after the semicolon directs Excel to display negative numbers in red. The zeroes at the end limit the display to two decimal places.

4. In the Type box, click after the "d" in "Red", press **[Backspace]** three times, then type **Blue**
   See Figure 10-1.

5. Click **OK**

6. Drag the **cell B21 fill handle** to include cell **H21**, then click any blank cell
   See Figure 10-2.

 close Bikes03.xls

Step 2
Custom formats apply to the workbook in which you created them. To make them available in another workbook, copy and paste a number with a custom format to the new workbook.

Figure 10-1: Customized format

Preview of selected cell value with custom format applied

Clicking Custom category displays available custom formats

Edit selected format in type box

Format you edited above

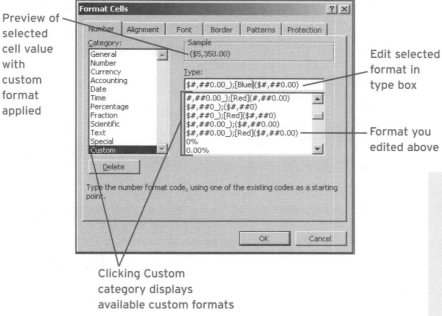

Figure 10-2: Worksheet with custom format applied

10	Sales	12,000.00	18,000.00	9,900.00	3,300.00	6,600.00	27,000.00	76,800.00
11	**Total Projected Income**	$10,800.00	$16,500.00	$ 6,600.00	$ 3,000.00	$31,900.00	$74,400.00	143,200.00
12								
13	**Projected Expenses**							
14	Payroll	$ 7,450.00	$ 7,450.00	$ 7,450.00	$ 4,800.00	$ 7,450.00	$12,800.00	$ 47,400.00
15	Cost of Sales	7,200.00	10,800.00	5,940.00	1,980.00	3,960.00	16,200.00	46,080.00
16	Maintenance	400.00	400.00	400.00	400.00	400.00	400.00	2,400.00
17	Equipment Lease	400.00	400.00	400.00	400.00	400.00	400.00	2,400.00
18	Advertising	700.00	700.00	400.00	1,200.00	1,800.00	2,200.00	7,000.00
19	**Total Projected Expenses**	$16,150.00	$19,750.00	$14,590.00	$ 8,780.00	$14,010.00	$32,000.00	$ 105,280.00
20								
21	**Profit**	($5,350.00)	($3,250.00)	($7,990.00)	($5,780.00)	$17,890.00	$42,400.00	$37,920.00

2003 / 2004

Negative values are blue

Positive values are black, the default color

Skill Set 10

Formatting Numbers

Create and Apply Custom Number Formats

Create and Apply a Custom Date and Time Format

Excel supplies numerous date and time formats. To customize a date and time format on the Number tab of the Format Cells dialog box, you first select an existing custom format, then modify it. In date and time formats, Excel uses first letters to represent the month, date, year, hour, and minute (m, d, y, h, m). (The letter "m" can also stand for "month," but if you type it right after an "h", Excel interprets it as "minute.") Characters such as dashes and colons (-, :) appear as typed.

Activity Steps

 open Shuttle03.xls

1. Click **cell B6**

2. Click **Format** on the menu bar, click **Cells**, then click the **Number tab** (if it's not already selected)

3. Under Category, click **Custom**

4. Scroll through the Type list, then click **m/d/yyyy h:mm**
   The Sample above the Type box shows that this format displays an entered time as [month with 1 or 2 digits]/[day]/[year with 4 digits] [time in hours and minutes].

5. In the Type box, click after **mm** to place the insertion point there

6. Press **[Spacebar]**, then type **AM/PM**
   See Figure 10-3.

7. Click **OK**

8. Click the **Format Painter button** on the Standard toolbar, then drag to select the range **B7:B17**

9. Click cell **B6**, type **3/6**, press **[Spacebar]**, type **7:15**, then press **[Enter]**
   If you were going to use this sheet, you would need to enter dates in the remainder of the cells in the column.
   See Figure 10-4.

 close Shuttle03.xls

Step 9
Using this format, you would enter times after 11:59 am using a 24-hour clock, such as 13:15 for 1:15 p.m., and so forth.

Figure 10-3: Custom format in Format Cells dialog box

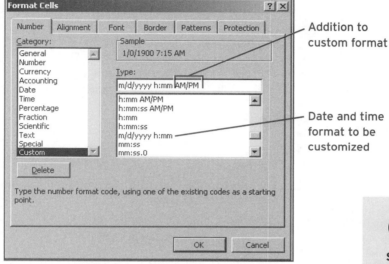

Addition to custom format

Date and time format to be customized

Figure 10-4: Custom format applied to worksheet cells

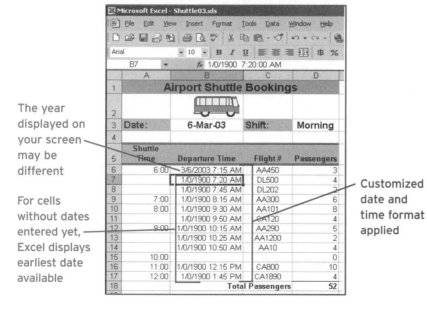

The year displayed on your screen may be different

For cells without dates entered yet, Excel displays earliest date available

Customized date and time format applied

extra!

Specifying date and time codes

You can repeat date and time codes to indicate how you want the values to display. For example, mm displays the month as a 2-digit number, such as 03 for March. The code mmmm (the maximum number of month code letters) displays the full month name, such as December. The code dd displays the third day of the month as 03, and dddd displays the first day of the week as Monday. If the code "m" follows an "h" code, Excel will interpret it as minutes instead of months. Similarly, if the code "d" follows a month code, it will be interpreted as date instead of day.

Skill Set 10

Formatting Numbers

Create and Apply Custom Number Formats
Create and Apply a Custom Format with Text

When you create a custom number format, you can add text or symbols that will appear in the formatted cell. Certain symbols, such as $, _, !, < and the space character will appear as you type them, but you need to enclose words in quotation marks. For example, the codes $0.00" OK" will display 4.50 as $4.50 OK in the worksheet cell. The custom formats $0.00" OK";$-0.00" Under target" will display positive numbers as $4.50 OK but negative numbers as $-4.50 Under target.

Step 5
Custom formats you add appear at the bottom of the Type list on the Number tab of the Format Cells dialog box. To delete a format you created, scroll to display it, click it once, then click Delete.

Activity Steps

 open Providers03.xls

1. Click cell **D3**, click **Format** on the menu bar, then click **Cells**

2. Click the **Number tab** (if it's not already selected), then under Category, click **Custom**

3. Under Type, click **0.00%** (the 15th format)

4. In the Type box, click after %

5. Type **"**, press **[Spacebar]**, type **Rate**, then type **"**
   The format should read 0.00%" Rate".
   See Figure 10-5.

6. Click **OK**

7. Click the **Format Painter button** on the Standard toolbar, drag down the range **D4:D13**, then click any blank cell
   See Figure 10-6.

 close Providers03.xls

Figure 10-5: Specifying text in a custom format

Text will appear
next to each
percentage

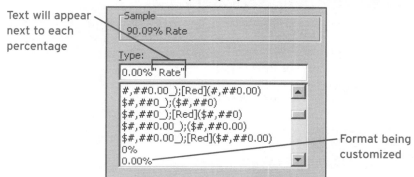

Format being
customized

Figure 10-6: Custom format with text applied to cells

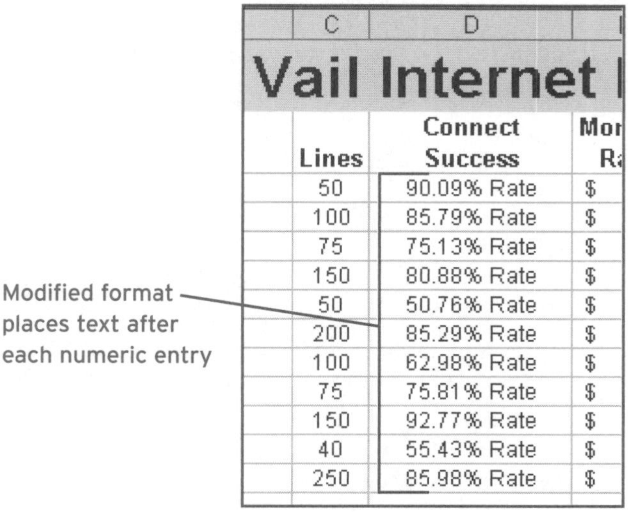

C	D	
Vail Internet		
	Connect	**Mo**r
Lines	**Success**	**R**a
50	90.09% Rate	$
100	85.79% Rate	$
75	75.13% Rate	$
150	80.88% Rate	$
50	50.76% Rate	$
200	85.29% Rate	$
100	62.98% Rate	$
75	75.81% Rate	$
150	92.77% Rate	$
40	55.43% Rate	$
250	85.98% Rate	$

Modified format
places text after
each numeric entry

Skill Set 10
Formatting Numbers

Use Conditional Formats
Apply Conditional Formats

A **conditional format** is a format you can have Excel apply only to cells whose values meet conditions you set. You can use any of the formats on the Fonts, Border, or Patterns tabs in the Format Cells dialog box. For example, in a schedule worksheet showing due dates, you can have Excel apply a bold, red format only to cells in which the date is later than a date you specify, such as >5/1 (which specifies dates later than May 1st). Or you could apply a shaded green format to values 20,000 and under (less than or equal to, or <=20,000). You can specify up to 3 conditional formats for a cell range.

Step 7
To delete a conditional format, select the range to which the formatting is applied, click Format, click Conditional Formatting, then click Delete. Click to place a check mark next to the format you want to delete, then click OK.

Activity Steps

 open Commissions02.xls

1. Select the range **C7:C37**, press and hold down **[Ctrl]**, then select the range **F7:F37**

2. Click **Format** on the menu bar, then click **Conditional Formatting**

3. In the leftmost list box, make sure **Cell Value Is** is selected

4. Click the **between list arrow**, click **less than**, click the rightmost box, then type **500**

5. Click **Format** to open the Format Cells dialog box

6. On the Font tab, select the **Bold** Font style, click the **Color list arrow**, click the **Violet color** (3rd row, 2nd color from the right), then click **OK**

7. Click **Add**, under Condition 2, specify that the Cell Value Is **greater than or equal to**, then type **1000** in the text box

8. Click **Format** for condition 2, specify **Bold** Font style, click **Red** color (3rd row, leftmost color), then click **OK**
   See Figure 10-7.

9. In the Conditional Formatting dialog box, click **OK**, click any blank worksheet cell, then scroll to view the top of the list if necessary
   See Figure 10-8.

 close Commissions02.xls

Figure 10-7: Specifying two conditional formats

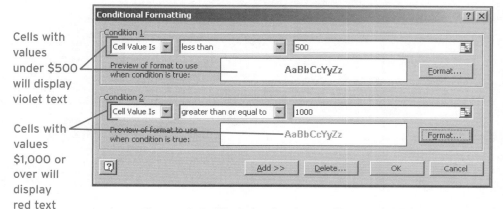

Cells with values under $500 will display violet text

Cells with values $1,000 or over will display red text

Figure 10-8: Worksheet values reflect conditional formats

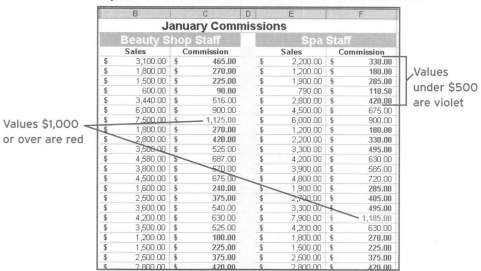

Values $1,000 or over are red

Values under $500 are violet

Skill Set 10

Formatting Numbers

Target Your Skills

 Water01.xls

1 Create four custom formats: for cell B3, modify the custom format mmm-yy as shown in Figure 10-9; for cell E7, modify the 0.00% format to delete the % sign, then add the word "HI" after the number, separated by a space; for cell E9, the same as E7 but have it add the word "LO" instead. Then in the range G7:G24, modify the 0.00% format so that negative numbers display in magenta.

 Guests05.xls

2 Using Figure 10-10 as a guide, create two conditional formats for the range B5:G15, one that displays numbers 1,000 and above in bold, italic, red, and another that displays numbers under 100 as bold, italic, blue.

Figure 10-9

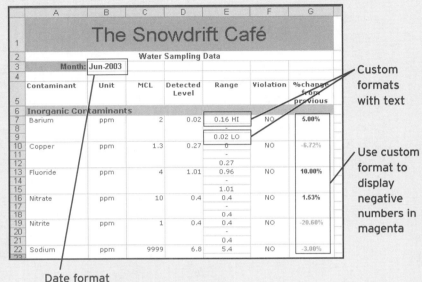

Figure 10-10

Skill Set 11
Working with Ranges

Skill List

1. Use named ranges in formulas
2. Use lookup and reference functions

Cell ranges, which are groups of adjacent cells, provide a convenient way of working with blocks of worksheet information. For example, if you want to total the values in the range E6 through E9, it's easier to refer to SUM(E6:E9), rather than to E6+E7+E8+E9. Excel simplifies the task of entering ranges further by allowing you to assign **range names**, which are names that represent groups of cells, such as "Sales" or "1997_Income." Once you name a cell range, you can use the name, instead of the range reference, in formulas.

You can name a range by typing, or you can direct Excel to use existing column or row labels as range names.

You can also use a range within a list to find list values. The VLOOKUP (vertical lookup) function searches down a list column and locates values, just as you would look down the names in a telephone book to locate a number. The HLOOKUP function looks across rows. These functions are especially useful in long lists of information.

Skill Set 11
Working with Ranges

Use Named Ranges in Formulas
Create a Cell or Range Name

Your Excel formulas usually contain references to other cells and ranges, such as =B5-C6 or =C2-SUM(C3:C10). While cell and range references will certainly do the job, formulas can become difficult to read in a large worksheet. You can simplify your formulas by using range names. A **range name** is a name that you assign to any cell or range; you can then use that name in formulas instead of the column and row references. For example, instead of =B6-B9, you could name cell B6 "Income" and cell B9 "Expenses", then create the formula =Income-Expenses. In a more complex example, you could assign the name "Salary" to range C3:C10, then use the name in the formula =C2-SUM(Salary). Range names you create are available on any worksheet in the workbook. You can assign names in the Name box on the left side of the Formula bar, or in the Define Name dialog box.

Step 3
You don't have to select a range before opening the Define dialog box. You can name the range, click the Collapse dialog box button , select the range, then click the Expand dialog box button .

Activity Steps

open Budget04.xls

1. Select the range B10:D11

2. Click the **Name box** on the left side of the Formula bar, type **Taxes**, then press **[Enter]**

3. Select the range B12:D17

4. Click **Insert** on the menu bar, point to **Name**, then click **Define**

5. Type **Other_Expenses**, check the range in the Refers to box, then click **Add**
   A range name cannot contain spaces, but it can contain letters, numbers, and the backslash (\) and underscore (_) characters.
   See Figure 11-1.

6. Click **Close**

7. Click the **Name list arrow**
   See Figure 11-2.

8. Click any blank worksheet cell

close Budget04.xls

Figure 11-1: Range name in the Define Name dialog box

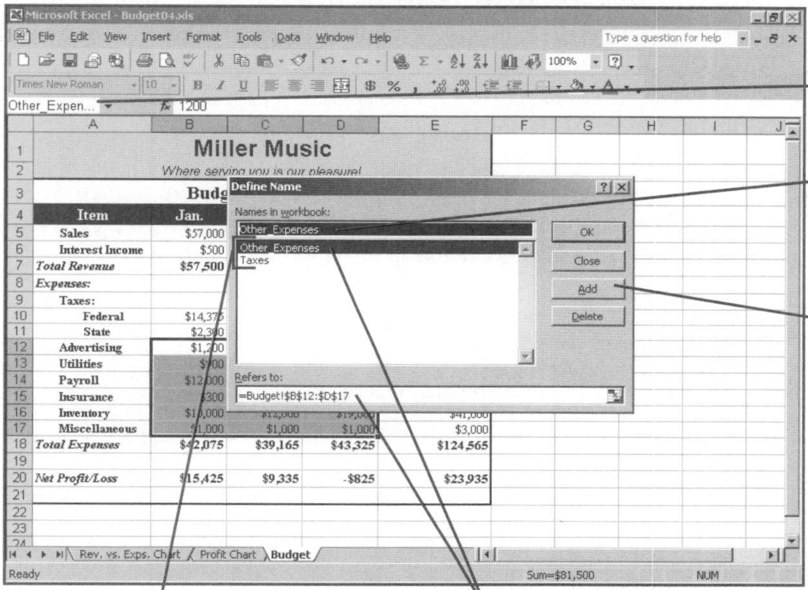

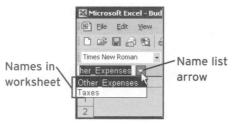

Name box

Type new range names here

Click to add new names to list

Range names appear here

Reference of selected name appears in bottom box

Figure 11-2: List of range names you created

Names in worksheet

Name list arrow

extra!

Navigating with Range Names

In a large worksheet, you can use names to select worksheet sections. Click the **Name list arrow** in the Formula bar, then choose the name of the range you want to select. Excel displays and selects that range. This can be a convenient way of checking the cell references of existing names. Excel also automatically lists range names in the Go To dialog box, so you can click **Edit** on the menu bar, click **Go To**, then select any range to select it and click OK.

Skill Set 11
Working with Ranges

Use Named Ranges in Formulas
Use Labels to Create Range Names

You can use column or row labels as range names, which saves time by allowing you to name several ranges at once. You begin by selecting the range containing the column or row labels and the values in those columns or rows, then using the Create Names dialog box to indicate which cells contain the label names. Since the purpose of creating range names is to use them as references and in formulas, be sure that all the cells in the named range contain values you will want to use later. If the column or label name contains spaces, Excel automatically replaces them with an underscore character to make them "legal" range names.

Step 5
To delete a range name, click Insert on the menu bar, point to Name, then click Define. Select the range name in the list, then click Delete. Repeat as necessary for each name you want to delete, then click OK.

Activity Steps

 open Instruments04.xls

1. Right-click the **column B heading** to select the column, then click **Delete**
   The column B information contains part numbers, which you don't want to include in your named range. When using cell labels to create range names, the labels and the data should be in contiguous columns.

2. Select the range **A7:C15**

3. Click **Insert** on the menu bar, point to **Name**, then click **Create**

4. Click the **Left column check box** to select it (if it's not already selected)
   See Figure 11-3.

5. Click **OK**, then click any blank worksheet cell

6. Click the **Name list arrow** in the formula bar, then click **Bass_Guitars**
   Excel has created a name for each row you selected, adding underscores in place of spaces. Notice that the name refers only to the cells containing values, not to the cells containing text.
   See Figure 11-4.

 close Instruments04.xls

Figure 11-3: Specifying the location of labels that will become range names

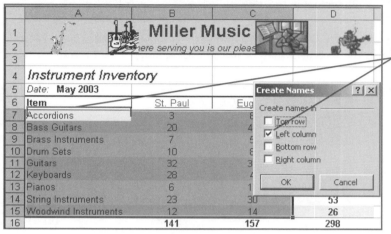

Excel will create range names for each row using item names in left column

Figure 11-4: Range names Excel created from row labels

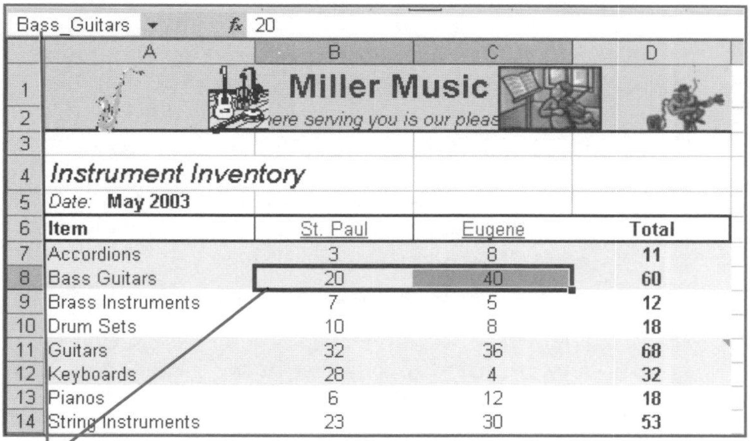

Selecting range name in list selects cells it refers to

extra!

Using range names for fixed values

Range names are also helpful when you have a value that doesn't change, called a **constant**, that you need to use repeatedly in a worksheet. For example, you might want to use a particular tax rate frequently in your formulas, such as a federal tax rate of 33%. In the Define Name dialog box, type a name, such as **Fed_Tax**, then type the constant, such as **=.33** in the Refers To box, then click **OK**. Then you can use the name Fed_Tax in formulas without having to recall the exact rate. Constant names do not appear in the Name list, but they do appear in the Define Name dialog box.

Skill Set 11
Working with Ranges

Use Named Ranges in Formulas
Use a Named Range Reference in One or More Formulas

After you have defined range names, you can use them in formulas so they are more readable. You can type the names or paste them using the Paste Names dialog box.

Activity Steps

 open Budget05.xls

1. Click cell **B22**

2. Type **=SUM(**

Step 5
Instead of pressing [F3] to display the Paste Name dialog box, you can click Insert on the menu bar, point to Name, click Paste, select the name you wish from the Paste name list, then click OK.

3. Type **taxes**, type **)**, notice that the range B10:D11 has a blue border, then press **[Ctrl][Enter]**
   Pressing [Ctrl][Enter] lets you enter the formula and leave the formula cell selected. The formula result uses the range name you entered—"taxes"—to calculate the total in cell B22. You don't have to type capital letters for Excel to recognize a range name.
   See Figure 11-5.

4. Click cell **B23**, then click the **Insert Function button** on the Formula bar
   If the Office Assistant appears, click "No, I don't need help right now."

5. Type **max**, press **[Enter]**, then double-click **MAX**

6. With the Number1 box highlighted, press **[F3]** to display the Paste Name dialog box
   See Figure 11-6.

7. Click **Other_Expenses**, then click **OK**

8. In the Function Arguments dialog box, click **OK**
   You have created a formula that finds the maximum, $19,000 value in the range named Other_Expenses.

 close Budget05.xls

Figure 11-5: Formula using typed range name

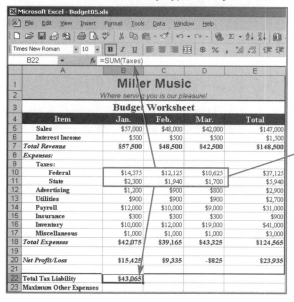

Formula uses range name to calculate total of B10:D11

Figure 11-6: Entering range name using the Paste Name dialog box

Click name to paste in Function Argument dialog box

extra!

Creating a name list
To help you keep track of worksheet names you've assigned, you can paste a list of names and related ranges anywhere in a worksheet. Click a cell that has blank cells below it and to its right. Press **[F3]** to display the Paste Name dialog box, then click **Paste List**. The Paste List button does not appear in the dialog box when Excel is in Enter or Edit mode. Be sure to leave enough blank cells, because the list will replace any data in the paste range.

Skill Set 11
Working with Ranges

Use Lookup and Reference Functions
Using VLOOKUP to Find Values in a List

You use an Excel **list** to record, manage, and analyze large amounts of data. In a list, if you need to search for a value, such as a customer number or a product price, you can save time by using the VLOOKUP function, which reads the list vertically and **returns** (finds and displays) a particular value based on information you enter. See Table 11-1 for an explanation of each of the VLOOKUP function arguments. The **comparison values**, the leftmost column in the search area, called the **table**, must be sorted in ascending order. The HLOOKUP function works just like the VLOOKUP function, but is used for tables arranged in rows. Instead of looking down a column to find comparison values, it reads across a row of information

Activity Steps

 open Roster02.xls

1. Copy the contents of cell **C4** and paste it in cell **H1**, then copy the contents of cell **F4** to cell **I1**

2. Type **Ramos** in cell **H2**, then press [Tab]
   You want to find the home town of the student with the last name of Ramos. Ramos is the lookup value.

3. Click the **Insert Function button** on the Formula bar, type **lookup**, press [Enter], then double-click **VLOOKUP**

4. With the insertion point in the Lookup_value box, click cell **H2** on the worksheet, moving the dialog box as necessary, then press [Tab]

5. With the insertion point in the Table_array box, drag to select the range **C5:G29**, then press [Tab]

6. In the Col_index_num box, type **4** to indicate you want to know the home town (which is in column 4 of the table array) for the last name you type in, then press [Tab]

7. In the Range_lookup box, type **FALSE** to indicate you want an exact match
   See Figure 11-7.

8. Click **OK**, then scroll up so you can see row 1
   Excel has found the home town of Portland for the student named Ramos.
   See Figure 11-8.

9. Type the name **Marks** in cell **H2**, press [Ctrl][Enter]; then check the result against the list

 close Roster02.xls

Step 5
You can also assign a name to the table range C5:G29 and use the name in the function in place of the range reference.

Figure 11-7: VLOOKUP arguments

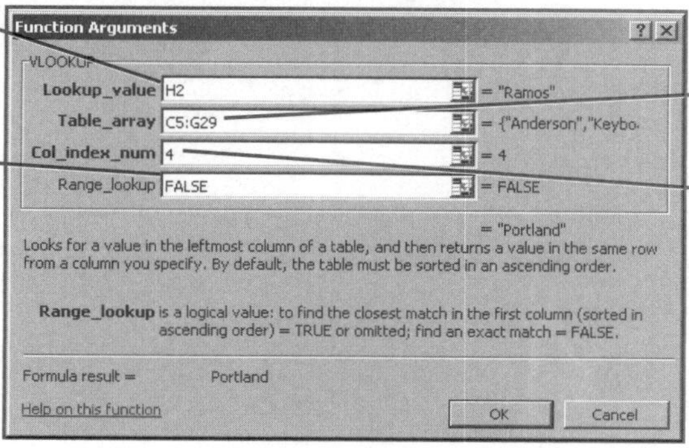

Location of value you want Excel to search for

Tells Excel to match lookup value exactly; a misspelled name will return an error value instead of a misleading one

Area of list to which the function applies

Tells Excel to return the value in 4th column of table

Figure 11-8: VLOOKUP function has located the home town for student named Ramos

List sorted by last name

Enter any other last name from table to display home town

Excel found correct home town for Ramos

Table 11-1: VLOOKUP function arguments

argument	meaning
Lookup_value	the cell reference containing the value you want Excel to search for in the list
Table_array	the list range you want to search, known as a **table**
Col_index_num	the column number of the column you want Excel to look in, counted from the left side of the table
Range_lookup	value is either TRUE, to find the closest match to the lookup_value (TRUE is the default), or FALSE, to find an exact match

Skill Set 11
Working with Ranges

Target Your Skills

 Sales03.xls

1 Assign the range names shown in the boxed area of Figure 11-9. Use names (using the Paste Function command) to create the formulas in cells C16 and C17. (*Hint*: the first formula divides E13 by B13; C17 uses the AVERAGE function for the range C7:C12.) Paste the name list, add its heading, then format your results as shown.

Figure 11-9

	A	B	C	D	E	F
1		**Miller Music**				
2		*Where serving you is our pleasure!*				
3						
4		**Current Sales of New Items**				
5						
6	**New Items**	**Qty Sold**	**Sales Price**	**Cost**	**Net Income**	
7	CDs	75,000	$13.99	$7.00	$524,250.00	
8	Records	42,336	$12.95	$5.95	$296,352.00	
9	Audio tapes	58,204	$9.95	$3.95	$349,224.00	
10	Blank tapes	15,467	$2.00	$0.50	$23,200.50	
11	T-shirts	1,897	$15.00	$2.00	$24,661.00	
12	Posters	1,352	$7.95	$2.95	$6,760.00	
13	**TOTAL**	194,256			$1,224,447.50	
14						
15				**Range Names**		
16	Average income per item		$ 6.30	Cost	='New Items'!$D$7:$D$12	
17	Average Sales Price		$ 10.31	Net_Income	='New Items'!$E$7:$E$12	
18				Qty_Sold	='New Items'!$B$7:$B$12	
19				Sales_Price	='New Items'!$C$7:$C$12	
20				Total_Income	='New Items'!$E$13	
21				Total_Quantity	='New Items'!$B$13	

Pasted list of all worksheet names, showing worksheet name and cell references

Use Paste Function command to create formulas in these cells; use range names in formulas

 Roster03.xls

2 As shown in Figure 11-10, use the VLOOKUP function so that you can type a number in cell H2, then have Excel return the last name of the student with that number. (Specify an exact match, and remember to sort the list by number first. Select the range A5:G29 before sorting.)

Figure 11-10

	A	B	C	D	E	F	G	H	I
1		**Miller Music**						**#**	*LastName*
2		*Where serving you is our pleasure!*						5	Mardell
3		***Student Roster***							
4	**#**	*FirstName*	*LastName*	*Instrument*	*Level*	*Home Town*	*Home State*		
5	1	Julie	Green	Flute	4	Portland	OR		
6	2	Edward	Mardell	Trombone	2	Phoenix	AZ		
7	3	Teri	Ham	Viola	1	Scottsdale	AZ		
8	4	Pilar	Marks	Trumpet	8	St. Petersburg	FL		
9	5	Bill	Mardell	Trombone	5	Sante Fe	NM		
10	6	Lori	Lippin	Drums	7	Los Angeles	CA		

Skill List

1. Customize toolbars and menus
2. Create, edit, and run macros

Customizing Excel

While Microsoft Excel supplies numerous features for almost any spreadsheet need, you may still find that you want to customize the program to help you work more efficiently. You can change the appearance of toolbars and menus and place commands and buttons in more convenient locations. For example, you can add buttons to any toolbar or reposition existing ones; you can also create a custom menu, place it anywhere on the menu bar, and fill it with commands you use frequently.

You can also customize your Excel workbooks using **macros**, which are special command sequences that you can create, name, and save to quickly and automatically perform specific tasks. For example, if you download a particular set of data from the Web to a worksheet daily or weekly, you could instantly format the worksheet data using one macro instead of selecting data and applying various formats each time.

The easiest way to create a macro is to use the **macro recorder**, which records your command sequence for later use. Once you create a macro, you can edit it to customize its actions further.

Skill Set 12

Customizing Excel

Customize Toolbars and Menus

Add a Custom Menu

While Excel menus contain most of the commands you need for standard worksheet tasks, you may find that commands you use frequently are not in convenient locations. For example, you might want to move a submenu command to a menu so you can display it more quickly. You can move commands to different menus or create an entirely new menu containing any Excel command, including some commands that do not appear on any standard menus. The Customize dialog box must be open any time you work with custom menus, which will then appear each time you use Excel. *If you are using a shared computer, check with your instructor or technical resource person before customizing any menus. Your system may not allow you to make changes. If you do have permission to change menus, you should delete any custom menus you create at the end of the activity.*

Step 6
You can also drag a menu command onto any toolbar. The command name will appear on the toolbar along with the buttons.

Activity Steps

1. With a blank workbook open, click **Tools** on the menu bar, click **Customize**; in the Customize dialog box, click the **Commands tab**, scroll to the bottom of the Categories list, then click **New Menu**

2. In the Commands area on the right side of the dialog box, click **New Menu**, hold down the mouse button, drag **New Menu** upward until the **position indicator**  and the **menu position pointer** are over the menu bar to the right of the Help menu, then release the mouse button

3. With the Customize dialog box still open, right-click **New Menu** in the menu bar, point to **Name: New Menu**, drag to select **New Menu**, then type **Special**
   See Figure 12-1.

4. Press **[Enter]**
   Your new menu is ready for you to add commands.

5. In the Categories list, click **Edit**, in the Commands list, drag the **Office Clipboard command** over the **Special menu** (you'll see a blank menu area appear under it), then down into the menu area to place the command on the menu
   See Figure 12-2.

6. Release the mouse button, drag the **Clear Contents command** onto the menu below the Office Clipboard command, then click **Close** in the Customize dialog box

7. Click **Special** on the menu bar, compare your screen to Figure 12-3, then click **Office Clipboard**

8. Click **Tools**, click **Customize**, drag the **Special menu** off the menu bar into the worksheet area, click **Close** in the Customize dialog box, then close the Office Clipboard

Figure 12-1: Customizing the new menu name

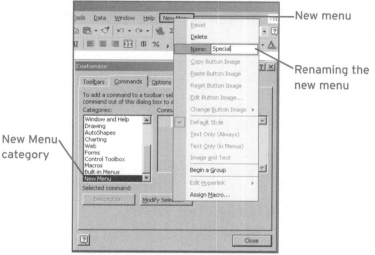

New menu

Renaming the new menu

New Menu category

Figure 12-2: Placing a command on the new menu

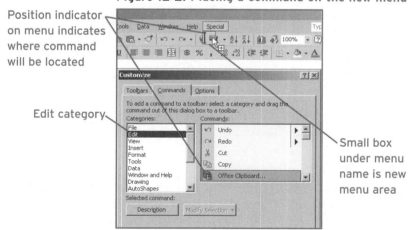

Position indicator on menu indicates where command will be located

Edit category

Small box under menu name is new menu area

Figure 12-3: New menu showing commands

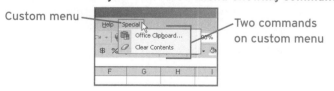

Custom menu

Two commands on custom menu

Skill Set 12

Customizing Excel

Customize Toolbars and Menus
Add and Remove Toolbar Buttons

Each Excel toolbar contains a default set of buttons, but you can add or delete buttons to suit your needs. For example, the Increase Font Size button does not appear by default on the Formatting toolbar, but if you want to use it frequently, you can add it to a toolbar. Or you may find that you use the [Ctrl][S] keyboard shortcut instead of the Save button on the Standard toolbar, so you could hide the Save button. Excel places buttons you add in a location the program determines, then hides a less-used button to make room. You can also move buttons to new locations, either on the same toolbar or on other displayed toolbars. *If you are using a shared computer, check with your instructor or technical resource person before customizing any toolbars. Your system may not allow you to make changes. If you do have permission to change them, return toolbars to their original arrangement at the end of the activity.*

Step 4
To return a toolbar to its default content and layout, click the Toolbar Options button ▾ on the toolbar, point to Add or Remove Buttons, point to Formatting, move the pointer to the bottom of the menu, then click the Reset Toolbar command.

Activity Steps

1. With a blank workbook open, click the **Toolbar Options button** ▾ on the right side of the Formatting toolbar

2. Point to **Add or Remove Buttons**, then point to **Formatting**

3. In the Formatting toolbar button list, click **Cells**, then compare your screen to Figure 12-4
   Any button image with a check mark next to it is currently displayed on the toolbar. You can check and uncheck any buttons to have them appear or not.

4. Click anywhere on the worksheet

5. Click the **Format Cells button** 🖺 on the Formatting toolbar
   See Figure 12-5.

6. Click **Cancel** in the Format Cells dialog box

7. Press and hold **[Alt]**, then drag the **Format Cells button** 🖺 from the Formatting toolbar to the worksheet area to remove it
   Pressing [Alt] is a shortcut for the "standard" way of removing toolbar buttons, which is to click Customize on the Toolbar Options/Add or Remove Buttons submenu. While the Customize dialog box is open, you can move buttons to new toolbar locations. You can also drag any button-and-command combination from the Customize dialog box onto any toolbar.

Figure 12-4: Buttons available for the Formatting toolbar

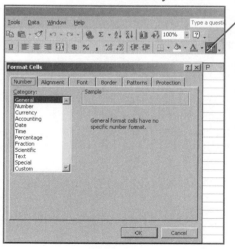

Check marks indicate buttons currently on toolbar

Format Cells button selected

Buttons available for the Formatting toolbar

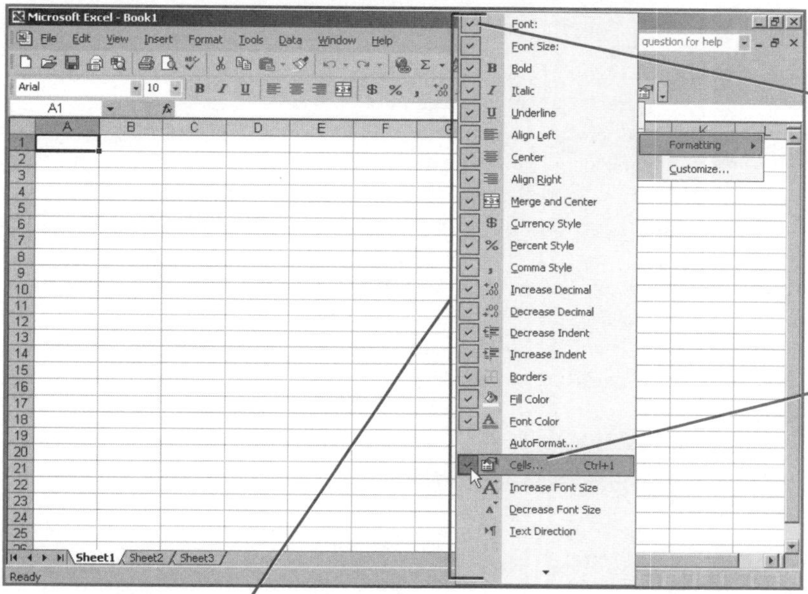

Figure 12-5: Format Cells button on the Formatting toolbar

Format Cells button on Formatting toolbar opens Format Cells dialog box

extra!

Customizing your toolbar display

To display or hide any toolbar, click **View** on the menu bar, point to **Toolbars**, then click next to any unchecked toolbar name to display it (clicking a checked toolbar name removes the check mark and hides the name). You can also open the Customize dialog box by clicking Customize at the bottom of the Toolbars submenu.

Skill Set 12

Customizing Excel

Create, Edit, and Run Macros

Record a Macro

A **macro** is a series of commands that performs one or more tasks. For example, if your company wants you to place the company name, logo, and your name in the footer of every worksheet you create, you could create a simple macro to perform those tasks. Macros save you time by performing repetitive tasks more quickly than you could using standard program tools. You can create macros in two ways. You can have the **macro recorder** record the task sequence, which automatically creates a macro in the **Visual Basic for Applications (VBA)** language. You can also type macro commands in the Visual Basic window. Often it's easiest to record a macro, then modify the recorded commands in the VBA window. *After you create a macro, you should run it to make sure it performs the actions you intended. In this activity you only create a macro; you run the macro in the next activity.*

Step 1
Clicking cell A1 at the beginning of the macro tells Excel that it should always place the company information there. Otherwise, the macro would place it in the high-lighted cell.

Activity Steps

 open Party02.xls

1. Click **Tools** on the menu bar, point to **Macro**, then click **Record New Macro**

2. Type **PowderTrails** to name the macro, then press **[Tab]**

3. Press **[Shift][N]** to assign a keyboard shortcut to run the macro, then compare your screen to Figure 12-6

4. Click **OK**
   The Stop Recording toolbar appears, meaning that every command you issue will now be recorded as part of the new macro.

5. Click cell **A1** (even though it's already selected), type **Powder Trails Resort**, press **[Enter]**, type **Vail, Colorado 81655**, press **[Enter]**, type **(970) 555-0888**, then press **[Enter]**

6. Click cell **A1**, click the **Font Size list arrow** [10 ▼], then click **18**

7. Click the **Bold button** [B] on the Formatting toolbar, click the **Font Color list arrow** [A ▼], then click **Blue** (2nd row, 3rd color from the right)
   See Figure 12-7.

8. Click the **Stop Recording button** [■] in the Stop Recording toolbar
   Although you can't see the macro you recorded, it is now attached to the Party02 workbook. In the next activity, you will open the Party03 workbook and run a PowderTrails macro that is identical to the one you created in this activity.

 close Party02.xls

Figure 12-6: Assigning a macro name and keyboard shortcut

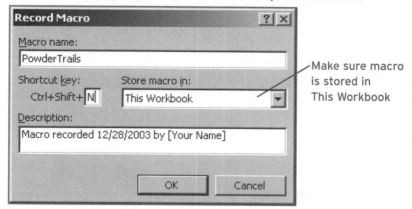

Make sure macro is stored in This Workbook

Figure 12-7: Recording the PowderTrails macro

Macro includes entry and formatting of this text in this location

	A	B	C	D	E
1	**Powder Trails Resort**				
2	Vail, Colorado 81655				
3	(970) 555-0888				
4					
5		**Staff Winter Party**			
6	**Expense**	**Unit**	**Unit Cost**	**Number**	**Total**
7	Catering	Person	$ 42.00	50	$2,100.00
8	Entertainment	DJ	$1,200.00	1	$1,200.00
9	Decorations	Table	$ 5.00	15	$ 75.00
10	Door Prizes	Each	$ 15.00	10	$ 150.00
11	Beverages	Bottle	$ 9.00	40	$ 360.00
12					
13					
14				**Total Expense**	$3,885.00
15	**Scheduling:**				
16	Meet with Caterers	1/10/2003			
17	Set up room	1/12/2003			
18	Party date	1/13/2003			
19					

Stop button

Stop Recording toolbar (your toolbar might be in a different location)

Skill Set 12
Customizing Excel

Create, Edit, and Run Macros
Run a Macro

When you **run** a macro, Excel performs all the actions in the macro rapidly. You can run a macro by selecting it in the Macros dialog box and clicking Run, or by using the keyboard shortcut you specified when you created the macro. When you open a workbook containing a macro, Excel displays a dialog box explaining that macros can contain dangerous computer viruses and asking whether you want to enable or disable macros. If you are sure of the macro source, click Enable Macros. You will see this message only if your macro security level is set to Medium. *In this activity, you open the Party03 workbook, which contains a PowderTrails macro identical to the one you created in the last activity.*

Step 1
The Macros dialog box lists macros for all open workbooks. Macros from other open workbooks are listed with the workbook name first, followed by an exclamation point (which Excel uses to separate outside workbook sources), then the macro name.

Activity Steps

1. With Excel running, click the **Open button** 📂 on the Standard toolbar, navigate to the drive and folder where your Project Files are stored, click **Party03.xls**, then click **Open**

2. Click **Enable Macros**
   If you don't see a warning message, then your security level is set to high. To check, click Tools, point to Macro, click Security, click the medium option button, then click OK.

3. Click **Tools** on the menu bar, point to **Macro**, then click **Macros**
   See Figure 12-8.

4. Click the **PowderTrails macro** (if it's not already selected), then click **Run**
   The macro places the company information in the range A1:A3, then formats it.
   See Figure 12-9.

5. Select cells **A1:A3**, click **Edit** on the menu bar, point to **Clear**, click **All**, then click any cell outside the selected range

6. Press **[Ctrl][Shift]N**
   The assigned keyboard shortcut runs the macro. When you use a keyboard shortcut to run a macro, the Macro dialog box does not open.

    close Party03.xls

Figure 12-8: Macro dialog box

Commands in the selected macro are executed when you click Run

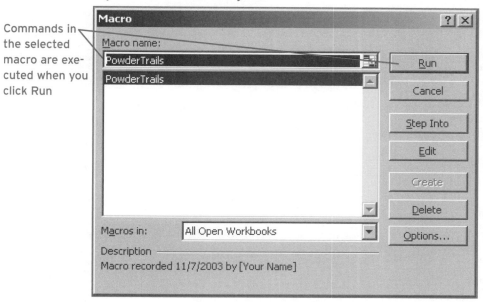

Figure 12-9: Company information inserted by the PowderTrails macro

Macro entered and formatted text

	A	B	C	D	E
1	**Powder Trails Resort**				
2	Vail, Colorado 81655				
3	(970) 555-0888				
4					
5		**Staff Winter Party**			
6	**Expense**	**Unit**	**Unit Cost**	**Number**	**Total**
7	Catering	Person	$ 42.00	50	$ 2,100.00
8	Entertainment	DJ	$ 1,200.00	1	$ 1,200.00
9	Decorations	Table	$ 5.00	15	$ 75.00

Skill Set 12

Customizing Excel

Create, Edit, and Run Macros
Run a Header and Footer Macro

You can also use macros to insert custom text and formatting in document headers and footers. As a macro runs, the screen may flicker slightly; the status bar will display "Ready" when the macro is finished running.

Step 1
In the Macro dialog box, the Macros in list arrow lets you choose and run macros from other open workbooks. It also lets you store macros in a workbook called Personal.xls, which will then open and make these macros available every time you start Excel. To hide the Personal workbook, click **Window** on the menu bar, then click **Hide**.

Activity Steps

 open Quarters02.xls (Enable Macros)

1. Click the **Print Preview button** on the Standard toolbar
   You can see in the Preview window that the worksheet does not contain a header or footer.

2. Click **Close**

3. Click **Tools** on the menu bar, point to **Macro**, then click **Macros**
   See Figure 12-10.

4. Click the **HeaderFooter macro** (if it's not already selected), then click **Run**

5. Click the **Print Preview button** on the Standard toolbar
   See Figure 12-11.

6. Click the **Zoom pointer** at the top of the worksheet, then scroll down to view the bottom of the worksheet

7. Click **Close**

 close Quarters02.xls

Figure 12-10: Macro dialog box

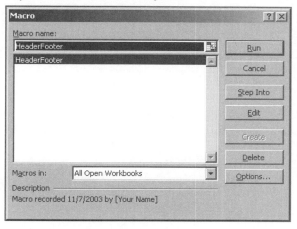

Figure 12-11: Macro results in Print Preview

Macro
added
header
and
footer

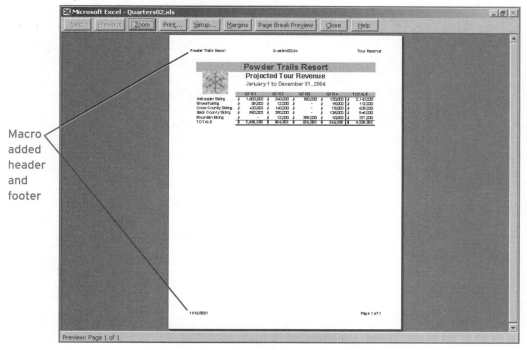

Skill Set 12
Customizing Excel

Create, Edit, and Run Macros
View Macro Code

While you would need an entire book to learn macro programming details, you can learn about a macro's general structure by viewing its **code**, or programming commands. **Visual Basic for Applications**, called **VBA**, is a programming language that runs in its own program window, called the **Visual Basic Editor**. When you record a macro, VBA interprets each command you issue and converts it to VBA program lines. The code for each macro is stored in a separate storage area in your workbook called a **module**. Each line in VBA code is called a **statement**; a sequence of statements that performs an action is called a **procedure**.

Activity Steps

 open Party04.xls (Enable Macros)

1. Click **Tools** on the menu bar, click **Macro**, then click **Macros**

2. Click **PowderTrails** if it's not already selected, then click **Edit**

3. In the Project – VBAProject window, click **Module1** if it's not already selected
   See Figure 12-12.

Step 6
There are over 100 kinds of **objects** (items that are acted upon) in VBA. An object called *range* is followed by an action, in this case, *select*, which is called a **method**. An object is like the noun in a sentence, and a method is like the verb. The Range lines illustrate a common type of statement.

4. Click the **Project Explorer button** 🖳 on the Visual Basic toolbar
   The Project Explorer window becomes highlighted, showing the project, which is the VBA name for a workbook.

5. Click the **Properties Window button** 🖳 on the Visual Basic toolbar
   The name of the selected module is Module1, the default name. The code window on the right shows the code. The first line begins with Sub, which stands for Sub procedure, a series of statements that performs an action. The last line, End Sub, is the end of the procedure.

6. Click in the line that begins **' Macro recorded**
   Lines with green text that begin with apostrophes are comments, which are notes that describe the code; they do not perform actions.

7. Click anywhere in the first line that reads **Range("A1").Select**
   This statement selects cell A1.

8. Click anywhere in the line that reads **ActiveCell.FormulaR1C1 = "Powder Trails Resort"**
   This line enters the text "Powder Trails Resort" in the selected cell.

9. Click **File** on the menu bar, then click **Close and Return to Microsoft Excel** to return to the worksheet

 close Party04.xls

Figure 12-12: Visual Basic Editor window

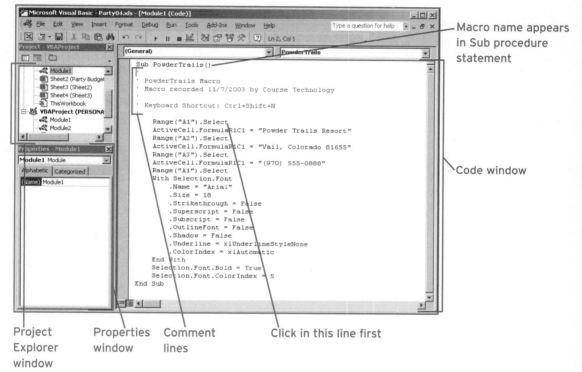

Macro name appears in Sub procedure statement

Code window

Project Explorer window

Properties window

Comment lines

Click in this line first

extra!

Describing VBA objects

Visual Basic objects can have **properties** that describe their characteristics. Properties are like adjectives. Under the With Selection statement, you see a list of properties relating to the range, such as `.size=18`. In this case, it sets the font size to 18 points.

Skill Set 12

Customizing Excel

Create, Edit, and Run Macros
Edit a Macro

You can modify any macro in the Visual Basic for Applications window by editing the program code. When you edit a macro, it's good practice to **document** your changes by inserting a comment line with your name and the date so other users will know whom to contact if they have questions. *Make sure your comment line begins with an apostrophe, or your macro will not run correctly.* Be careful when you edit macros; if you alter the syntax (the exact arrangement and structure of statements) the macro may not run.

Activity Steps

 open Rentals04.xls (Enable Macros)

1. Click **Tools** on the menu bar, click **Macro**, then click **Macros**

2. With the FormatLogo macro name highlighted, click **Run**
   The macro formats the company name in 14-point type, bolds the text in cell A2, shades the range A1:E2, then selects cell A1. You will edit the macro to change the point size and the cell the macro selects. *See Figure 12-13.*

3. Click **Tools** on the menu bar, click **Macro**, then click **Macros**

4. With the FormatLogo macro name highlighted, click **Edit**

5. Click in the comment line under Macro Recorded, then type **Edited by [Your Name]** followed by the **date**

6. In the Size line, double-click **14**, then type **18**; in the second-to-last line (which selects cell A1), double-click **A1**, then type **B8**
   See Figure 12-14.

7. Click **File** on the menu bar, then click **Close and Return to Microsoft Excel**

8. Select the range **A1:E2**, click **Edit** on the menu bar, point to **Clear**, then click **Formats**

9. Click any worksheet cell, then press **[Ctrl][Shift][F]**
   See Figure 12-15.

 close Rentals04.xls

Step 7
You could also return to the workbook by clicking the **Microsoft Excel – Rentals04.xls button** on the taskbar. Saving the workbook would also save the edited version of the macro.

Figure 12-13: Results of macro before editing

FormatLogo macro applied formatting to A1:E2

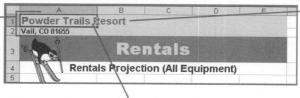

FormatLogo macro made company name 14-point bold green Arial

Macro selected cell A1 after formatting A1:E2

Figure 12-14: Edited macro

Your documentation

Font size increased from 14 to 18 points

The macro will select cell B8 after it enters and formats text

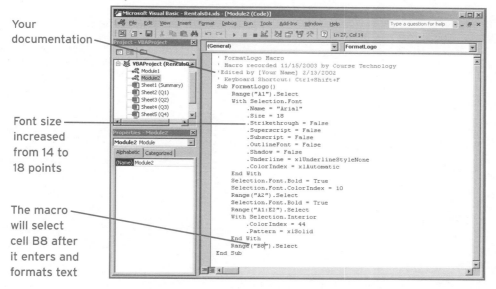

Figure 12-15: Results of edited macro

Title now 18-point type

Cell B8 selected

Skill Set 12

Customizing Excel

Target Your Skills

1 Create the custom menu and display the toolbar buttons shown in Figure 12-16. Then reset the toolbars and remove the custom menu.

file > Revenues01.xls

2 Create a macro called FormatRooms that formats the worksheet as shown in Figure 12-17, using the keyboard shortcut [Ctrl][Shift][R]. Edit the macro to make the modifications shown to cell A1. Clear the formats from the data, then run your revised macro.

Figure 12-16

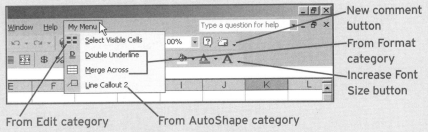

From Edit category   From AutoShape category

Figure 12-17

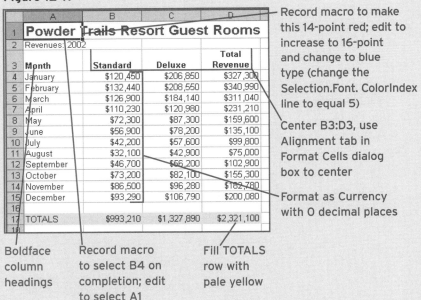

Record macro to make this 14-point red; edit to increase to 16-point and change to blue type (change the Selection.Font. ColorIndex line to equal 5)

Center B3:D3, use Alignment tab in Format Cells dialog box to center

Format as Currency with 0 decimal places

Boldface column headings

Record macro to select B4 on completion; edit to select A1

Fill TOTALS row with pale yellow

Skill Set 13

Auditing Worksheets

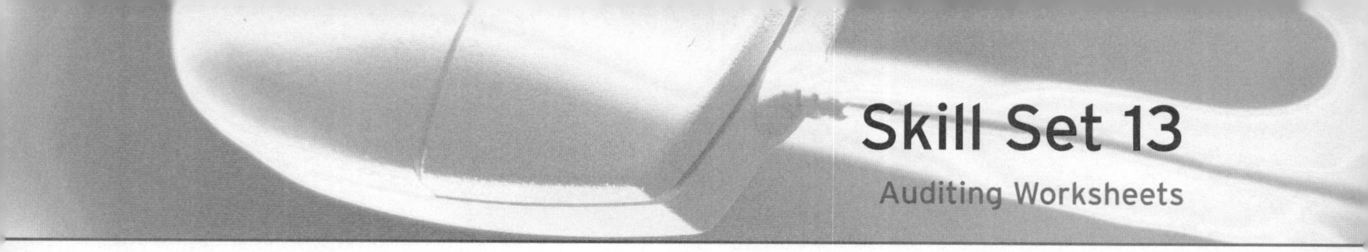

Skill List

1. Audit formulas
2. Locate and resolve errors
3. Identify dependencies in formulas

Most of the formulas that you create in Microsoft Excel contain cell references. When a formula refers to another cell, you can say it *depends on* that cell. While this interconnected relationship adds power to your worksheets, it also adds complexity. If you build a worksheet that has many "layers" of formulas and references, you will need a way to check them easily.

Excel provides several **auditing** features that can help you analyze your worksheet and formula structure to trace relationships between cells and formulas. You can find all the cells that formulas refer to, or you can locate all the formula cells that use a particular cell.

Worksheet auditing is most useful when your worksheet contains an error and you need to find its source. Excel recognizes several types of errors and helps you identify their cause.

Skill Set 13

Auditing Worksheets

Audit Formulas
Find Cell Dependents

In a complex worksheet, it can be difficult to keep track of the flow of data among cells. For example, a profit formula might use a total expenses figure, which might, in turn, use individual expenses figures, which themselves use values from other cells. This chain effect creates "levels" of dependency. To understand a worksheet's structure and find errors, you will often need to know what cells a formula uses, either directly or indirectly. In such cases, you will find it helpful to **trace**, or find, dependents. A **dependent** is a cell that uses the values in the selected cell(s). For example, if cell B6 contains the formula =B4+B5, cell B6 is a dependent of those cells. You can trace cells that are **direct dependents** of the selected cell (those which use the cell's value in a formula) and those that are **indirect dependents** (which depend on the cell, but only via other cells). The Formula Auditing toolbar lets you find dependents quickly by displaying blue **tracer arrows** between a selected cell and any dependents.

Step 5
Double-clicking a line to change the active cell is especially useful in large worksheets, where dependent cells may not be visible on the screen. This feature can save you a lot of time because the worksheet will automatically scroll to the location of the other cell.

Activity Steps

 open Advertising04.xls

1. If the Formula Auditing Toolbar is not already displayed, click **Tools** on the menu bar, point to **Formula Auditing**, then click **Show Formula Auditing Toolbar**
2. Click cell **B8**
3. Click the **Trace Dependents button** ⬚ on the Formula Auditing Toolbar
   Blue tracer arrows point to the cells that use the selected cell in its formulas; they are the dependents of cell B8.
4. Click the **Trace Dependents button** ⬚ on the Formula Auditing Toolbar again
   Another tracer arrow appears, from cell C19 to D19, showing another dependency level.
   See Figure 13-1.
5. Double-click the **blue tracer arrow** between cells B8 and C19
   The cell at the other end of the tracer arrow becomes selected.
   See Figure 13-2.
6. Double-click the **blue tracer arrow** again
7. Verify that cell B8 is selected, click the **Remove Dependent Arrows button** ⬚ on the Formula Auditing Toolbar to remove the arrow to the indirect dependent of the selected cell
8. Click the **Remove Dependent Arrows button** ⬚ on the Formula Auditing Toolbar again to remove the arrows to the direct dependents of the selected cell

 close Advertising04.xls

Figure 13-1: Dependent arrows show relationships among cells

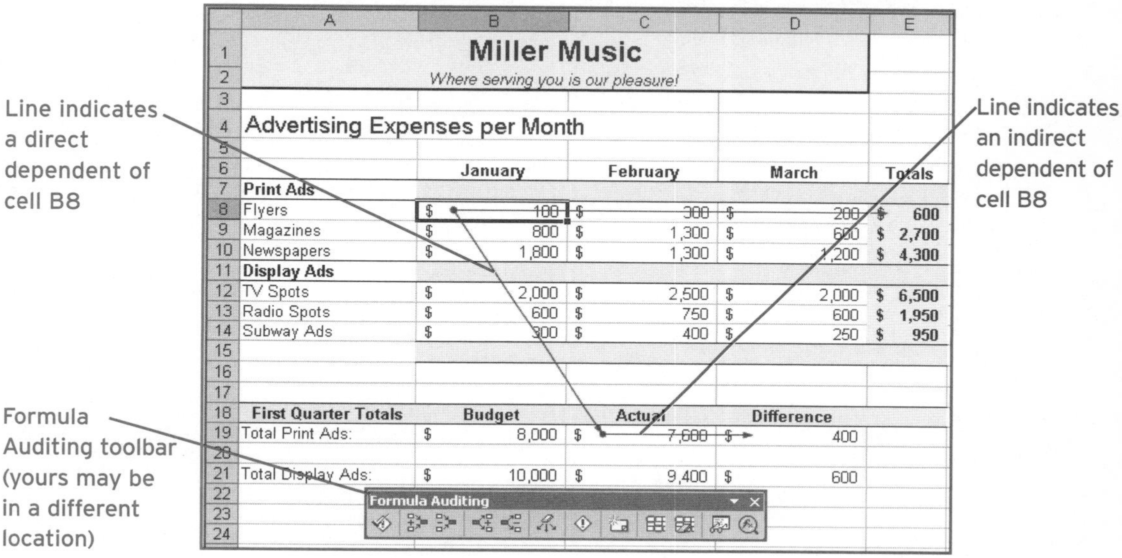

Line indicates a direct dependent of cell B8

Line indicates an indirect dependent of cell B8

Formula Auditing toolbar (yours may be in a different location)

Figure 13-2: Changing the selected cell using the tracer arrow

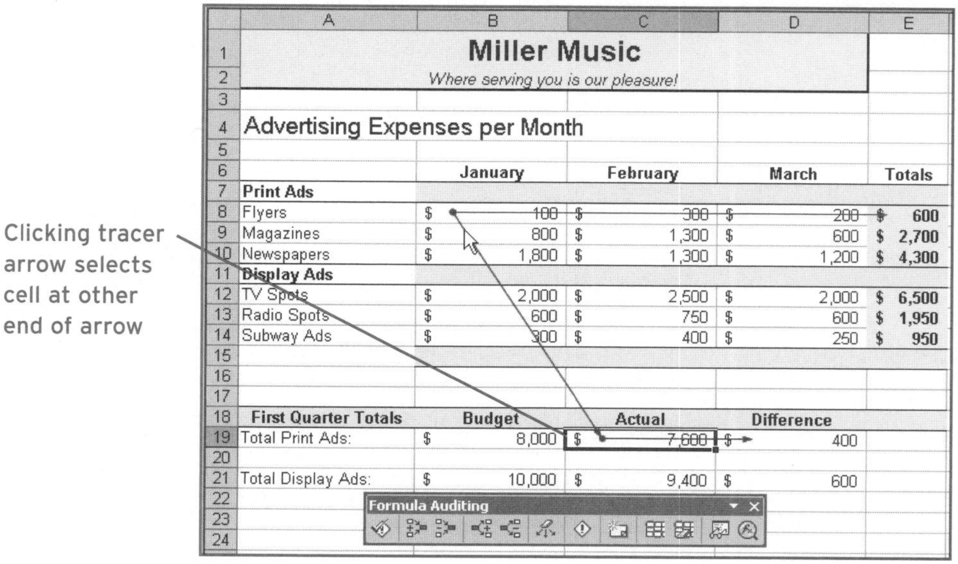

Clicking tracer arrow selects cell at other end of arrow

Skill Set 13

Auditing Worksheets

Audit Formulas
Trace Precedents

Another way to help you audit your worksheet formulas is to **trace**, or find, precedents. For a cell containing a formula, any cells referred to and used in that formula are called the formula cell's **precedents**. As with tracing dependents, tracing precedents is useful in finding the cause of worksheet errors. If a precedent is located in another worksheet or workbook, an arrow with a dotted line leads to a small worksheet icon; double-click the dotted line to go to that location using the Go To dialog box. If the reference is to another workbook, that workbook must be open.

Activity Steps

 open Summary04.xls

1. If the Formula Auditing Toolbar is not already displayed, click **Tools** on the menu bar, point to **Formula Auditing**, then click **Show Formula Auditing Toolbar**

2. Click cell **G17**

3. Click the **Trace Precedents button** on the Formula Auditing toolbar
   Excel displays a blue tracer arrow and outlines the entire range of cells that are precedents of cell G17.

4. Click the **Trace Precedents button** on the Formula Auditing toolbar again
   Tracer arrows appear from the other cells that are precedents of the selected range.
   See Figure 13-3.

5. Double-click the **blue tracer arrow** between cell G7 and G17
   See Figure 13-4.

6. Double-click the **blue tracer arrow** again to move the cell highlight again

7. Click the **Remove Precedent Arrows button** on the Formula Auditing Toolbar to remove the arrows to the indirect precedents

8. Click the **Remove Precedent Arrows button** on the Formula Auditing Toolbar again to remove the arrows to the direct precedents

 close Summary04.xls

Step 4
Each time you click the Trace Precedents button or the Remove Precedent Arrows button, you move to the next level of precedence.

Figure 13-3: Precedent arrows

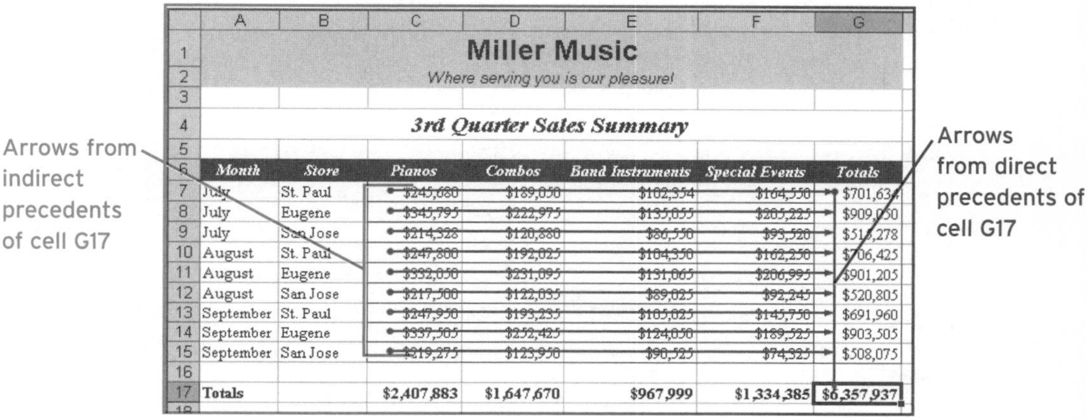

Arrows from indirect precedents of cell G17

Arrows from direct precedents of cell G17

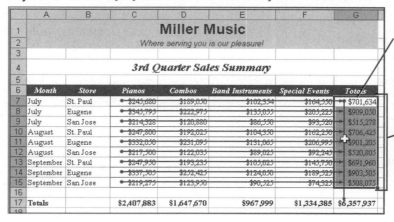

Figure 13-4: Changing the selected cell using the tracer arrow

Cell at other end of arrow becomes selected

Precedents of cell G17 become shaded

Skill Set 13
Auditing Worksheets

Locate and Resolve Errors
Locate and Resolve Formula Errors

In a complicated worksheet, you may have formulas that contain errors. Excel helps you find and correct those errors. If a cell contains an error that Excel recognizes, you will see a green triangle in the upper left corner of the cell and a code that describes the type of error. See Table 13-1 for a summary of the most common formula errors. See the online help topic "Find and Correct Errors in Formulas" for a more complete description. If you select the cell with the error, you will see a smart tag that you can click to display options for diagnosing and correcting the problem.

Step 1
You can have Excel select each error consecutively by clicking the Error Checking button on the Formula Auditing Toolbar. The Error Checking dialog box offers the same options as the Smart Tag actions menu, and contains Previous and Next buttons to move from one error to another.

Activity Steps

 open Drums04.xls

1. If the Formula Auditing Toolbar is not already displayed, click **Tools** on the menu bar, point to **Formula Auditing**, then click **Show Formula Auditing Toolbar**

2. Click cell I18, which shows #DIV/0!

3. Move the pointer over the **smart tag** ⟐ , then, when the smart tag changes to ⟐ ▾, click once
   See Figure 13-5.

4. In the Smart Tag actions menu, click **Help on this error**

5. Read the instructions, then click the Help window **Close button** ☒

6. Click the **Trace Error button** ⟐ in the Formula Auditing toolbar
   As shown in Figure 13-6, tracer arrows show that the formula precedents include cell I16, which is correct, and cell H17, which is blank. This produces an error because division by zero (a cell with no value) is impossible.

7. In the Formula bar, double-click the reference to cell **H17**, click cell **H16** on the worksheet, then click the **Enter button** ☑ on the Formula bar

 close Drums04.xls

Figure 13-5: Smart tag actions menu

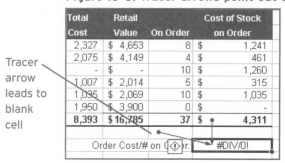

Smart tag actions menu

Smart tag

#DIV/0! indicates error

Figure 13-6: Tracer arrows point out error

Total Cost	Retail Value	On Order	Cost of Stock on Order
2,327	$ 4,653	8	$ 1,241
2,075	$ 4,149	4	$ 461
-	$ -	10	$ 1,260
1,007	$ 2,014	5	$ 315
1,035	$ 2,069	10	$ 1,035
1,950	$ 3,900	0	$ -
8,393	$ 16,785	37	$ 4,311
Order Cost/# on Order:			#DIV/0!

Tracer arrow leads to blank cell

Table 13-1: Common formula errors

error	meaning	example
#VALUE	Incorrect operand, value, or argument	Entering range in a function that requires one value
#DIV/0!	Value is divided by zero, which is impossible	Divisor refers to a blank cell
#NAME	Excel does not recognize text	Name used in formula does not exist
#N/A	Value is not available to formula	Function argument is missing
#REF	Incorrect cell reference	Deleting cells a formula refers to
#NUM	Incorrect formula numbers	Function requires number argument, not text

Skill Set 13

Auditing Worksheets

Identify Dependencies in Formulas
Locate Dependencies in Formulas

In a complex worksheet, your formulas may become long and difficult to analyze. The Evaluate Formula dialog box lets you step through the formula levels to help you understand the formula's structure. You can click the Evaluate button to display the results of a function or a function argument; clicking Evaluate repeatedly cycles through the levels of your formula so you can analyze each one.

Activity Steps

 open Practice03.xls

1. If the Formula Auditing Toolbar is not already displayed, click **Tools** on the menu bar, point to **Formula Auditing**, then click **Show Formula Auditing Toolbar**

2. Click cell I11

3. Click the **Evaluate Formula button** on the Formua Auditing toolbar
   See Figure 13-7.

4. Click **Step In** to view the formula that calculates the highlighted argument
   See Figure 13-8.

5. Click **Step Out** to display the value in cell I11
   The Step In and Step Out buttons are useful when part of a formula refers to another formula. The buttons let you evaluate the parts of a "nested" formula in the order in which they are calculated.

6. Click **Evaluate** to view the value of the second underlined argument, which is FALSE

7. Click **Evaluate** again to display the final value in the cell, which is Below average

8. Click **Close** to close the Evaluate Formula dialog box

 close Practice03.xls

Step 7
To begin the analysis again, click Restart. To proceed directly through the arguments without viewing the underlying formula, do not click Step In.

Figure 13-7: Evaluate dialog box showing "top level" formula

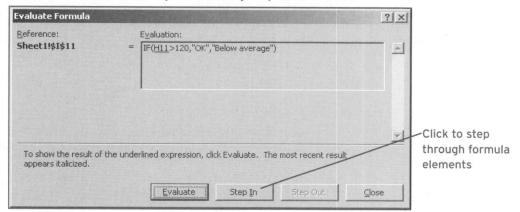

Click to step through formula elements

Figure 13-8: Revealing formula underlying function argument

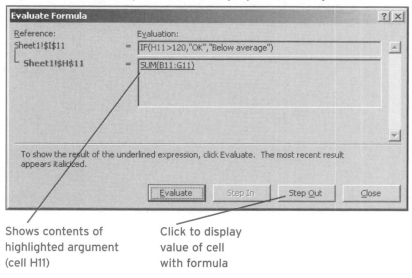

Shows contents of highlighted argument (cell H11)

Click to display value of cell with formula

extra!

Watching formulas
In a large or complex worksheet or workbook, you may want to monitor the status of one or more formulas. Instead of repeatedly clicking the cell to display it, you can keep it visible at all times by using the Watch Window. Click the cell you want to watch, click the **Show Watch Window button** on the Formula Auditing tool-bar. Click **Add Watch**, then click **Add** in the Add Watch dialog box. The Watch Window displays the cell address, its value, and its formula. Any changes you make to the formula will be reflected in the window.

Skill Set 13

Auditing Worksheets

Identify Dependencies in Formulas
Remove All Tracer Arrows

Although you can remove the most recent level of tracer arrows using Remove Precedent Arrows and Remove Dependent Arrows buttons, you may want to remove all arrows at once.

Activity Steps

 open Budget06.xls

Step 3
Tracer arrows are not saved when you close a worksheet.

1. If the Formula Auditing Toolbar is not already displayed, click **Tools** on the menu bar, point to **Formula Auditing**, then click **Show Formula Auditing Toolbar**

2. Click cell **E20**

3. Click the **Trace Precedents button** on the Formula Auditing toolbar four times
   See Figure 13-9.

4. Click the **Remove All Arrows button** on the Formula Auditing toolbar
   See Figure 13-10.

 close Budget06.xls

Figure 13-9: All precedents' arrows displayed

Click to remove all tracer arrows

	A	B	C	D	E
1		**Miller Music**			
2		*Where serving you is our pleasure!*			
3		**Budget Worksheet**			
4	**Item**	**Jan.**	**Feb.**	**Mar.**	**Total**
5	Sales	$57,000	$48,000	$42,000	$147,000
6	Interest Income	$500	$500	$500	$1,500
7	*Total Revenue*	$57,500	$48,500	$42,500	$148,500
8	*Expenses:*				
9	Taxes:				
10	Federal	$14,375	$12,125	$10,625	$37,125
11	State	$2,300	$1,940	$1,700	$5,940
12	Advertising	$1,200	$900	$800	$2,900
13	Utilities	$900	$900	$900	$2,700
14	Payroll	$12,000	$10,000	$9,000	$31,000
15	Insurance	$300	$300	$300	$900
16	Inventory	$10,000	$12,000	$19,000	$41,000
17	Miscellaneous	$1,000	$1,000	$1,000	$3,000
18	*Total Expenses*	$42,075	$39,165	$43,325	$124,565
19					
20	*Net Profit/Loss*	$15,425	$9,335	-$825	$23,935
21					
22	Total Tax Liability	$43,065			
23	Maximum Other Expenses	$19,000			

Figure 13-10: Worksheet without precedents' arrows

	A	B	C	D	E
1		**Miller Music**			
2		*Where serving you is our pleasure!*			
3		**Budget Worksheet**			
4	**Item**	**Jan.**	**Feb.**	**Mar.**	**Total**
5	Sales	$57,000	$48,000	$42,000	$147,000
6	Interest Income	$500	$500	$500	$1,500
7	*Total Revenue*	$57,500	$48,500	$42,500	$148,500
8	*Expenses:*				
9	Taxes:				
10	Federal	$14,375	$12,125	$10,625	$37,125
11	State	$2,300	$1,940	$1,700	$5,940
12	Advertising	$1,200	$900	$800	$2,900
13	Utilities	$900	$900	$900	$2,700
14	Payroll	$12,000	$10,000	$9,000	$31,000
15	Insurance	$300	$300	$300	$900
16	Inventory	$10,000	$12,000	$19,000	$41,000
17	Miscellaneous	$1,000	$1,000	$1,000	$3,000
18	*Total Expenses*	$42,075	$39,165	$43,325	$124,565
19					
20	*Net Profit/Loss*	$15,425	$9,335	-$825	$23,935
21					

Skill Set 13

Auditing Worksheets

Target Your Skills

 Sales04.xls

1 Locate and resolve the errors in cells B13 and B17 so that the results appear as in Figure 13-11. (*Hint:* For the error in cell C17, examine the range names.) Then display the tracer arrows shown to each cell's precedents and dependents. Remove all tracer arrows.

Figure 13-11

	New Items	Qty Sold	Sales Price	Cost	Net Income	
	Miller Music					
	Where serving you is our pleasure!					
	Current Sales of New Items					
6	New Items	Qty Sold	Sales Price	Cost	Net Income	
7	CDs	75,000	$13.99	$7.00	$524,250.00	
8	Records	42,336	$12.95	$5.95	$296,352.00	
9	Audio tapes	58,204	$9.95	$3.95	$349,224.00	
10	Blank tapes	15,467	$2.00	$0.50	$23,200.50	
11	T-shirts	1,897	$15.00	$2.00	$24,661.00	
12	Posters	1,352	$7.95	$2.95	$6,760.00	
13	TOTAL	194,256			$1,224,447.50	

Range Names

Cost	='New Items'!$D$7:$D$12	
16	Average income per item	$ 6.30
17	Average Sales Price	$ 10.31
Net_Income	='New Items'!$E$7:$E$12
Qty_Sold	='New Items'!$B$7:$B$12
Sales_Price	='New Items'!$C$7:$C$12
Total_Income	='New Items'!$E$13
Total_Quantity	='New Items'!$B$13

 Tickets04.xls

2 See Figure 13-12. Use the Step In button in the Evaluate Formula dialog box to evaluate the formula in cell F11. Use the Smart Tag action menu, the Formula Auditing toolbar, and tracer arrows to locate and resolve the problem in cell F21.

Figure 13-12

	A	B	C	D	E	F
1			**Miller Music**			
2			*Where serving you is our pleasure!*			
3			*Ticket Sales by Employee*			
5	Folk Festival ticket price		$15			
6	Concert ticket price		$30			
9			*Number of Tickets Sold*		*Total*	
10	*Employee*		*Folk Festival*	*Concert*	*Sales*	*Commission*
11	Davis	Jan	110	143	$5,940	$594
12	Gibson	Carol	132	87	$4,590	$459
13	Johnson	Chris	89	92	$4,095	$410
14	Kniepp	Gordon	44	74	$2,880	$288
15	Kramer	Joan	78	117	$4,680	$468
16	McHenry	Bill	67	108	$4,245	$425
17	Miller	George	0	0	$0	$0
18	Wallace	Pat	35	97	$3,435	$344
19	TOTALS		555	718	$ 29,865	$ 2,987
20	Total # of Employees:	8				
21					Total Commission/#employees:	$ 373.31

Skill List

1. Use subtotals with lists and ranges
2. Define and apply filters
3. Add group and outline criteria to ranges
4. Use data validation
5. Retrieve external data and create queries
6. Create extensible markup Language (XML) Web queries

An Excel spreadsheet lets you analyze lists of data. A **list** consists of labeled columns and rows of organized data. When information is in list format, you can use the Excel Data menu commands to work with it.

You can **sort**, or reorder, the information based on the contents of any text or numeric column. You can also subtotal numeric list information to view selected group totals, or **filter** a list to display only selected information. Lists that have the same information in more than one record (for example, a list with several sales rep names listed with many sales transactions) can easily be grouped and used to view summary information.

If other people will enter data in your list, you may want to use **data validation** to limit cell entries to acceptable values.

Though you can type list data into Excel, you will often want to import it from another source, such as the World Wide Web. You can use one of the Web queries Excel supplies or create your own query to a Web site or Extensible Markup Language **(XML)** data (a universal file standard), on the Web or on a network. You can also share list information by saving files in XML format to send to others.

Skill Set 14

Summarizing Data

Use Subtotals with Lists and Ranges

Sort a List by One Field

An Excel **list** consists of columns and rows of related information with column labels in the first row. For example, a customer list might consist of names and addresses along with related sales information for each customer. A **field** is a column that contains one type of information (such as Last Name); a **record** is a row that contains the information for one item (such as one customer). See Table 14-1 for guidelines to follow when creating a list. You can **sort**, or change the order of, list data. An **ascending sort** orders column information beginning with the letter A or the number 0; a **descending sort** starts with the letter Z or with the highest number in a column.

Activity Steps

 open Packages01.xls

1. Click any cell in the list range A5:H14

2. Click **Data** on the menu bar, then click **Sort**

3. Click the **Sort by list arrow**, then click **Customer**

4. Click the **Ascending option button** (if it's not already selected)
   See Figure 14-1.

5. Click **OK**
   The list is sorted by Customer name. In a list, the data in each row stays together when you sort it.

6. Click **Data** on the menu bar, then click **Sort**

7. Click the **Sort by list arrow**, then click **Revenue**

8. Click the **Descending option button**, then click **OK**
   See Figure 14-2.

 close Packages01.xls

Step 1
Excel recognizes your range as a list when it has formatted column labels and contains no blank rows or columns within the range.

**Figure 14-1: Specifying an ascending
sort by Customer**

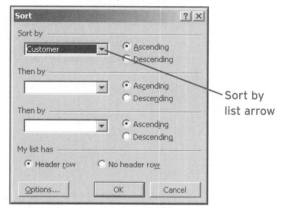

Sort by
list arrow

Figure 14-2: List sorted in descending order by Revenue amount

Information
in each row
stays
together
after sorting

List sorted
by Revenue
amount in
descending
order

	Sales Rep	Customer	City	State	Package	# people	# days	Revenue
				Powder Trails Resort				
				Package Sales				
				First Quarter, 2003				
6	Mercede	Laird Corp.	Lowell	MA	Deluxe	17	5	$ 18,700
7	Clayton	Hitech Corp.	Cleveland	OH	Deluxe	20	3	$ 15,000
8	Clayton	Mill College	Vincent	PA	Deluxe	20	3	$ 15,000
9	Clayton	Lloyd Publishing Co.	Chicago	IL	Basic	9	5	$ 5,400
10	Randall	Mather High School	York	CT	Basic	15	3	$ 5,250
11	Mercede	Lefevre School	Las Vegas	NV	Basic	13	3	$ 4,550
12	Randall	Donald Marino	Boston	MA	Deluxe	5	3	$ 3,750
13	Randall	Kato & Sons	Seattle	WA	Basic	10	3	$ 3,500
14	Clayton	Marymount Ski Club	Tulsa	OK	Basic	5	5	$ 3,000

TABLE 14-1: Guidelines for creating lists

elements	guideline
Worksheet	Only include one list on a worksheet
Labels	Format column headings to help Excel separate them from the data
Rows	Do not include blank rows or columns within a list; do separate your list from other worksheet data using blank columns and rows
Spaces	Don't add extra spaces in data that could interfere with sorting
Columns	Place the same type of data in each column

Skill Set 14
Summarizing Data

Use Subtotals with Lists and Ranges
Sort a List by Two Fields

Excel lets you sort list information by more than one field at once. For example, you might want to sort a Supplier list by State, then within each state by the amount you ordered. You can think of each sort field as a level: the first sort field is the highest level, followed by the second field, which sorts data within each of the higher-level fields.

Step 5
You can specify up to three sort levels in a list.

Activity Steps

 open Packages02.xls

1. Click any cell in the range **A5:H14**

2. Click **Data** on the menu bar, then click **Sort**

3. Click the **Sort by list arrow**, then click **Package**

4. Click the **Ascending option button** (if it's not already selected)

5. Click the first **Then by list arrow**, then click **Revenue**

6. Click the **Descending option button** for the Revenue sort field
   See Figure 14-3.

7. Click **OK**
   See Figure 14-4.

 close Packages02.xls

Figure 14-3: Sorting by two fields

Sort within each Package type in descending order by Revenue —

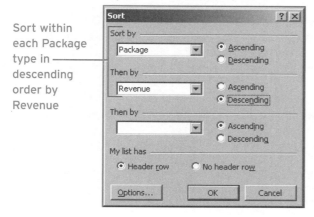

Figure 14-4: List sorted by Package type and Revenue

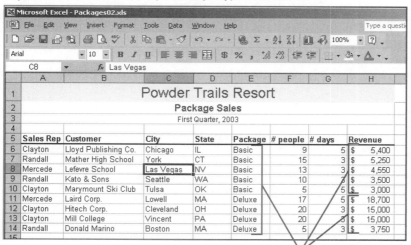

List sorted first by Package then in descending order by Revenue within each Package type

extra!

Sorting by multiple fields

When you sort by multiple fields, make sure that the first sort field occurs often enough to make the other sort levels meaningful. For example, if your list has many entries for each state, then you can sort by name or amount within each state. But if you only have one entry for each state, don't make State your first sort field; it won't group data in a way that is easily sorted on another field.

Skill Set 14
Summarizing Data

Use Subtotals with Lists and Ranges
Subtotal a List

An Excel list usually contains numeric data, such as budget or invoice amounts. You can use the Excel **subtotal** feature to calculate the total of each budget category or each region's invoices. Before you subtotal a list, you must first sort the list by the same category you want to subtotal. For example, if you want to calculate the amount of sales per store, first sort the list by the Store Name field. When Excel subtotals a list, it also outlines the list by placing brackets on the left side of the data. You can click the plus and minus signs on the brackets to hide or display list data. (For more information on outlining, see the Group and Outline Structured Data activity later in this skill set.)

Activity Steps

 open Tours03.xls

1. Click anywhere in the list range **A4:E12**, click **Data** on the menu bar, then click **Sort**

2. Click the **Sort by list arrow**, click **Course Title**, make sure the **Ascending option button** is selected, then click **OK**

3. Click **Data**, then click **Subtotals**

4. Click the **At each change in list arrow**, then click **Course Title** (if it's not already selected)

5. Click the **Use function list arrow**, then click **Sum** (if it's not already selected)

6. In the Add subtotal to list, click to place a check next to **Total Revenue** (if it's not already selected)

7. Check the **check boxes** shown in Figure 14-5 (if they're not already selected), then click **OK**
   See Figure 14-6.

8. Click **Data**, click **Subtotals**, then click **Remove All**

 close Tours03.xls

Step 5
You can subtotal a list using one of 11 standard functions, including COUNT, MAX, MIN, and AVERAGE. You can subtotal lists with nonnumeric data using the COUNT function.

Figure 14-5: Subtotaling the list by Course Type using the SUM function

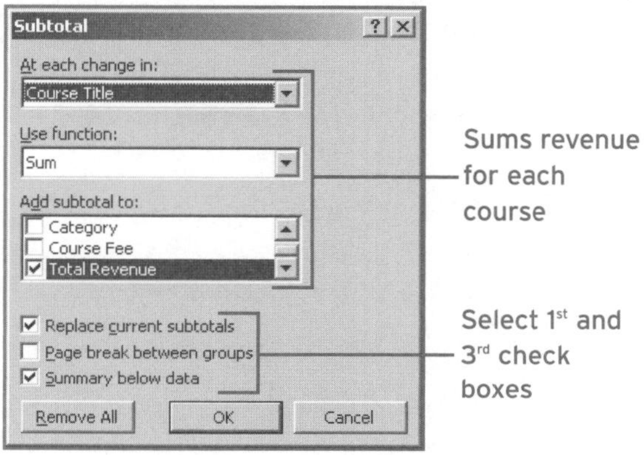

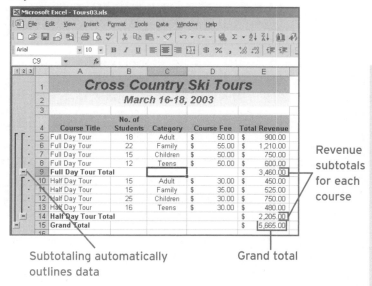

Sums revenue for each course

Select 1st and 3rd check boxes

Figure 14-6: Subtotaled list

extra!

Modifying a subtotaled list
To modify a subtotaled list, click in the list, click **Data** on the menu bar, click **Subtotals**, then select a different function or field name. To display more than one subtotal (for example, a subtotal and an average of the same field), deselect the **Replace current subtotals check box**. To make subtotals stand out, click **Format**, click **Autoformat**, then choose a format with contrasting subtotal lines.

Subtotaling automatically outlines data

Revenue subtotals for each course

Grand total

Skill Set 14

Summarizing Data

Define and Apply Filters
Create a Custom Filter

In a long Excel list, it can be difficult to view only the data you want. Excel lets you **filter** lists to display only a **subset**, or portion, of the data. In addition to AutoFilter, you can use a custom filter that lets you specify **criteria**, or conditions, you want the program to use in displaying records. For example, you might want to display only data where the Sales amount is higher than a certain number. You can also specify more than one criterion for a field: if you specify AND between the two criteria, Excel will display only records that meet both criteria. If you specify OR between them, Excel will display records that meet either criterion.

Step 4
To display all records for a field after a custom filter, click its AutoFilter list arrow, then click All. If you have filtered on more than one field, click Data on the menu bar, point to Filter, then click Show All. To clear all AutoFilter arrows, click Data on the menu bar, point to Filter, then reselect AutoFilter.

Activity Steps

 open Wages01.xls

1. Click **Data** on the menu bar, point to **Filter**, then click **AutoFilter**
   List arrows appear next to each field name.

2. Click the **AutoFilter list arrow** next to **Hourly Wage**, then click **(Custom)**

3. In the Custom AutoFilter dialog box, click the **Hourly Wage list arrow**, then click **is greater than**

4. Click in the top right box, type **7**, then click **OK**
   Excel displays records for employees who make over $7 an hour. The Hourly Wage list arrow is blue, indicating that an AutoFilter is in effect.

5. Click the **Department list arrow**, then click **(Custom)**

6. Click the **Department list arrow**, click **equals** (if it's not already selected), click the **top right list arrow**, then choose **Housekeeping**

7. Click the **Or option button**

8. Click the **bottom left list arrow**, click **equals**, click the **bottom right list arrow**, then click **Front Desk**
   See Figure 14-7.

9. Click **OK**
   Excel displays employees who make more than $7 per hour and who work in either Housekeeping or at the Front Desk.
   See Figure 14-8.

 close Wages01.xls

Figure 14-7: Specifying two criteria using Or

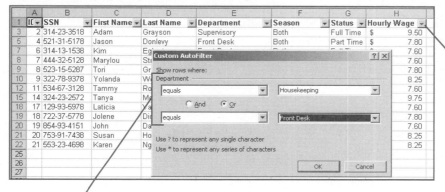

Current AutoFilter will be in addition to Hourly Wage filter

Displays rows where Department is Housekeeping or Front Desk

Figure 14-8: List filtered on two fields

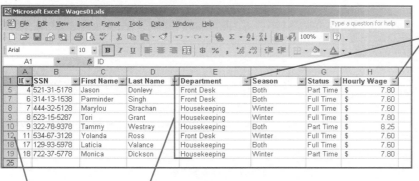

Blue arrows indicate sort on two fields

Blue row numbers indicate filter is in effect

Employees who work in Housekeeping or at Front Desk and who make more than $7.00 per hour

extra!

Using wildcards in a custom filter

You can use the wildcard characters * and ? in the Custom AutoFilter dialog box. Use * to represent any number of characters and use ? to represent any one character. To display all records beginning with the letter c, you could create a filter where "Last Name is equal to C*".

Skill Set 14

Summarizing Data

Define and Apply Filters
Create an Advanced Filter

While AutoFilter is useful for many types of data, it does not let you specify more complex criteria. An **advanced filter** lets you have three or more criteria for one field. In an advanced filter, you place criteria on the worksheet in a range above the list. Then in the Advanced Filter dialog box, you indicate the **criteria range**, which is the location where Excel should look for the criteria when filtering the list range. In the criteria range, you place criteria for AND conditions (where both criteria are true) on the same row, and criteria for OR conditions (where one criterion or the other is true) on different rows.

Activity Steps

 open Wages02.xls

1. Right-click the **row 1 heading**, click **Insert**, then press **[F4]** twice to repeat the action and insert another 2 rows

2. Right-click the **row 4 header**, click **Copy**, right-click the **row 1 header**, then click **Paste**

Step 8
After you filter your data using Advanced Filter, you don't need to display all data again before your next filter. Excel will automatically refilter the entire list. But if you need to clear all filters, click Data on the menu bar, point to Filter, then click Show All.

3. Click cell **E2**, type **Housekeeping**, click cell **H2**, type **>7**
You have created a criteria range in A1:H2, asking Excel to display only employees who are in Housekeeping *and* who make more than $7 an hour.

4. Click anywhere in the list range (A4:H27), click **Data** on the menu bar, point to **Filter**, then click **Advanced Filter**

5. Verify that the List Range box contains **$A$4:$H$27**, click the **Criteria range box**, then drag across the range **$A$1:$H$2** on the worksheet
See Figure 14-9.

6. Click **OK**, then press **[Ctrl][Home]** to select cell A1
See Figure 14-10.

7. Click cell **H2**, then move its contents to cell **H3** to create an Or condition

8. Click anywhere in the list range A4:H27, click **Data** on the menu bar, point to **Filter**, then click **Advanced Filter**

9. Verify that the List range box contains **$A$4:$H$27** and modify the Criteria range to read **$A$1:$H$3**, click **OK**, then press **[Ctrl][Home]**
The list displays those who work in Housekeeping or who earn more than $7 per hour.

 close Wages02.xls

Figure 14-9: Creating an Advanced Filter

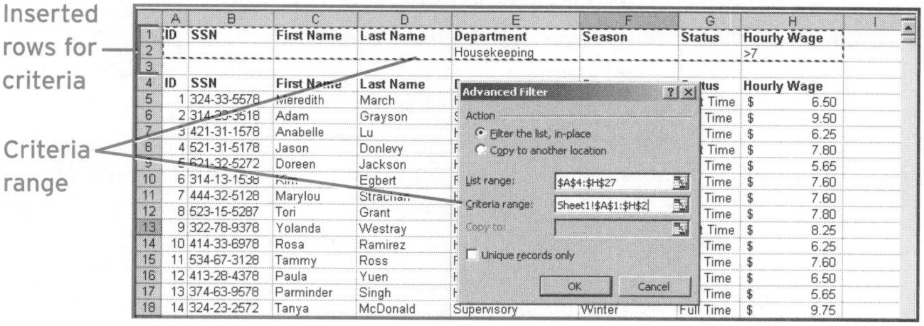

Inserted rows for criteria

Criteria range

Figure 14-10: Results of Advanced Filter with AND criteria

Records that meet above criteria

Blue row numbers indicate filter is in effect

Criteria range specifies Housekeeping employees earning over $7 per hour

extra!

Ensuring success with Advanced Filters
Clicking in the list range before opening the Advanced Filter dialog box ensures that the list range will automatically appear in the dialog box. Always check the criteria range in the dialog box to make sure it includes any additional criteria you have added. It's also important to make sure your criteria range doesn't include any blank lines, which can happen if you're changing an OR filter to an AND filter by moving a criterion up to the first line. *If you have blank lines included in the criteria range, Excel will not filter the data.*

Skill Set 14
Summarizing Data

Add Group and Outline Criteria to Ranges
Group and Outline Structured Data

An Excel list is an example of structured data: it contains column labels in the top row, followed by data rows containing similar types of information. If a list spans several screens or pages, it can be difficult to get the overall "picture" of your data. Excel lets you **group and outline** your list data to show summary information and hide detail. You can use the Hide and Show Details buttons to hide or expand rows or columns in any data grouping. The Row and Column Level buttons will hide or show particular levels on the entire worksheet.

Step 2
To use grouping and outlining, your data must be organized like a list, with no blank columns or rows. You may need to sort your data as well, so that rows with similar types of information are next to each other.

Activity Steps

 open Marketing01.xls

1. Click anywhere in the list range A5:I13
   The data is in list format: it has formatted column headings, no blank rows, and has similar data (sales figures) in each column.

2. Click **Data** on the menu bar, point to **Group and Outline**, then click **Auto Outline**
   Excel displays the worksheet in outline view, as shown in Figure 14-11.

3. Click the **Hide Detail button** 🔳 (above column E), which then becomes the Show Detail button

4. Click the **Show Detail button** ➕ above column E

5. Click the **Row Level 1 button** 1️⃣
   See Figure 14-12.
   Only Level 1, summary information, is visible.

6. Click the **Row Level 2 button** 2️⃣ to redisplay the row details

7. Click the **Column Level 1 button** 1️⃣

 close Marketing01.xls

Figure 14-11: Worksheet with outlining brackets

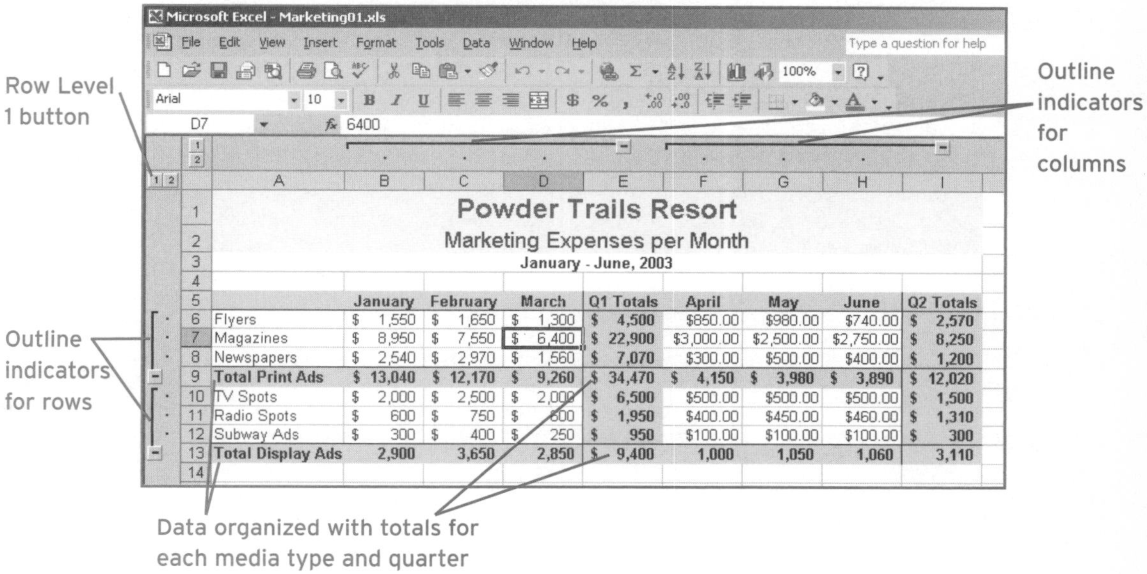

Row Level 1 button

Outline indicators for columns

Outline indicators for rows

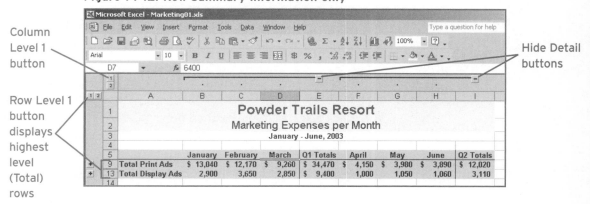

Data organized with totals for each media type and quarter

Figure 14-12: Row summary information only

Column Level 1 button

Hide Detail buttons

Row Level 1 button displays highest level (Total) rows

Skill Set 14
Summarizing Data

Use Data Validation
Validating Entered Data

When you create an Excel list, you usually want each column to contain a particular type of data. For example, a Price column should contain only values under $100, or a Customer column should contain only text. To help ensure list accuracy, you can use Excel **data validation** to limit the data users enter in any cell or range. In the Data Validation dialog box, you enter **criteria** that describe acceptable values, such as a date range, a number of decimal places, or a series of values you specify. If a user enters invalid data, an error message appears. You can customize the error message.

Activity Steps

 open Reservations01.xls

Step 9
If the acceptable values are listed on the worksheet, you can click the Collapse dialog box button , drag across the range to enter it, then click the Redisplay dialog box button.

1. Select the range **B14:B18**, click **Data** on the menu bar, then click **Validation**; click the **Allow list arrow**, then click **Whole number**

2. Click the **Minimum box**, type **1**, click the **Maximum box**, type **10**, then click **OK**

3. Select the range **H14:H18**, click **Data** on the menu bar, then click **Validation**

4. Click the **Allow list arrow**, then click **List**

5. Click the **Source box**, type **Check, Charge, Not Paid**, then compare your screen to Figure 14-13

6. Click the **Error Alert tab**, make sure the check box is selected, click the Error message box, type **Use the list arrow to enter allowable entries**, then click **OK**

7. Click cell **B14**, type **10**, then press **[Enter]**

8. Click cell **H14**, type **15**, then press **[Enter]**, read the error message, then click **Retry**

9. Press **[Delete]**, click the **cell H14 list arrow**, compare your screen to Figure 14-14, click **Check**, then press **[Enter]**
   When you have limited data to a specific list, users can either use the list arrow or type an acceptable entry. The AutoComplete feature will enter the rest of the item after the user types enough characters to distinguish it from other acceptable entries.

 close Reservations01.xls

Figure 14-13: Entering data validation criteria

Selected cells will only allow values from this list

Click to remove validation criteria from selected cells

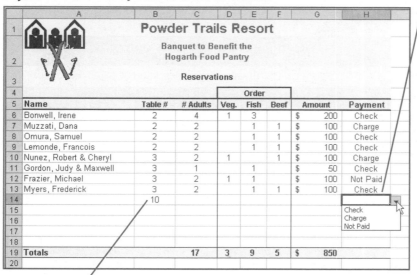

Cell entries limited to values in list

Figure 14-14: Limiting data to a list of entries

	A	B	C	D	E	F	G	H
1			**Powder Trails Resort**					
2			**Banquet to Benefit the Hogarth Food Pantry**					
3			**Reservations**					
4					Order			
5	**Name**	**Table #**	**# Adults**	**Veg.**	**Fish**	**Beef**	**Amount**	**Payment**
6	Bonwell, Irene	2	4	1	3		$ 200	Check
7	Muzzati, Dana	2	2		1	1	$ 100	Charge
8	Omura, Samuel	2	2		1	1	$ 100	Check
9	Lemonde, Francois	2	2		1	1	$ 100	Check
10	Nunez, Robert & Cheryl	3	2	1		1	$ 100	Charge
11	Gordon, Judy & Maxwell	3	1		1		$ 50	Check
12	Frazier, Michael	3	2	1	1		$ 100	Not Paid
13	Myers, Frederick	3	2		1	1	$ 100	Check
14		10						
15								Check
16								Charge
17								Not Paid
18								
19	**Totals**		17	3	9	5	$ 850	
20								

Value limited to numbers between 1 and 10

extra!

Adding screen tips
You can also add screen tip messages that users see after they select cells. Select a cell or range, click **Data** on the menu bar, click **Validation**, then click the **Input Message tab**. Select the **Show input message when cell is selected check box**, type a message title and a message, then click **OK**. You can use screen tips to tell users the type of data they should enter.

Skill Set 14

Summarizing Data

Retrieve External Data and Create Queries

Import Web Data Using an Existing Web Query

Just as you retrieve data from an external database, you can use a **query**, a reusable request saved in .iqy file format, to retrieve data from the World Wide Web. You can use the saved query to **refresh**, or update, imported Web data, also called the **external data range**. You can use one of the existing Excel queries to retrieve a variety of information. *In order to perform all the steps in this lesson, your computer needs to have access to the World Wide Web.*

Step 4
In the Import Data dialog box, you can click Properties to set refresh options; you can have Excel refresh the query every time you open the file or after a specified number of minutes.

Activity Steps

1. With a blank workbook open, click Data on the menu bar, point to Import External Data, then click Import Data

2. In the Select Data Source dialog box, click MSN MoneyCentral Investor Currency Rates.iqy
   See Figure 14-15.

3. Click Open
   See Figure 14-16.

4. Click OK
   The name of each country and its currency unit appears in column A in the form of a hyperlink, specially formatted text you can click to display more information on the subject from the Web.

5. Click the Save button 🖫 on the Standard toolbar, navigate to the location where your Project Files are saved, change the filename in the File name text box to Currency01, then click Save

6. If you do not see the External Data toolbar, right-click any toolbar, then click External Data
   See Figure 14-17.

7. Click the Refresh Data button ⏻ on the External Data toolbar, then watch the Status bar at the bottom of the screen
   Text and a rotating globe appear briefly to inform you that the program is going to the Web to refresh the worksheet data. *When you import Web data, check the Web page's legal statement to ensure that you are not violating any copyright restrictions.*

8. Click cell A2, Click here to visit MSN MoneyCentral Investor, scroll to the bottom of the page, click Terms of Use, then click the Close button ☒ on your browser window

 close Currency01.xls

Figure 14-15: Queries supplied with Microsoft Excel

My Data Sources folder opens automatically

Your dialog box contents may differ

Select this query

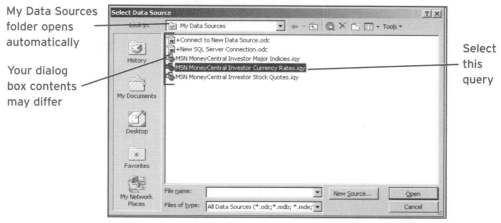

Figure 14-16: Specifying the destination of imported data

Retrieved data will be placed in the range starting in cell A1

Existing worksheet is default destination

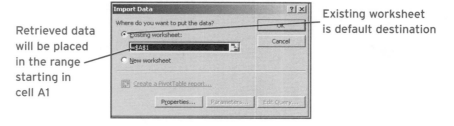

Figure 14-17: Imported data saved in Excel workbook format

External Data toolbar lets you manipulate and refresh data

Your query results will differ because data is updated regularly

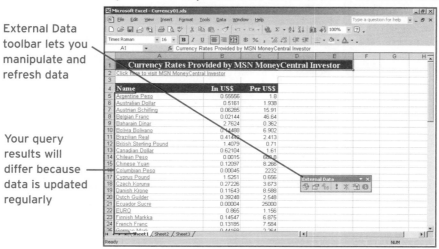

Skill Set 14

Summarizing Data

Retrieve External Data and Create Queries
Create a Web Query to Import Web Data

You can create a **Web query**, a reusable request with an .iqy file extension, to import information from the Internet and the World Wide Web into an Excel worksheet. You might use a Web query to obtain updated information on stocks, the weather, or the books a company currently publishes on a particular subject. As with any query, you can **refresh**, or update, the imported information at any time. *To perform all the steps in this lesson, your computer needs access to the World Wide Web. If the Web page in this lesson has become unavailable since this book was printed, use any other Web address, such as www.course.com.*

Activity Steps

1. With a blank workbook open, click **Data** on the menu bar, point to **Import External Data**, then click **New Web Query**
   The New Web Query dialog box displays your current home page.

2. In the Address box, select the current address if it isn't already highlighted, then type **http://weather.noaa.gov/weather/current/KASE.html**
   See Figure 14-18.
   Because this service is not on the World Wide Web, you do not need to type www in the address.

3. Click **Go**

4. Move the pointer over any yellow arrow box and observe the ScreenTip and the heavy outline that surrounds the area

5. Click the yellow arrow box next to **Current Weather Conditions**
   See Figure 14-19.

6. In the New Web Query dialog box toolbar, click the **Save Query button** , navigate to the location where your Project Files are saved, change the filename to **Weather Query**, then click **Save**

7. In the New Web Query dialog box, click **Import**, make sure the **Existing worksheet option button** is selected, then click **OK**
   The current weather conditions for Aspen, Colorado, appear.

8. Click **File** on the menu bar, click **Save**, navigate to the location where your Project Files are stored, change the filename to **Weather01**, then click **Save**
   When you import Web data, be sure to check the Web page's legal statement so that you are not violating any copyright or usage restrictions.

 close Weather01.xls

Step 1
If your browser is Internet Explorer, you can also right-click any Web page, then click Export to Microsoft Excel, which starts a new Excel session and creates a new Web Query.

Figure 14-18: Specifying Web address for the query

Type Web address from which you want to import data

Your home page may differ

Click to display page whose address you typed

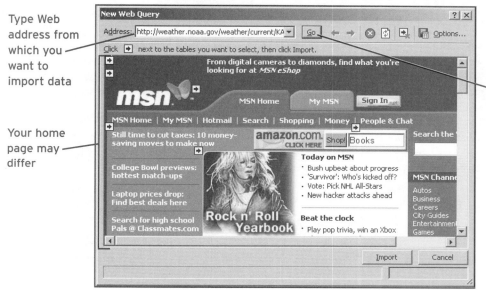

Figure 14-19: Specifying the information to include in the query

Click this arrow to include all page areas

Click any yellow arrow box to include area in query

Yellow arrow box becomes green check box after you click it

Page content will differ depending on when you access this site

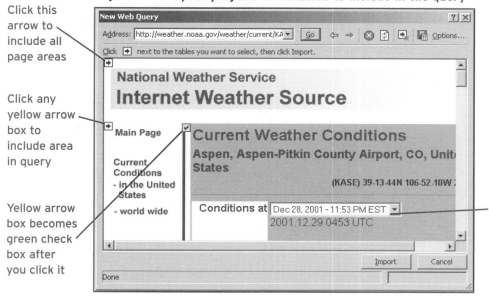

Skill Set 14
Summarizing Data

Retrieve External Data and Create Queries
Use XML to Share Excel Data on the Web

Extensible Markup Language, or **XML**, is a file standard that Web designers and organizations use for structured data, such as the data in Excel spreadsheets. XML is a universal format for sharing data. XML files are text files that can be easily exchanged either over the the Internet or an Intranet. Unlike text files, however, XML files are "marked up" with **tags** that describe the type of data they contain. The files do not contain formatting. Formatting is placed in **stylesheets** that Web developers apply to the XML file. Excel lets you save workbook files in XML format. You cannot see the XML code unless you open the file in a program designed for that purpose, called an **XML parser**, such as the parser in Internet Explorer 5.5.

Activity Steps

 open Media04.xls

1. Click **File** on the menu bar, click **Save As**, click the **Save in list arrow**, then if necessary navigate to the location where your Project Files are stored

2. Click the **Save as type list arrow**, then click **XML Spreadsheet (*.xml)**

3. Select the filename, then type **Media05**
   See Figure 14-20.

4. Click **Save**

5. Start the **Internet Explorer** program, click **File** on the menu bar, then click **Open**

6. Click **Browse**, then navigate to the location where your Project Files are stored

7. Click the **Files of type** list arrow, click **All Files**, click **Media05.xml**, then click **Open**

8. In the Open dialog box, click **OK** to view the XML file in Internet Explorer
   See Figure 14-21.

9. Click the **Close button** on the Internet Explorer title bar

 close Media05.xls

Step 3
When you save an Excel file in XML format, certain features are lost, including graphic objects, charts, and custom views.

Figure 14-20: Saving a worksheet in XML format

Your save location and file list may differ

XML file type

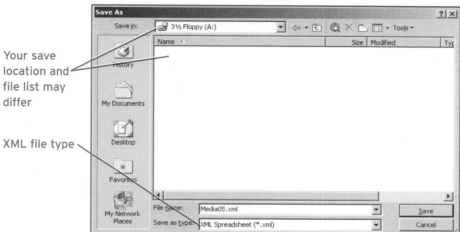

Figure 14-21: XML code for the Media04.xml file

XML code

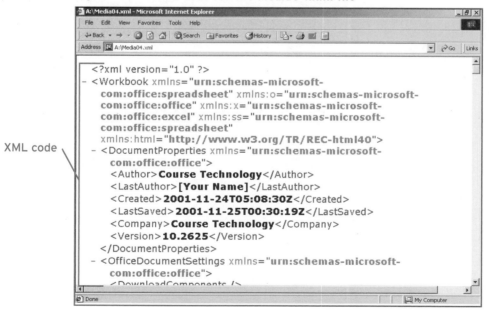

Skill Set 14

Summarizing Data

Create Extensible Markup Language (XML) Web Queries

Create XML Web Queries

You may want to retrieve XML data regularly from the Web or from a network. To do this, you can create a query to an XML file on the Web using the same techniques you would use to query a database file. *Web sites with XML data exist, but it would be difficult to supply a stable Web site that users can access months after this book is published. In this activity, you will create a Web Query to an existing XML file in your Project Files location. The procedure is the same as if you were going to a Web site.*

Step 4
Unlike most Web pages you would view in the New Web Query dialog box, the XML file contains only one arrow, which selects the entire page. You don't need to click the arrow; clicking Import will automatically import the entire page.

Activity Steps

1. With a blank workbook open, click **Data** on the menu bar, point to **Import External Data**, then click **New Web Query**

2. In the Address box of the New Web Query dialog box, type the path to your Project File location, followed by **Providers04.xml**
   For example, if your Project Files are stored on a floppy disk in the A: drive, type A:\Providers04.xml. If they are on your hard drive, designated C: in a folder called Project Files, type C:\Project Files\Providers04.xml.
   See Figure 14-22.

3. Click **Go**
   The XML code appears in the New Web Query window, as shown in Figure 14-23.

4. Click **Import**, making sure the Import Data dialog box has the **Existing worksheet option** selected and cell **$A$1** designated as the destination

5. Click **OK**

6. Save the file as **XML Query.xls**

   close XML Query.xls

Figure 14-22: XML Query

Type path to
XML file
(normally
this would be
a Web or
intranet site
address)

Click to
display
XML code

Figure 14-23: XML code in New Web Query window

XML code
for file
named in
Address box

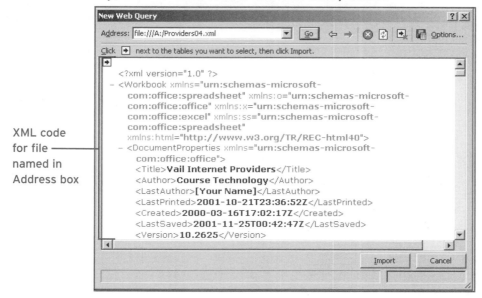

Skill Set 14
Summarizing Data

Target Your Skills

 Wages03.xls

1 Sort the list by Department and Last Name in ascending order. Use a Custom Filter to display employees who make more than $6 *and* less than $8. Clear the AutoFilter, then create an Advanced Filter above the data as shown in Figure 14-24. Save the file in XML format as Wages04.xml. Close the file, then open it in your Web browser.

Figure 14-24

	A	B	C	D	E	F	G	H
1	ID	SSN	First Name	Last Name	Department	Season	Status	Hourly Wage
2				>f	Housekeeping	Winter	Full	<7
3								
4	ID	SSN	First Name	Last Name	Department	Season	Status	Hourly Wage
12	10	414-33-6978	Adam	Grayson	Housekeeping	Winter	Full Time	$ 6.25
14	3	421-31-1578	Anabelle	Lu	Housekeeping	Winter	Full Time	$ 6.25
20	12	413-28-4378	Paula	Yuen	Housekeeping	Winter	Full Time	$ 6.50
28								

2 Use a Web Query to import the information in School02.xml from your Project File location, then save the file as School02.xls. Format it as shown in Figure 14-25. Use Data Validation to restrict data entered in cells C2:C13 to the three options that appear in the column, then create the Category subtotals shown. Collapse then expand the outline levels.

Figure 14-25

	A	B	C	D	E
1	Course	Students	Category	Course	Total Revenue
2	Half Day Beginners	45	Adult	30	$ 1,350
3	Full Day Beginners	50	Adult	50	$ 2,500
4	Half Day Intermediate	21	Adult	35	$ 735
5	Full Day Intermediate	28	Adult	55	$ 1,540
6			Adult Total		$ 6,125
7	Half Day Beginners	50	Children	30	$ 1,500
8	Full Day Beginners	46	Children	50	$ 2,300
9	Half Day Intermediate	29	Children	35	$ 1,015
10	Full Day Intermediate	20	Children	55	$ 1,100
11			Children Total		$ 5,915
12	Half Day Beginners	40	Teens	30	$ 1,200
13	Full Day Beginners	30	Teens	50	$ 1,500
14	Half Day Intermediate	22	Teens	35	$ 770
15	Full Day Intermediate	18	Teens	55	$ 990
16			Teens Total		$ 4,460
17	Total	399			$ 16,500
18			Grand Total		$ 33,000
19					

Skill List

1. Create PivotTable reports and PivotChart reports
2. Forecast values with what-if analysis
3. Create and display scenarios

Excel worksheets let you track large amounts of information; Excel analysis tools let you explore data relationships in your worksheets. **What-if analysis** lets you explore how a change in worksheet values affects formula results.

In a long data list with many fields, simple column totals or subtotals only tell part of the story. **PivotTable reports** let you drag list fields in a special table layout to create automatic grouping and totals quickly. **PivotChart reports** let you use the same technique to create charts that summarize your data. These easy-to-use features let you explore data relationships quickly and efficiently.

While changing formula values is a simple type of what-if analysis, chart **trendlines** help you project data based on past trends. Excel scenarios are another type of what-if analysis. **Scenarios** let you create and save named sets of formula input values so you can apply them to your worksheet and view their effect on formula results.

Skill Set 15

Analyzing Data

Create PivotTable Reports and PivotChart Reports

Create a PivotTable Report

In a long Excel list, it can be difficult to see trends in your data. A **PivotTable report** is an interactive grid that lets you quickly rearrange data fields to combine and analyze list data. For example, you could create a PivotTable report from a long list of sales figures for each sales rep and district, then drag fields to "pivot" that data and see totals for each rep and district. This flexibility makes PivotTable reports a useful analysis tool, especially for long lists of information. The PivotTable and PivotChart Wizard helps you set up a report in three steps.

Step 6

As you drag fields over drop areas, the pointer displays a miniature PivotTable with the current drop area highlighted. For example, if the pointer is over the row area, the leftmost area of the pointer is blue.

Activity Steps

 open Report04.xls

1. Click anywhere within the list range **A7:E29**

2. Click **Data** on the menu bar, then click **PivotTable and PivotChart Report**
   If the Office Assistant appears, click **No, I don't need help now.**

3. In the Step 1 of 3 dialog box, make sure that the **Microsoft Excel list or database** and the **PivotTable option buttons** are selected, then click **Next**

4. In the Step 2 of 3 dialog box, make sure that the list range **$A$7:$E$29** appears in the Range box, then click **Next**

5. In the Step 3 of 3 dialog box, make sure the **New worksheet option** is selected, then click **Finish**
   A new worksheet appears, containing PivotTable **drop areas** surrounded by blue lines and a **PivotTable Field List** showing all of the list fields. The PivotTable toolbar appears on the worksheet.

6. Drag the **Begin Date field** from the Field List to the **Drop Row Fields Here area**, releasing the mouse button when the pointer becomes ↓
   See Figure 15-1.

7. Drag the **Item field** from the Field List to the **Drop Column Fields Here area**

8. Drag the **Amount field** from the Field List to the **Drop Data Items Here area**
   You can see expense totals by date and totals for each expense item.
   See Figure 15-2.

 close Report04.xls

Figure 15-1: Begin Date in row fields area

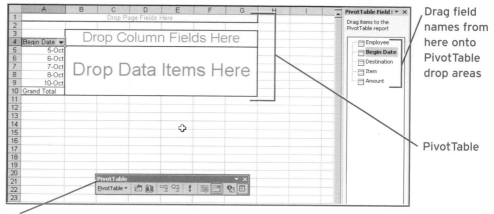

Drag field names from here onto PivotTable drop areas

PivotTable

Your PivotTable toolbar may be in a different position

Figure 15-2: Completed PivotTable

Item field in column area

Begin Date in row area

Amount field in data area

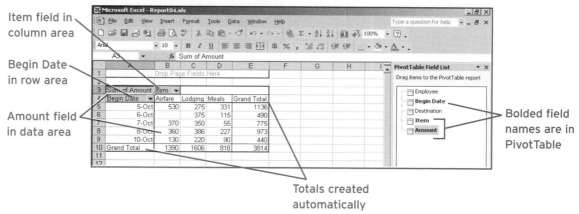

Bolded field names are in PivotTable

Totals created automatically

Skill Set 15
Analyzing Data

Create PivotTable Reports and PivotChart Reports
Modify a PivotTable Report

Once you have created a PivotTable report, you will want to use it to explore relationships in your data, which is the real power of a PivotTable. To do this, you drag fields to row, column, data, and page field "drop areas" and view the results. Excel immediately recalculates the summary information. A **page field** is the area at the top of the PivotTable report where you can place any field to filter the PivotTable data. For example, if you have data for different years, you could place a Year field in the page field area, then select a particular year to show only data for that year.

Step 4
In the PivotTable field list window, fields that have already been placed in the PivotTable are boldfaced; unused fields are in light type.

Activity Steps
 open Report05.xls

1. Drag the **Item field** from the column area on the left side of the PivotTable to any blank worksheet area outside the PivotTable, releasing the mouse button when the pointer becomes

2. Drag the **Destination field** from the row drop area on the left to the **column drop area** (the cell above "Total")

3. Drag the **Item field** from the PivotTable Field List to the **row area** (below the Sum of Amount field)
   You can see the total for each expense item for each city.
   See Figure 15-3.

4. Drag the **Employee field** from the field list to the **Drop Page Fields Here** area
   By default, the PivotTable displays data for all employees.

5. Click the **Employee list arrow** in the page field area, click **Harris**, then click **OK**
   The item and destination information for Harris appears in the PivotTable.
   See Figure 15-4.

6. Click the **Employee list arrow** in the page field area, click **(All)**, then click **OK**

 close Report05.xls

Figure 15-3: Rearranged PivotTable

Item field in row area

Totals for each item by destination

Destination field in column area

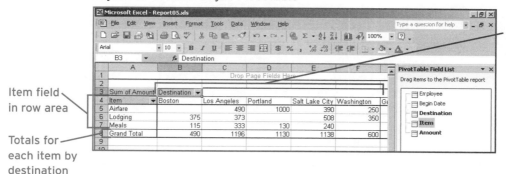

Figure 15-4: Page field filters PivotTable data

Selecting one name shows expenses for only that employee

Employee field in page area

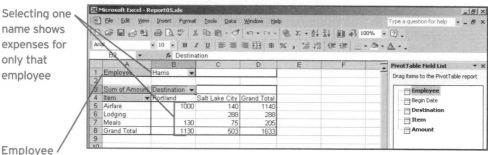

Skill Set 15

Analyzing Data

Create PivotTable Reports and PivotChart Reports

Update a PivotTable Report

While Excel charts automatically reflect changes to the source worksheet information, PivotTables do not update automatically. If you change underlying worksheet data, display the PivotTable, then click the **Refresh Data button** on the PivotTable toolbar. The PivotTable amounts update to include the new information. See Table 15-1 for a summary of the buttons on the PivotTable toolbar.

To remove the Field List from your screen, click the Hide Field List button 🔳 on the PivotTable toolbar. This button is a toggle, meaning that you click it once to display the Field List and click it again to hide the Field List.

Activity Steps

file open Songbooks01.xls

1. On the PivotTable, notice that the sales total for Educators, Inc. is $1,046.00
   See Figure 15-5.

2. Click the **Sales Data sheet tab**

3. Click cell **H8**

4. Type **15**, then press **[Enter]**

5. Click the **PivotTable sheet tab**, then notice that the Educators, Inc. total has not changed

6. Watch the sales amounts for Educator's Inc., then click the **Refresh Data button** on the PivotTable toolbar
   See Figure 15-6.

file close Songbooks01.xls

Table 15-1: Selected PivotTable toolbar buttons		
button	**name**	**use to**
📊	Format Report	Apply one of 21 table and report formats
📶	ChartWizard	Create a PivotChart report from your PivotTable
❗	Refresh Data	Update PivotTable report after changing source data
🔢	Field Settings	Change summary function of selected fields
🔳	Show/Hide Field List	Close Field List window

Figure 15-5: PivotTable before editing worksheet

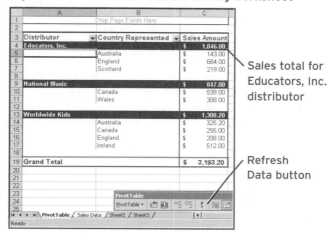

Sales total for Educators, Inc. distributor

Refresh Data button

Figure 15-6: PivotTable after updating

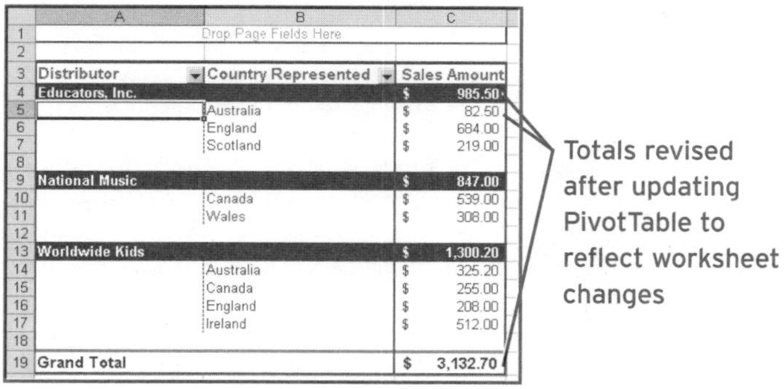

Totals revised after updating PivotTable to reflect worksheet changes

Skill Set 15

Analyzing Data

Create PivotTable Reports and PivotChart Reports

Format a PivotTable Report

The default PivotTable report contains minimal formatting, but you can apply AutoFormats to enhance its appearance. You can choose from **table formats**, which apply shading and fonts, or **report formats** (also called **indented formats**). Indented formats apply shading and fonts and move column fields to the row area; they also indent each row field and show data in a single column. To format PivotTable numbers, you use the Field Settings button on the PivotTable toolbar.

Step 3
To remove all formatting from a PivotTable, click None at the bottom of the AutoFormat dialog box, then click OK. To restore a previous format, click the Undo button immediately after applying a format.

Activity Steps

 open Classes01.xls

1. Click any cell inside the PivotTable
   The PivotTable field list appears.

2. Click the **Format Report button** 🖼 on the PivotTable toolbar
   See Figure 15-7.

3. In the AutoFormat dialog box, scroll down and click the format labeled **Table 2**, click **OK**, then click any PivotTable cell
   See Figure 15-8.

4. Click the **Format Report button** 🖼 on the PivotTable toolbar

5. Click the **Report 6** AutoFormat, click **OK**, then click any PivotTable cell in column C

6. Click the **Field Settings button** 🔢 on the PivotTable toolbar, then click **Number**

7. Click **Currency**, verify that the Decimal places box contains 2, click **OK**, then click **OK** again
   See Figure 15-9.

 close Classes01.xls

Figure 15-7: PivotTable formats

Format
Report button

Figure 15-8: Table 2 AutoFormat applied

AutoFormat
adds fonts
and fills

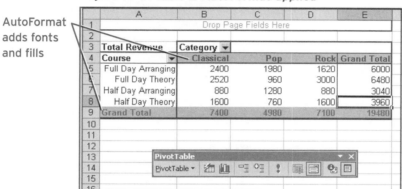

Figure 15-9: Report 6 AutoFormat applied

Summary
figures
appear in
one column

Row fields
indented

Column
fields move
to row area

Numbers
formatted
as currency

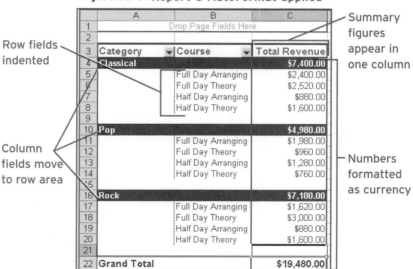

Skill Set 15

Analyzing Data

Create PivotTable Reports and PivotChart Reports

Create and Modify a PivotChart Report

PivotChart reports are useful for creating graphical representations of list data. You can pivot the data the same way you would in a PivotTable report, by dragging fields to different locations to explore data relationships. Like an Excel chart, a PivotChart report has data markers, series, categories, and axes, as well as a field representing each element. It also has a page field area. When you use the Wizard to create a PivotChart report, Excel creates the corresponding PivotTable on a separate sheet. *When you create a PivotTable, carefully check the range that Excel suggests. If there is no space between your worksheet title information and the column headings, the suggested range may be incorrect.*

Step 9
To view a chart of selected series data, click the Course list arrow, click the (Show All) box to deselect it, click one or more of the Course types to select them, then click OK.

Activity Steps

 open Classes02.xls

1. Click **Data** on the menu bar, then click **PivotTable and PivotChart Report**

2. Make sure the **Microsoft Excel list or database option button** is selected, click the **PivotChart report (with PivotTable report) option button**, then click **Next**

3. On the worksheet, drag to select the correct range, **A3:E15**
   If you include the worksheet title or any information outside the list range, the PivotChart report will not appear.
   See Figure 15-10.

4. Click **Next**

5. Make sure the **New worksheet option button** is selected, then click **Finish**

6. Drag the **Type field** to the **Drop Category Fields** Here area at the bottom of the chart area (you may need to move the PivotTable toolbar)

7. Drag the **Course Fee field** to the **Drop Page Fields Here** area

8. Drag the **Total Revenue field** to the **Drop Data Items Here** area

9. Drag the **Course field** to the **Drop Series Fields Here** area (depending on how your system is set up, you may need to move the PivotTable Field List box to the far right in order to view the Drop Series Fields Here area)
   See Figure 15-11.

 close Classes02.xls

Figure 15-10: Selecting the list range

Headings not included in list range

Drag to insert sheet name and correct range reference

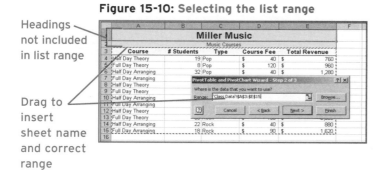

Figure 15-11: Completed PivotChart report

Use Chart type command on Chart menu to choose a different chart type

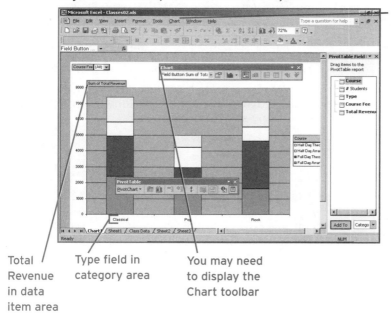

Total Revenue in data item area

Type field in category area

You may need to display the Chart toolbar

extra!

Modifying PivotChart options

You can change the chart type and options for any PivotChart. Click the **ChartWizard button** on the PivotTable toolbar, select a chart type, click **Next**, click a tab to modify any chart element, then click **Finish**. To change a PivotChart's summary function (which is SUM by default), double-click the **Sum of Total Revenue button**, select a **function**, then click **OK**.

Skill Set 15

Analyzing Data

Forecast Values with What-If Analysis
Create a Trendline

In an Excel chart, you might want to display not only a graphical representation of the data but also of the overall tendency in one or more series. To do this, you can display a **trendline**, which is used to make mathematical predictions about data trends using the principles of **regression analysis**, a statistical measure. When you add a trendline to a chart, Excel uses the data in your selected series and the mathematical formula for the trendline you chose to calculate the trendline position. You can use trendlines to project data levels based on existing trends. A **linear trendline** assumes that the trend will continue at a steady rate. An **exponential trendline** is curved, indicating that the series will increase or decrease at an increasing rate over time. You format a trendline by double-clicking it and selecting options, as you would any chart data series.

Step 3
To delete a trendline, select it on the chart, then press [Delete].

Activity Steps

 open Projection01.xls

1. Click the **Lesson Revenue Chart sheet tab**

2. Click **Chart** on the menu bar, then click **Add Trendline**

3. In the Add Trendline dialog box, click the **Type tab** (if it's not already selected), then, under Trend/Regression type, click **Linear** (if it's not already selected)
   See Figure 15-12.

4. Click **OK**

5. Click **Chart** on the menu bar, then click **Add Trendline**

6. In the Add Trendline dialog box, click **Exponential**, then click **OK**
   If the sales increase trend follows the same pattern it did in the first six months, December lesson revenues are projected to be about $37,000. If revenues are expected to increase exponentially, December revenues are projected to be about $43,000.
   See Figure 15-13.

 close Projection01.xls

Figure 15-12: Choosing a trendline

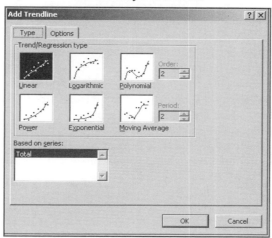

Figure 15-13: Chart showing linear and exponential trendlines

Exponential trendline

Linear trendline

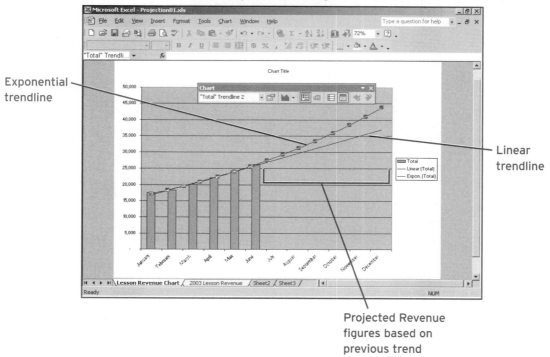

Projected Revenue figures based on previous trend

Skill Set 15

Analyzing Data

Forecast Values with What-If Analysis
Create a One-Input Data Table

When performing what-if analysis using Excel, you might want to investigate many different levels of an **input value** (a value that is used in a formula) on a formula result. For example, for a car payment calculation, you might want to substitute many different interest rates in the payment formula and examine the payment for each rate. It would be time-consuming to type each rate in a cell and see its effect on the payment. An Excel **data table** lets you quickly examine the effect of many levels of a changing value (often called a **variable**) on formula results. You create a table that contains the varying rates in a column and the formula, which you usually hide to make the table easier to read. The Data Table command uses the formula to calculate results for each input value level you list.

Step 7
A custom format has four sections representing positive numbers, negative numbers, zero values, and text, separated by semicolons. Entering only the semicolons means that nothing will display for any value, effectively hiding the cell value.

Activity Steps

 open Computer02.xls

1. Click cell C11 and view its formula, noting that the input value for the interest rate is in cell C8

2. Click cell F6, type 6.25%, press [Enter], type 6.50%, then press [Enter]

3. Drag to select the range F6:F7, then drag its fill handle to cell F17 until the screen tip reads 9.00%

4. Click cell F5, then type Rate

5. Click cell G5, type =, click cell C11, click the Enter button ☑ on the Formula bar, then compare your screen to Figure 15-14

6. With cell G5 selected, click Format on the menu bar, then click Cells

7. Click the Number tab (if it's not already selected), under Category click Custom, double-click the Type box, type ;;; (three semicolons) to indicate no format and hide the formula, then click OK

8. Drag to select the range F5:G17, click Data on the menu bar, then click Table

9. Click the Column input cell box, click cell C8 on the worksheet, click OK, then click any blank cell
   See Figure 15-15.

 close Computer02.xls

Figure 15-14: Setting up a data table

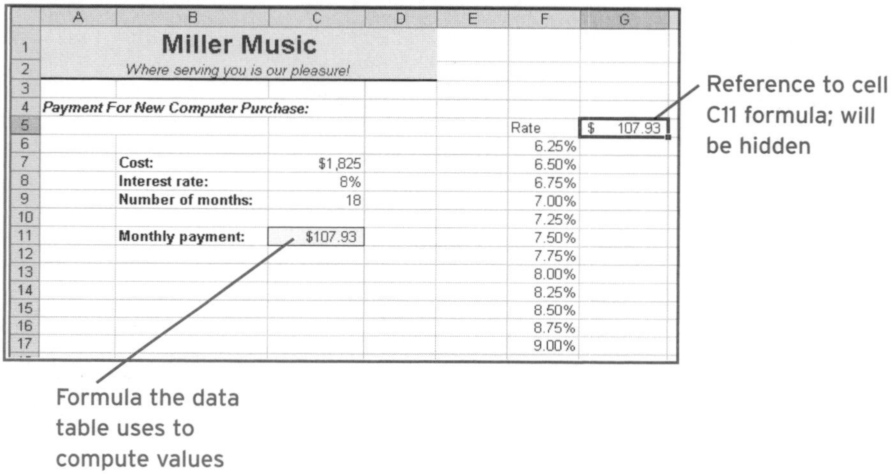

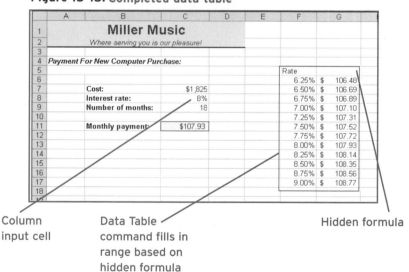

Reference to cell
C11 formula; will
be hidden

Formula the data
table uses to
compute values

Figure 15-15: Completed data table

Column
input cell

Data Table
command fills in
range based on
hidden formula

Hidden formula

extra!

Creating a two-input data table

To create a two-input data table, place the values of a second variable, such as months, across the top of the table, and place the formula reference at the intersection of the variable 1 column and the variable 2 row (which now reads "Rate"). Select the entire table, click **Data** on the menu bar, then click **Table**. The Row input cell would contain the months cell reference, and the Column input cell would contain the rate cell reference.

Skill Set 15

Analyzing Data

Forecast Values with What-If Analysis
Use Goal Seek

When using trendlines and data tables, you work with given input values in order to calculate an end result in a dependent formula cell. But when you want to determine the input level that will create a known result, you can use an Excel feature called **Goal Seek**. For example, you might want to determine an item's inventory level that will produce a profit of $10,000. With Goal Seek, Excel rapidly substitutes different input values until it reaches the result you want.

Activity Steps

 open Tickets05.xls

1. Click cell **E19**
   Cell E19 is an indirect dependent of the ticket price, $30, in cell C6. You use Goal Seek to see what concert ticket price would produce $35,000 in total sales.

2. Click **Tools**, then click **Goal Seek**

3. Verify that the Set Cell box contains **E19**

4. Click the **To value box** then type **35000**

5. Click the **By changing cells box**, then click cell **C6**
   See Figure 15-16.

6. Click **OK**
   See Figure 15-17.

7. If necessary, drag the Goal Seek Status dialog box so you can see cells C6 and E19

8. In the Goal Seek Status dialog box, click **OK**
   Goal Seek found that a ticket price of $37 would produce your goal of $35,000 in Total Sales. It substitutes these values in the worksheet.

 close Tickets05.xls

Step 6
Instead of replacing worksheet values with the Goal Seek result, you could click Cancel to return to the original values.

Figure 15-16: Goal Seek dialog box

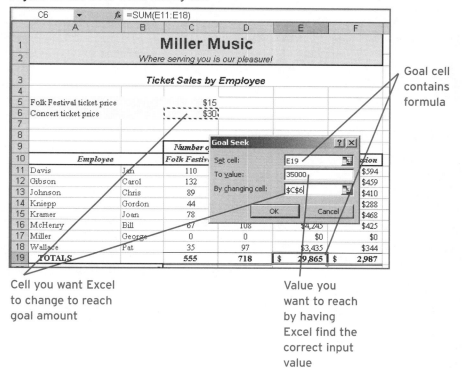

Goal cell
contains
formula

Cell you want Excel
to change to reach
goal amount

Value you
want to reach
by having
Excel find the
correct input
value

Figure 15-17: Goal and modified input value substituted in worksheet

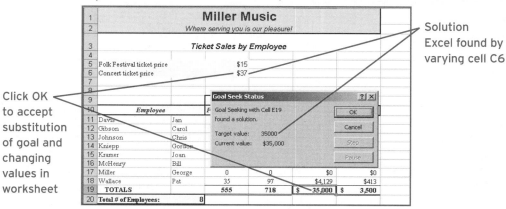

Solution
Excel found by
varying cell C6

Click OK
to accept
substitution
of goal and
changing
values in
worksheet

Skill Set 15

Analyzing Data

Create and Display Scenarios
Create Two or More Scenarios

In a **what-if analysis**, you can manually change formula input values, then view the effect of your change on formula results. This analysis method, however, can be slow and difficult to manage. To keep track of varying values, you can use an Excel **scenario**, which is a named set of values that Excel will substitute in your worksheet. For example, you might want to create a scenario where revenues are $10,000 per month higher than their current values. You could save this value in a scenario called "High Revenue," then show the scenario in a worksheet to see its effect on profit formula results.

Activity Steps

 open Band02.xls

1. Click cell **E15**, click **Tools**, then click **Scenarios**
   The Formula bar shows that cell E15 calculates the monthly payment based on the amount in B9 and the rate in B18. You will create scenarios for two interest rates and see their effect on the payment.

2. Drag the Scenarios dialog box as necessary so you can see the worksheet range **A1:E15**

3. Click **Add**, click the **Scenario name box**, then type **High Rate**

4. Click the **Changing cells box**, delete any text there, click cell **B18**, see Figure 15-18, then click **OK**
   You now define the new value that this scenario will substitute in cell B19.

5. Type **.12**, see Figure 15-19, then click **OK**

6. Click **Add**, type **Low Rate**, make sure the Changing cells box contains **B18**, then click **OK**

7. In the $B$18 box, type **.05**, then click **OK**

8. Repeat steps 6 and 7 to enter a Scenario called **Current Rate**, using a rate of **.08**

9. In the Scenario Manager dialog box, click **High Rate**, then watch cell E15 as you click **Show**
   The value of the High Rate scenario is inserted in the worksheet, and the formula output in cell E15 changes to reflect the higher rate.
   See Figure 15-20.

10. Click **Low Rate**, click **Show**, click **Current Rate**, click **Show**, then click **Close**

 close Band02.xls

Step 8
The worksheet values will display the values of whichever scenario you last selected.

Figure 15-18: Creating a scenario

Name for first scenario

First scenario will "try out" a higher value in cell B18

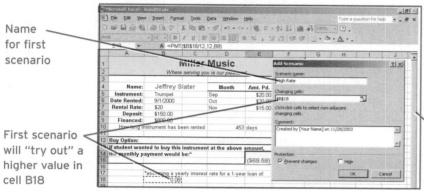

Formula result will be affected by higher interest rate scenario

Figure 15-19: Defining a scenario value

Scenario will substitute 12% rate in cell B18

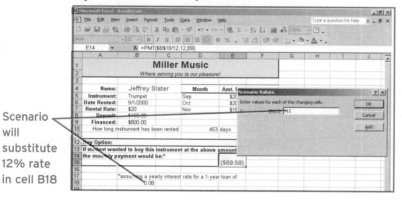

Figure 15-20: Worksheet with High Rate Scenario values displayed

High Rate scenario substituted higher rate and shows effect on payment

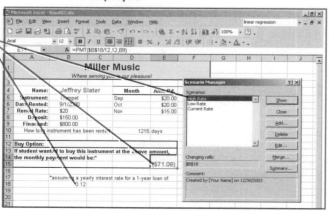

extra!

Creating a scenario summary

Often you will want to see the results of all your scenarios at the same time. In the Scenario Manager dialog box, click **Summary**. Click the **Scenario summary option button**, make sure the Results cells box contains the location of the formula, then click **OK**. Excel creates a new worksheet displaying the results of all scenarios that relate to the formula you indicated.

Skill Set 15

Analyzing Data

Target Your Skills

 Instruction01.xls

1 Create and format the PivotTable shown in Figure 15-21, using the Table 4 AutoFormat. Change the Data Items from "Paid" to "Minutes." Create a PivotChart report from the table, then position the fields using the instructions on the figure.

Figure 15-21

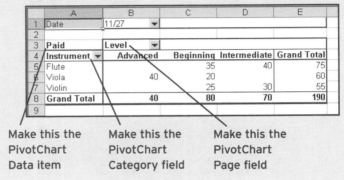

Make this the PivotChart Data item

Make this the PivotChart Category field

Make this the PivotChart Page field

 Budget07.xls

2 On the Projection chart, click the Total Revenue series, then create an Exponential trendline. Create a Linear trendline for Total Expenses series. Double-click the Exponential trendline and select a heavier line weight. On the Budget worksheet, create the three scenarios for cell B5 shown in Figure 15-22.

Figure 15-22

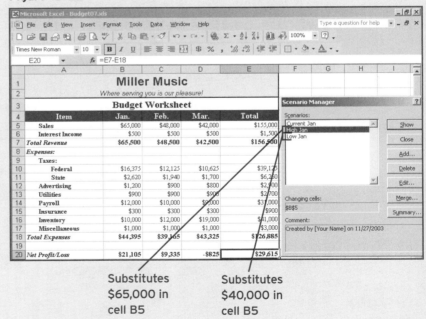

Substitutes $65,000 in cell B5

Substitutes $40,000 in cell B5

Skill Set 16
Workgroup Collaboration

Skill List

1. Modify passwords, protections, and properties
2. Create a shared workbook
3. Track, accept, and reject changes to workbooks
4. Merge workbooks

Working collaboratively on spreadsheets used to be a laborious undertaking. You could distribute workbook copies on a floppy disk, then examine each co-worker's changes and type them into your master. Like all Microsoft Office programs, Microsoft Excel is designed to help you work efficiently in a workgroup.

In a shared work environment, it is important to think about the types of information you want to share with users. Sensitive payroll information, for example, should be available only to those who have approval to access it. Excel lets you protect cells, worksheets, and entire workbooks, depending on your needs. You can hide information and use passwords to customize the amount of information available to others.

When you work with many shared documents, it is often helpful to catalog information by using document properties.

You can share workbooks to solicit feedback and changes from other users, using either a shared file on a central file server or multiple copies of the same shared workbook. Then you can keep track of feedback and accept or reject suggested changes. You can also merge user changes into one master copy, then choose which to accept or reject.

Skill Set 16
Workgroup Collaboration

Modify Passwords, Protections, and Properties
Protect Worksheet Cells

While workbook sharing can speed your work, it also offers two challenges: protecting confidential information and preventing unauthorized changes. You might not want all users to see all your data, formulas, or worksheets, or you might want them to see data but not change it. Excel protection commands let you **hide** information from view and **lock** cells to prevent changes. Locking and hiding only take effect if you also **protect** the worksheet from changes using the Protection command on the Tools menu. By default, Excel locks all worksheet cells. In an unprotected workbook, you are not aware of this. But you can unlock any cells you want, such as an area reserved for data entry. See Table 16-1 for other hiding and protecting options.

Step 3
To hide a worksheet formula, click the cell containing the formula, click Format on the menu bar, click Cells, click the Protection tab, then select the Hidden check box. As with cell locking, formulas are hidden only if you then protect the worksheet using the Protection command on the Tools menu.

Activity Steps

   open Helicopters03.xls

1. Drag to select the range **B7:D7**, press and hold down **[Ctrl]**, then select the range **B11:D11**

2. Click **Format** on the menu bar, click **Cells**, then click the **Protection tab**

3. Click the **Locked check box** to remove the check mark and unlock the selected cells
   See Figure 16-1.

4. Click **OK**

5. Click **Tools** on the menu bar, point to **Protection**, then click **Protect Sheet**

6. Click to select the **Protect worksheet and contents of locked cells check box** (if it's not already selected)
   You don't need to enter a password. Other users, however, will still be able to unprotect the sheet.

7. Click **OK**

8. Click cell **B11**, type **110**, then press **[Enter]** to edit the unlocked cell

9. Click cell **B14** (which is still locked), press any key, then read the message that appears
   See Figure 16-2.

10. Click **OK**

   close Helicopters03.xls

Figure 16-1: Unlocking selected cells

Removing check mark unlocks selected cells

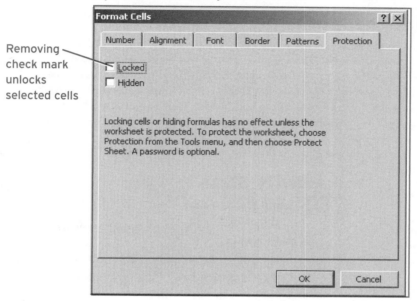

Figure 16-2: Attempting to modify a locked cell

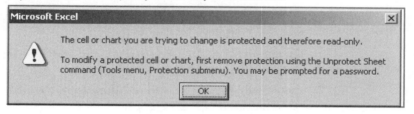

TABLE 16-1: Selected options for hiding and protecting

to	click
Hide a worksheet	Format/Sheet/Hide
Hide a row	Format/Row/Hide
Hide a column	Format/Column/Hide
Hide a formula	Format/Cells/Protection tab, select Hidden, click OK

Skill Set 16
Workgroup Collaboration

Modify Passwords, Protections, and Properties
Protect Worksheets

Excel lets you protect an entire worksheet from changes by others. You can also assign a **password**, a confidential sequence of letters and/or numbers that will unprotect the sheet. Password-protecting a sheet blocks unauthorized users from using locked cells. (By default, all worksheet cells are locked; you can unlock them using the Protection tab in the Format Cells dialog box.) *But be sure to keep track of any passwords you assign. If you lose a password, you will not be able to use the worksheet.* If you want finer control over the types of changes users can make, you can allow or prevent use of specific worksheet features.

Activity Steps

 open Wages04.xls

1. Click **Tools** on the menu bar, point to **Protection**, then click **Protect Sheet**

2. Click to place a check in the **Protect worksheet and contents of locked cells check box** (if it's not already selected)

3. In the Password to unprotect sheet box, type **bluedog**
   Excel masks the characters you type with asterisks as added protection.

4. Scroll down the feature list, click to place a check mark next to **Use AutoFilter**, compare your screen to Figure 16-3, then click **OK**

5. In the Confirm Password dialog box, type **bluedog**, then click **OK**

6. Click any worksheet cell, press any letter or number key, read the message shown in Figure 16-4, then click **OK**

7. Click the **Department list arrow**, then click **Front Desk**

8. Click **Tools** on the menu bar, point to **Protection**, then click **Unprotect sheet**

9. Type **bluedog**, then click **OK**

 close Wages04.xls

Step 3
You must type passwords exactly as they were created, including upper- and lower-case letters. Excel passwords can contain up to 255 letters, numbers, or characters. For added security, use a combination of letters and numbers.

Figure 16-3: Allowing access to selected worksheet features

Password masked with asterisks

Allows users to use AutoFilter lists

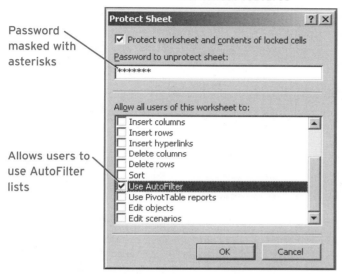

Figure 16-4: Worksheet protection message

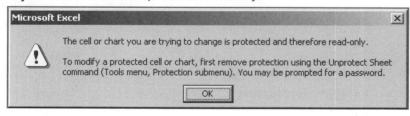

extra!

Giving access to specific users

If your operating system is Windows 2000, you can allow selected users to modify ranges you specify. In an unprotected workbook, click **Tools** on the menu bar, point to **Protection**, then click **Allow Users to Edit Ranges**. Click **New**, then enter a title, range, and password for the range. Click **Permissions**, click **Add**, select the names of users who should have access, then click **OK** twice.

Skill Set 16

Workgroup Collaboration

Modify Passwords, Protections, and Properties
Protect Workbooks

When you share your workbooks with others, Excel lets you assign varying protection levels. You can protect entire workbooks to prevent others from opening or editing them or changing their structure.

Step 9
Be sure to type passwords exactly as you entered them, including upper- and lower-case letters, or the workbook will not open. Write down your passwords and keep them in a secure location.

Activity Steps

 open Bikes03.xls

1. Click **File** on the menu bar, click **Save As**

2. On the Save As dialog box toolbar, click **Tools**, then click **General Options**

3. In the Password to open box, type **icebox**, then press **[Tab]** twice

4. In the Password to modify box, type **redhouse**

5. Compare your screen to Figure 16-5, click **OK**, reenter **icebox**, click **OK**, then reenter **redhouse** in the next two dialog boxes

6. Click the **Save in list arrow**, then navigate to the location where your Project Files are stored, if it is not already visible

7. In the File name text box, edit **Bikes03.xls** to read **Bikes04.xls**

8. Click **Save**, then click the **Close Window button** ⊠ on the menu bar

9. Click the **Open button** on the Standard toolbar, double-click **Bikes04.xls**, in the Password dialog box shown in Figure 16-6, type **icebox**, press **[Enter]**, type **redhouse**, then press **[Enter]**
   See Figure 16-7.

 close Bikes04.xls

Figure 16-5: Setting workbook passwords

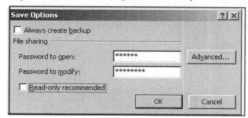

Figure 16-6: Using a password to open a workbook

Type **icebox**

Figure 16-7: Opened workbook after entering passwords

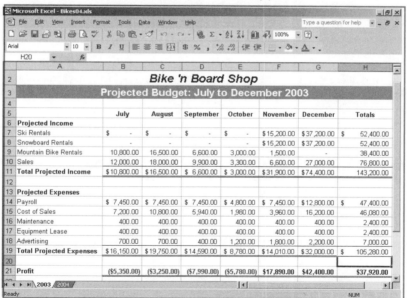

Skill Set 16

Workgroup Collaboration

Modify Passwords, Protections, and Properties

Protect Workbook Elements

Instead of protecting an entire workbook from all changes, you can protect particular aspects of the workbook, such as its structure, window size, and position. When you protect a workbook's *structure*, users cannot add, delete, move, rename, or insert worksheets. When you protect a workbook's *windows*, the workbook window is the same size every time you open it. To prevent others from deleting workbook protection, you can enter a password.

Step 4
To assign a password to a shared workbook, you must first unshare the workbook. You learn more about workbook sharing in the next lesson.

Activity Steps

 open Reservations02.xls

1. Click **Tools** on the menu bar, point to **Protection**, then click **Protect Workbook**

2. In the Protect Workbook dialog box, make sure there is a check next to **Structure**, then click to place a check mark next to **Windows**

3. Click the **Password box**, type **apple**, compare your screen to Figure 16-8, then click **OK**

4. Type **apple**, then click **OK**
The title bar only displays Minimize, Maximize, or Close buttons for the program. There is no extra set of buttons for the workbook.

5. Right-click any **sheet tab**, and note that the worksheet commands are unavailable
See Figure 16-9.

6. Click **Tools**, point to **Protection**, click **Unprotect Workbook**, type **apple**, then click **OK**

 close Reservations02.xls

Figure 16-8: Protecting workbook elements

Figure 16-9: Workbook with protected structure and windows

Sheet manipulation commands not available

No workbook window control buttons

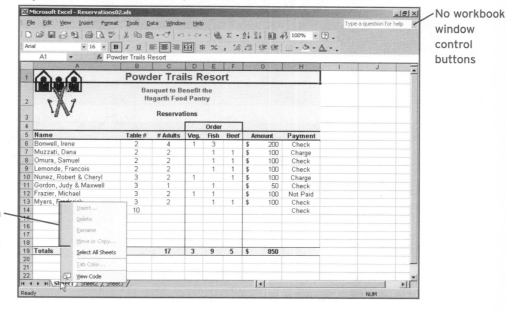

Skill Set 16

Workgroup Collaboration

Modify Passwords, Protections, and Properties

Modify Workbook Properties

Every Excel workbook has **properties**, which include identifying features such as the author and when it was created and last modified. Excel updates some properties automatically, such as the modification date, every time you save a file. You can set some properties, including the Author and Company, and add detailed information about the document that will help others who might use your workbook later. Some properties apply to all workbooks you open in Excel, while others apply only to an individual workbook. Companies that keep file libraries for employees to share on an intranet or the Internet can use properties to help users find and organize files.

If you are working on a shared computer on a network, you may not have permission to change Excel or workbook properties. Check with your technical resource person.

Step 1
You can also display the Properties dialog box from the Tools menu in the Open and Save As dialog boxes. At the Windows desktop, you can right-click any filename, then click Properties.

Activity Steps

 open Rentals05.xls

1. Click **File** on the menu bar, then click **Properties**

2. Click the **Summary tab** (if it's not already selected)

3. Click the **Category box**, then type **Forecasts**

4. Click the **Comments box**, then type **Q1 Rental and Profit Projections**
   See Figure 16-10.

5. Click **OK**

 close Rentals05.xls

Figure 16-10: Properties dialog box

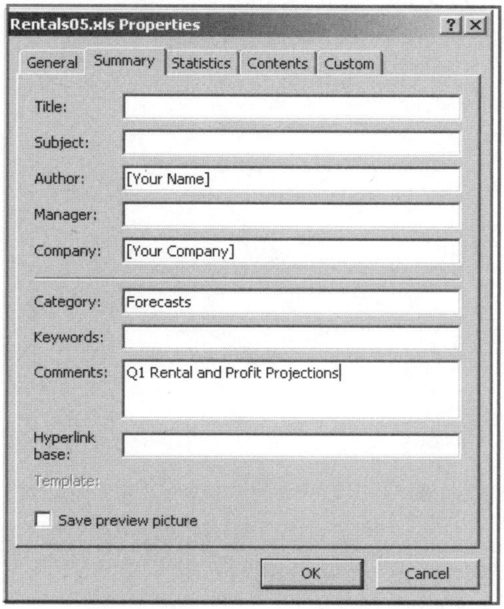

extra!

Viewing properties

You can also view selected properties for any document in the Open or Save dialog box. Click **File** on the menu bar, click **Open** or click **Save As**, click the **Views list arrow** on the dialog box toolbar, then click **Properties**. The properties of any filename you click in the dialog box will appear in the Preview pane.

Skill Set 16
Workgroup Collaboration

Create a Shared Workbook
Create Workbooks for Shared Use

Shared workbooks offer users a way of working together on the same project. For example, you may have a financial analysis worksheet where various accounting employees contribute and update different pieces of data, such as payables or receivables. You can resave any workbook as a shared workbook, then place it on a network for others to access. See Table 16-2 for a summary of features that you cannot change after you save a workbook as shared. Also, if you want to track changes by other users later on, be sure Change tracking is turned on before saving it as a shared workbook. (Change tracking is covered in the next lesson.)

Be sure you are working on a copy of the Statement02.xls file in case you want to repeat this activity. Saving a workbook in shared format automatically overwrites the original shared workbook.

Step 4
After you save a workbook as shared, you can use the Save As command on the File menu to save it to a network server, but not a Web server.

Activity Steps

 open Statement02.xls

1. Click **Tools** on the menu bar, click **Share Workbook,** then click the **Editing tab** if it's not already selected

2. Click to select the **Allow changes by more than one user at the same time. This also allows workbook merging. check box**
   See Figure 16-11.

3. Click **OK**

4. In the dialog box that asks if you want to continue by saving the workbook, click **OK**
   See Figure 16-12.

 close Statement02.xls

TABLE 16-2: Features to set before sharing a workbook

graphics	Web	data & analysis	formatting & layout
Charts	Hyperlinks	Scenarios	Conditional formats
Pictures		Outlines & subtotals	Merged cells
Drawing objects		PivotTable Reports	Cell block changes
		Data validation	Delete sheets

Figure 16-11: Saving a workbook as shared

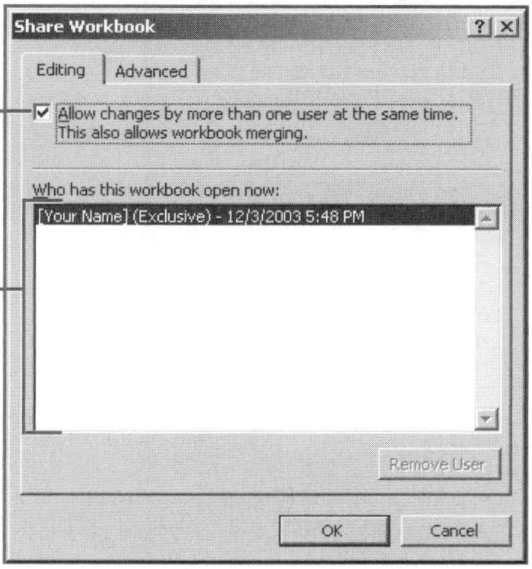

Select to create shared workbook

Lists people using this workbook now

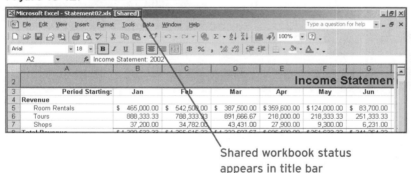

Figure 16-12: Shared workbook

Shared workbook status appears in title bar

extra!

Sharing workbooks
After you save a workbook as shared and place it on a network server, others can open the workbook, change it, then save it. All users have their own settings for viewing, filtering, and printing the workbook. When a user saves, the shared workbook is automatically upated with changes others have made. If your changes conflict with changes another user has made to the same cell, Excel opens a conflict resolution dialog box, in which you indicate changes you want to keep.

Skill Set 16

Workgroup Collaboration

Track, Accept, and Reject Changes to Workbooks

Track Worksheet Changes

When sharing workbooks with others, it is often helpful to automatically **track**, or keep a record of, changes that each person makes to a workbook. Tracked changes are highlighted on the worksheet with a different color representing each user. You can display a list of tracked changes that Excel creates on a separate worksheet called a **change history**. You can also decide which changes to accept and reject, either individually or in a dialog box that will display each change for your evaluation. When you turn on change tracking, Excel automatically resaves the workbook as shared.

If you want to repeat the steps in the activity, be sure you are working on a copy of the Party03.xls file, because you must save your changes for change tracking to take effect.

Step 8
The History sheet tab will disappear after you save your workbook again, but the workbook is still tracking changes. Reopen the Track Changes dialog box, deselect the When option, then select List changes on a new sheet again to redisplay the sheet.

Activity Steps

 open Party03.xls

1. Click **Tools** on the menu bar, point to **Track Changes**, then click **Highlight Changes**

2. In the Highlight Changes dialog box, click to select **Track changes while editing. This also saves your workbook.** to share your workbook

3. Click the **When option** to deselect it, then make sure the **Who option** is deselected and reads **Everyone**
See Figure 16-13.

4. Click to select the **Highlight changes on screen** (if it's not already selected), click **OK**, then click **OK** again
To appear in the change history, changes must first be saved.

5. Click cell **C9**, type **10**, press **[Enter]**, then click the **Save button** on the Standard toolbar

6. Point to cell **C9**, then view the screen tip

7. Click **Tools** on the menu bar, point to **Track Changes**, then click **Highlight changes**

8. Click to select **List changes on a new sheet**, then click **OK**
See Figure 16-14.

 close Party03.xls

Figure 16-13: Setting change tracking

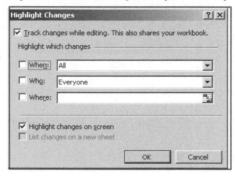

Figure 16-14: Change History sheet

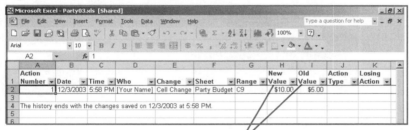

Change history sheet
shows new and old values

extra!

Learning more about change tracking
Change history does not record formatting changes. You can specify that you want to track changes only in a particular range if you select the **Where option** in the Highlight Changes dialog box, click the **Where box**, then drag to select the range. To set the number of days to track changes, click **Tools** on the menu bar, click **Share Workbook**, click the **Advanced tab**, then, under **Track changes**, set the number of days.

Skill Set 16

Workgroup Collaboration

Track, Accept, and Reject Changes to Workbooks

Review, Accept, and Reject Changes

If you activate change tracking when you save a workbook for sharing, you can review user changes to accept or reject each one. To have Excel automatically display a dialog box with each change for your evaluation, you specify that you want to see all changes "not yet reviewed." The dialog box summarizes the change, its author, and when the change was made. After you have accepted or rejected all changes, you cannot review them again, but you can still view them on the Change History worksheet.

If you want to repeat this activity, make sure you are working on a copy of the Holiday02.xls file, because you can only accept or reject changes once.

Step 7
Remember that Excel erases change history items older than the number of days in effect the last time you saved the workbook. For example, if you are keeping 10 days of change history and you open the workbook after 30 days, you'll be able to view the changes from 30 days before, but when you close the workbook, the history from 11 to 30 days is deleted.

Activity Steps

 open Holiday02.xls

1. Click **Tools** on the menu bar, point to **Track Changes**, then click **Accept or Reject Changes**
   The Select Changes to Accept or Reject dialog box opens.

2. In the When box, make sure **Not yet reviewed** is selected, then click **OK**
   See Figure 16-15.

3. Click **Accept**
   See Figure 16-16.

4. Click **Reject**

5. Accept the remainder of the changes in the workbook, then click the **Save button** ▣ on the Standard toolbar

6. Click **Tools** on the menu bar, point to **Track Changes**, then click **Highlight Changes**

7. Under Highlight which changes, make sure **When** is checked and that the When box says **All**, click to select **List changes on a new sheet**, then click **OK**
   Notice that any rejected changes appear under a line on the change history.
   See Figure 16-17.

 close Holiday02.xls

Figure 16-15: Evaluating the first tracked change

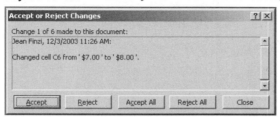

Figure 16-16: Evaluating the second tracked change

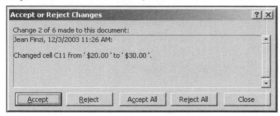

Figure 16-17: Change history shows all changes

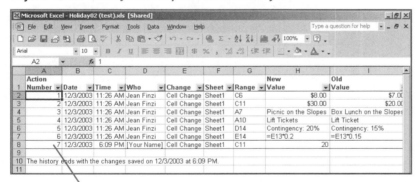

Rejected change (scroll right
to see accept/reject status)

extra!

**What changes
Excel tracks**

When tracking changes,
Excel records changes
to cell contents, as well
as row and column
changes. It does not
track sheet name
changes, formatting,
cell comments, formula
result changes, or any
changes unavailable in
shared workbooks (see
Table 16-2).

Skill Set 16
Workgroup Collaboration

Merge Workbooks
Merge Workbook Revisions

In workgroups without a shared file server, not everyone can work on one file at the same time. In these cases, you can save a workbook as shared, then distribute copies to people you want to review it. Reviewers edit the workbook and return their copies to you. You then open the original workbook and **merge**, or combine, all their changes into your copy. You can accept or reject any merged change. When you save the workbook as shared, make sure you allow enough days on the Advanced tab of the Share Workbook dialog box for all users to return their changes. To be safe, use a large number such as 300.

If you want to repeat this activity, make sure you are working on a copy of the Early01.xls file, because the merged information will remain in the master file even if you don't save changes. If you are using Excel 2002 version 1.0, you may see an error message regarding a sharing violation. If you do, click Save Temporary file and continue with the unit. To avoid this error, you must download and install Office XP Service Pack 1.

Activity Steps

 open Early01.xls

1. Click **Tools** on the menu bar, then click **Compare and Merge Workbooks**

2. In the Select Files to Merge Into Current Workbook dialog box, navigate to the location where your Project Files are stored, click **Early02.xls**, press and hold down **[Ctrl]**, click **Early03.xls**, then click **Early04.xls**
See Figure 16-18.

3. Click **OK**
After a moment, the new information appears in the Early01.xls file.

4. Click **Tools** on the menu bar, point to **Track Changes**, then click **Highlight Changes**

5. Click the **When list arrow**, then click **All**

6. Click to select the **List changes on a new sheet check box**, then click **OK**
See Figure 16-19.

7. Click the **Sheet 1 sheet tab**, then move the pointer over each cell with a triangular change marker, observing how changes appear in a different color for each reviewer
See Figure 16-20.

 close Early01.xls

Step 1
You can only merge workbooks that you saved while file sharing was turned on.

Figure 16-18: Selecting workbooks to merge into the master workbook

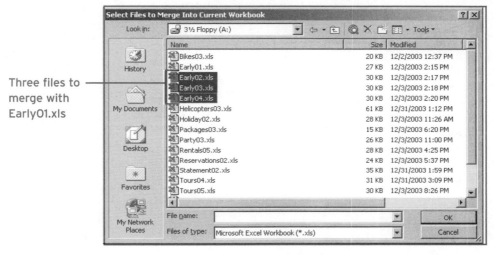

Three files to merge with Early01.xls

Figure 16-19: Change history sheet shows all reviewers' changes

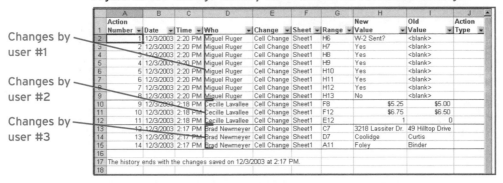

Changes by user #1

Changes by user #2

Changes by user #3

Figure 16-20: Review changes display in different colors

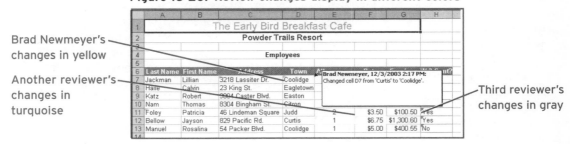

Brad Newmeyer's changes in yellow

Another reviewer's changes in turquoise

Third reviewer's changes in gray

Skill Set 16

Workgroup Collaboration

Target Your Skills

 Packages03.xls

1 Unlock the range shown, then protect the worksheet, using the password "packages." Save the workbook as Packages04, but specify the password "desktop" to open it and "picture" to edit it. Add a comment in the workbook properties that reads "First quarter group sales." Share the workbook and make sure change tracking is turned on.

Figure 16-21

	A	B	C	D	E	F	G	H
1			Powder Trails Resort					
2			Package Sales					
3			First Quarter, 2003					
4								
5	Sales Rep	Customer	City	State	Package	# people	# days	Revenue
6	Clayton	Lloyd Publishing Co.	Chicago	IL	Basic	9	5	$ 5,400
7	Randall	Mather High School	York	CT	Basic	15	3	$ 5,250
8	Mercede	Lefevre School	Las Vegas	NV	Basic	13	3	$ 4,550
9	Randall	Kato & Sons	Seattle	WA	Basic	10	3	$ 3,500
10	Clayton	Marymount Ski Club	Tulsa	OK	Basic	5	5	$ 3,000
11	Mercede	Laird Corp.	Lowell	MA	Deluxe	17	5	$ 18,700
12	Clayton	Hitech Corp.	Cleveland	OH	Deluxe	20	3	$ 15,000
13	Clayton	Mill College	Vincent	PA	Deluxe	20	3	$ 15,000
14	Randall	Donald Marino	Boston	MA	Deluxe	5	3	$ 3,750
15								

Unlock this range

 Tours04.xls

2 With Tours04.xls open, merge the workbook revisions in the files Tours05.xls, Tours06.xls, and Tours07.xls. Save your changes, then review all changes, accepting all changes. Create the change history shown in Figure 16-22. Remove the workbook from shared status, then protect the workbook's structure and windows, using the password "merged."

Figure 16-22

	A	B	C	D	E	F	G	H	I	J	
1	Action Number	Date	Time	Who	Change	Sheet	Range	New Value	Old Value	Action Type	Los Act
2	1	1/21/2003	9:47 PM	Ben Soclowsky	Row Auto-Insert	Sheet1	13:13				
3	2	1/21/2003	9:47 PM	Ben Soclowsky	Cell Change	Sheet1	D13	Total	<blank>		
4	3	1/21/2003	9:47 PM	Ben Soclowsky	Cell Change	Sheet1	E13	=SUM(E5:E12)	<blank>		
5	4	1/21/2003	9:46 PM	Carla Owens	Cell Change	Sheet1	B12	20	18		
6	5	1/21/2003	9:46 PM	Janelle Levertov	Cell Change	Sheet1	C7	Kids	Children		
7	6	1/21/2003	9:46 PM	Janelle Levertov	Cell Change	Sheet1	C11	Kids	Children		
8	7	1/21/2003	9:46 PM	Janelle Levertov	Cell Change	Sheet1	D5	$50.00	$55.00		
9											
10	The history ends with the changes saved on 1/21/2003 at 9:46 PM.										
11											

If you are using Excel 2002 version 1.0, you may see an error message regarding a sharing violation. If you do, click Save Temporary file and continue with the unit. To avoid this error, you must download and install Office XP Service Pack 1.

Excel 2002 Core Projects Appendix

Projects List

Project 1 – Sales Projection for Alaska Adventures

Project 2 – Invoice for Art Rentals to Movies

Project 3 – Budget for Into Thin Air Balloon Tours

Project 4 – Price Lists for Keeping the Beat Drum Shop

Project 5 – Maui Resorts Time Share Vacation Options

Project 6 – Sales Information for Fanfloratastic Flowers

Project 7 – Sales Report for Splashdown Rafting

The Excel Core skill sets include the features and functions you need to create and modify spreadsheets for a variety of purposes. In the following projects, you will format a sales projection, create an invoice, modify a budget, organize price lists, calculate mortgage options, present sales information with charts and graphics, and save a sales report created in Excel as a Web page.

Project for Skill Set 1

Working with Cells and Cell Data

Sales Projection for Alaska Adventures

You work for Alaska Adventures, a small company based in Juneau, Alaska, that offers sea kayaking, mountain biking, and hiking tours. You've received a workbook containing a sales projection for the sea kayaking tours that the company hopes to sell in the busy summer months of June, July, and August. In this project, you will complete and format this worksheet. The workbook also contains a second worksheet that includes a list of the guests who purchased sea kayaking tours on a single day during the previous summer. You'll use the AutoFilter features on this list to determine the number of customers who came from countries other then the United States and Canada.

Activity Steps

 open EC_Project1.xls

1. Clear the contents and formats of cell **A3**, drag cell **A4** up to cell **A3**, then delete cell **D14** and shift the cells left

2. Merge cell **A3** across cells **A3** to **E3**, then check the spelling in the worksheet and correct any errors

3. Enter **Total** in cell **E5**, use the **Go To** command to navigate to cell **C13**, then change the value in cell **C13** to **1200**

4. Use the **SUM** function in cell **E12** to add the values in cells **B12** through **D12**, then copy the formula to cells **E13** through **E15**

5. Select cells **B12** through **B16**, then use the **AutoSum button** to calculate the totals required for cells **B16** through **E16**

6. In cell **B18**, enter the formula required to subtract the value in cell **B16** from the value in cell **B9**, then copy the formula to cells **C18** through **E18**

7. Use **Find and Replace** to locate all instances of **1500** and replace them with **500**

8. Format cells **B7** through **E7**, **B9** through **E9**, **B12** through **E12**, **B16** through **E16**, and **B18** through **E18** with the **Currency style**, format cells **B8** through **E8** and cells **B13** through **E15** with the **Comma** style, then compare the completed worksheet to Figure EP 1-1

9. Switch to the **Customers worksheet**, then use AutoFilter to show only the **International** customers in the Category column The filtered list appears as shown in Figure EP 1-2.

 close EC_Project1.xls

Step 8
To save time, press and hold the [CTRL] key, select each group of cells, and then click the Currency Style button.

Figure EP 1-1: **Completed Projections worksheet**

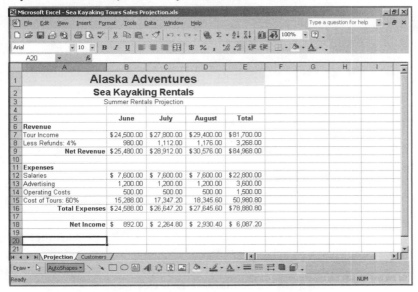

Figure EP 1-2: **AutoFiltered list in Customers worksheet**

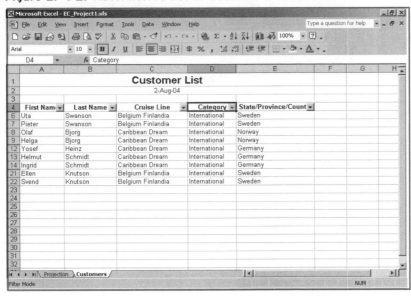

Project for Skill Set 2

Managing Workbooks

Invoice for Art Rentals to Movies

Max Brenner, an artist friend of yours, frequently rents his paintings, drawings, and sculptures to movie crews for use on film sets throughout Vancouver, British Columbia—the new "Hollywood North." Max has asked you to help him create and manage Excel workbooks he can use to track his rental contracts. In this project, you will first create a folder in which to store all of the files related to Max's rental contracts and then save an existing workbook listing information about Max's most recent rental contracts to the new folder. You will then create a workbook in Excel that Max can use to generate invoices. You will create this invoice form from an Excel template and save it into the new folder.

Activity Steps

 open EC_Project2.xls

1. Create a new folder called **Art Rentals** on your floppy disk or hard drive

2. Save the current workbook, **EC_Project2.xls**, as **Rentals List** into the Art Rentals folder, then close the workbook

3. Open the New Document task pane, click **General Templates**, then click the **Spreadsheet Solutions tab** in the Templates dialog box

4. Select the **Sales Invoice template**
   You may need to wait for a few minutes while the template is loaded.

5. Complete the invoice as shown in Figure EP 2-1
   Note that you need to press [Alt][Enter] to enter multiple lines in the top cell of the invoice. When you type the amounts in the Unit Price column, the totals will automatically appear in the Total column. To delete the Farewell Statement at the bottom of the page, click Edit, point to Clear, then click Contents.

6. Save the invoice as **Invoice101** to the Art Rentals folder

 close Invoice101.xls

Figure EP 2-1: Completed invoice

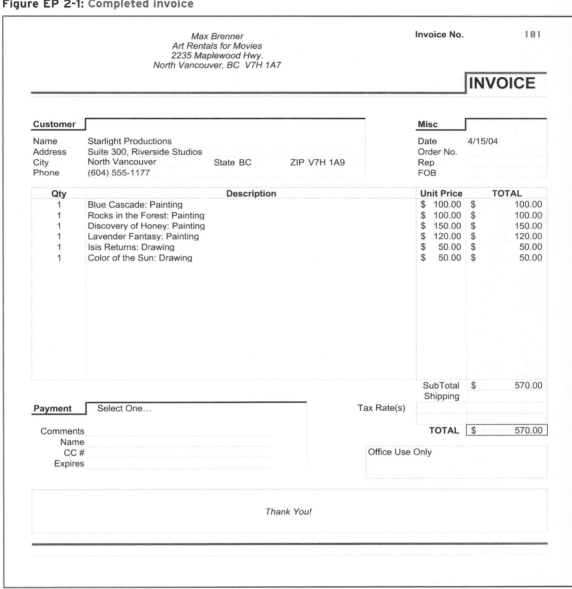

	Max Brenner Art Rentals for Movies 2235 Maplewood Hwy. North Vancouver, BC V7H 1A7		Invoice No.	101

INVOICE

Customer			**Misc**	
Name	Starlight Productions		Date	4/15/04
Address	Suite 300, Riverside Studios		Order No.	
City	North Vancouver	State BC ZIP V7H 1A9	Rep	
Phone	(604) 555-1177		FOB	

Qty	Description	Unit Price		TOTAL	
1	Blue Cascade: Painting	$	100.00	$	100.00
1	Rocks in the Forest: Painting	$	100.00	$	100.00
1	Discovery of Honey: Painting	$	150.00	$	150.00
1	Lavender Fantasy: Painting	$	120.00	$	120.00
1	Isis Returns: Drawing	$	50.00	$	50.00
1	Color of the Sun: Drawing	$	50.00	$	50.00

		SubTotal	$	570.00
		Shipping		

Payment	Select One…	Tax Rate(s)		

		TOTAL	$	570.00

Comments
Name
CC #
Expires

Office Use Only

Thank You!

Project for Skill Set 3

Formatting and Printing Worksheets

Budget for Into Thin Air Balloon Tours

You work for Into Thin Air Balloon Tours, a company based in Phoenix that takes tourists on spectacular hot air balloon tours over the deserts and canyons of Arizona. You've been asked to format the company's budget for January to June 2004 and then to print various views of the budget data. The printed budget appears as shown in Figure EP 3-1.

Activity Steps

 open EC_Project3.xls

1. Unhide **column E** (the totals for March), set the width of **columns B through I** to **15**, set the height of **row 1** to **30**, then format cell **A1** with **Bold**, the **Arial** font syle, and **24 pt**

2. Insert a new row following the first row, enter **Projected Budget: January to June 2004** in the new cell **A2**, center the text across cells A2 through I2, decrease the font size to **16 pt**, then remove the shaded fill

3. Delete **column B**, freeze panes at cell **B5**, then change the Equipment Rentals for June to **9000**

4. Click cell **B19**, create a style called **Profit** that formats cell contents with **Bold**, **Grey 25%** shading, a **Single top** border, and a **Double bottom** border, then apply the Profit style to cells **B19** through **H19**

5. Unfreeze the panes, apply the **Classic 2 AutoFormat** to cells **A4** through **H17**, then right-align the label in cell **A19**

6. In the Page Setup dialog box, change the orientation of the worksheet to **Landscape**, then set the worksheet to print on one page

7. Create a custom header containing the **current date** at the left margin, nothing in the center, and **your name** at the right margin, then create a custom footer containing the **tab name** in the center

8. Print a copy of the worksheet
   The printed worksheet appears in landscape orientation, as shown in Figure EP 3-1.

9. Set the print areas as cells **B4 through B19** and cells **G4 through G19**, then preview and print the two areas
   The two areas print on separate pages.

 close EC_Project3.xls

Figure EP 3-1: Printed budget worksheet in landscape orientation

9/24/2004   [Your Name]

Into Thin Air Balloon Tours

Projected Budget: January to June 2004

	January	February	March	April	May	June	Totals
Projected Income							
Balloon Tours	$ 15,500.00	$ 18,000.00	$ 17,500.00	$ 21,000.00	$ 10,000.00	$ 9,000.00	$ 91,000.00
Equipment Rentals	11,800.00	12,900.00	13,000.00	23,000.00	9,000.00	9,000.00	78,700.00
Sales	12,000.00	18,000.00	9,900.00	3,300.00	6,600.00	9,000.00	49,800.00
Total Projected Income	$ 39,300.00	$ 48,900.00	$ 40,400.00	$ 47,300.00	$ 25,600.00	$ 27,000.00	$ 201,500.00
Projected Expenses							
Payroll	$ 7,450.00	$ 7,450.00	$ 7,450.00	$ 4,800.00	$ 7,450.00	$ 7,451.00	42,051.00
Cost of Sales	7,200.00	10,800.00	5,940.00	1,980.00	3,960.00	5,400.00	35,280.00
Balloon Maintenance	1,500.00	1,500.00	1,500.00	1,500.00	1,500.00	1,500.00	9,000.00
Equipment Lease	400.00	400.00	400.00	400.00	400.00	400.00	2,400.00
Advertising	1,200.00	1,200.00	1,200.00	1,200.00	1,200.00	1,200.00	7,200.00
Total Projected Expenses	$ 17,750.00	$ 21,350.00	$ 16,490.00	$ 9,880.00	$ 14,510.00	$ 15,951.00	$ 95,931.00
Profit	$ 21,550.00	$ 27,550.00	$ 23,910.00	$ 37,420.00	$ 11,090.00	$ 11,049.00	$ 105,569.00

Budget

Project for Skill Set 4

Modifying Workbooks

Price Lists for Keeping the Beat Drum Shop

As the office manager of Keeping the Beat Drum Shop, you have decided to use Excel to organize some of your price lists into various worksheets within one workbook. You can then use 3-D cell references to calculate totals for data contained in the various worksheets.

Activity Steps

 open EC_Project4.xls

1. Delete the **Hardware** worksheet

2. Insert a new worksheet called **Summary**

3. Move the Summary worksheet so it is the first worksheet in the workbook

Step 6
In each worksheet, the total to be used in the 3-D reference formula appears in cell D14.

4. Change the name of the **Miscellaneous** worksheet to **World Percussion**

5. Set up the Summary sheet so it appears as shown in Figure EP 4-1

6. Enter a formula in cell B7 that uses **3D cell references** to calculate the total value of the Cymbals, World Percussion, and Drums price lists
   The total value of all three price lists is $5,944.00 in cell B7, as shown in Figure EP 4-2.

 close EC_Project4.xls

Figure EP 4-1: Summary sheet setup

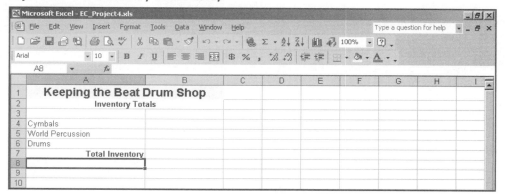

Figure EP 4-2: 3D total in cell B7

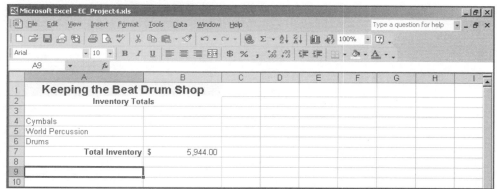

Project for Skill Set 5

Creating and Revising Formulas

Maui Resorts Time Share Vacation Options

You are thinking of purchasing a time share at a condominium resort complex in Maui, Hawaii. Several time share condos are available, so you decide to use Excel to help you determine which option best suits your budget. You'll also use formulas to help you calculate other vacation costs such as airfare, food, and recreation. The workbook you will use contains two worksheets. The Budget worksheet contains values related to your vacation budget and the Mortgage worksheet contains the calculations you'll use to determine the mortgage options on various time share condos.

Activity Steps

 open EC_Project5.xls

1. In the **Budget** worksheet, enter a formula in cell **E3** that multiplies the **Unit Cost** by the **Number**, copy the formula into cells **E4** through **E9**, then define cells **E3** through **E9** as a range called **Expenses**

2. In cell **E11** enter a **SUM** formula that adds all the values in the Expenses range

3. In the **Mortgage** worksheet, use the **PMT** function in cell C7 to calculate mortgage payments; use the value in cell **B4** as the Rate/12, the value in cell **B5** as the Nper*12, the value in cell **B7** as the PV (as a negative number), then make the **Rate** and **Nper** values absolute
   The PMT Argument Function dialog box should appear as shown in Figure EP 5-1.

4. Copy the PMT formula to cells **C8** through **C16**, then name cells **C7** through **C16** as a range called **Payments**

5. In cell **B18** enter the **MIN** function to determine which payment option is the lowest, then in cell **B19**, enter the **MAX** function to determine which payment is the highest

6. In cell **D7** enter an **IF** function that enters **YES** in cell D7 if the mortgage payment is less then $400 and **NO** if the mortgage payment is greater than or equal to $400
   Figure EP 5-2 shows how the IF function dialog box should appear.

7. Copy the formula from cell D7 to cells **D8** through **D16**, click cell **A3**, then use the **NOW** function to enter the current date and time
   The completed Mortgage worksheet appears as shown in Figure EP 5-3.

 close EC_Project5.xls

Figure EP 5-1: PMT function

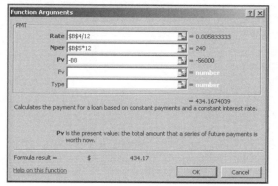

Figure EP 5-2: IF function

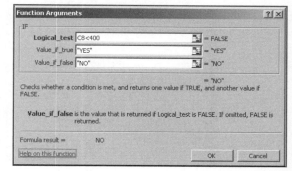

Figure EP 5-3: Completed Mortgage worksheet

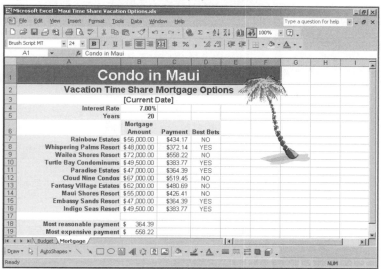

Project for Skill Set 6

Creating and Modifying Graphs

Sales Information for Fanfloratastic Flowers

Fanfloratastic is a small flower stall located at San Francisco's Fisherman's Wharf. The owner of the stall provides you with sales information and asks you to create a worksheet that includes two charts and some graphic enhancements. When printed, the worksheet appears as shown in Figure EP 6-1.

Step 7
Note that you must be connected to the Internet to insert this piece of clip art from the complete Microsoft Clip Gallery.

Activity Steps

 open EC_Project6.xls

1. Create a **Pie chart** from the data in cells **A6** through **B11**; accept all the default settings in the Chart Wizard except select the option to include a legend and show the Percentage labels

2. Modify the chart by changing the color of the **Roses wedge** to **Pink,** and then change the pie chart format to 3D format with an elevation of **45 degrees**

3. Re-size and position the chart as shown in Figure EP 6-1

4. Create a **Bar chart** from the data in cells **A24** through **F26**

5. Move the legend below the chart data, then size and position the chart as shown in Figure EP 6-1

6. Change the font size of the Y-axis and X-axis labels to **8-point** and the font size of the Legend text to **11-point**

7. Insert, size, and position the clip art picture of a rose shown in Figure EP 6-1

8. Draw a sun autoshape and fill it with Light Yellow, then size it and position it as shown in Figure EP 6-1

 close EC_Project6.xls

Figure EP 6-1: Completed sales information

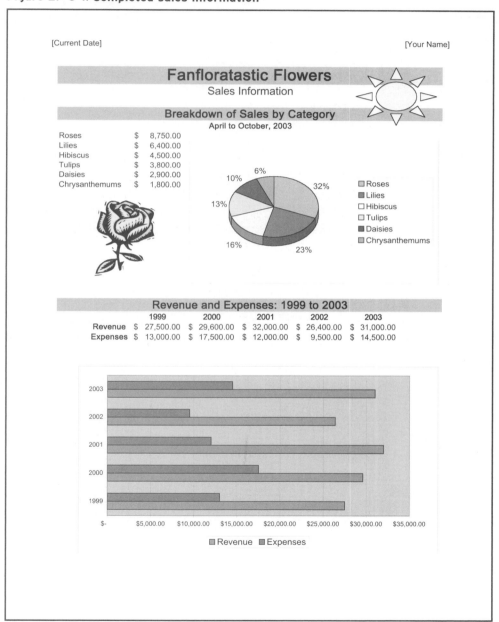

Project for Skill Set 7

Workgroup Collaboration

Sales Report for Splashdown Rafting

Splashdown Rafting takes thrill-seekers on wet-and-wild raft trips down the Snake River in Montana. You've agreed to help the company modify a Sales Report worksheet for viewing on the company intranet. The worksheet already includes a comment from the owner, Zack Barr. You respond to Zack's comment, add a comment of your own, insert a hyperlink to a second worksheet in the workbook, and then save the workbook for viewing on the intranet.

Activity Steps

 open EC_Project7.xls

1. Read Zack's comment in cell **E8**, make the change he requests, then delete his comment

2. Edit Zack's comment in cell **E12** by adding the sentence **I think this number is too low.**

3. Add a comment to cell **B9** with the text **Check out the chart in the Summary worksheet!**

4. Make cell **B9** a hyperlink to the **Summary** worksheet

5. Edit the hyperlink in cell **A19** so that it points to the company's new Web site at www.splashdownrafting.com

6. Preview the **2004 Tours** worksheet in your browser, test the link to the **Summary** worksheet, then click the **2004 Tours tab** to return to the 2004 Tours worksheet
   The Tours worksheet appears in the browser as shown in Figure EP 7-1 and the 2004 Summary worksheet appears in the browser as shown in Figure EP 7-2.

7. Save the EC_Project7.xls workbook as a Web page called **2004Tours.htm**

 close 2004Tours.htm

Figure EP 7-1: 2004 Tours worksheet displayed in the browser

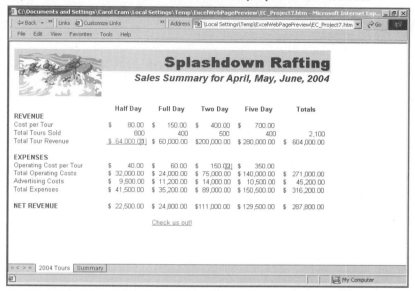

Figure EP 7-2: Summary worksheet displayed in the browser

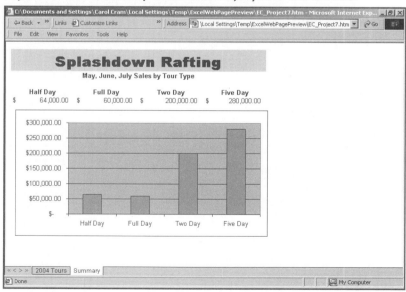

Excel 2002 Expert Projects Appendix

Projects List

The Excel Expert skill sets include the features and functions you use to perform advanced data analysis and summary functions, to apply custom features, and to collaborate with one or more other users. In the following projects, you will import and export data, manage workbooks, apply custom formats to numbers, work with ranges, automate Excel by creating macros, audit worksheets, summarize and analyze data, and finally use collaboration options to share workbooks between users.

Project for Skill Set 8

Importing and Exporting Data

E-Commerce Conference Itinerary

As the manager of a Web-based travel service, you've decided to attend a conference on E-Commerce issues being held in The Hague in the Netherlands. You need to compile a workbook that contains information about the trip and the conference. In this project, you will insert the trip itinerary from an existing text file and insert a picture file to enhance the appearance of the itinerary worksheet. You will then insert information about the conference sessions from an Access database table and obtain a map of the Netherlands from a Web site on the World Wide Web. Finally, you will save selected worksheets for use in other applications, including the Web browser and Access.

Activity Steps

 open EE_Project8A.xls

1. Import the **EE_Project8B.txt** file to cell **A7** in the **Itinerary worksheet**, accepting all defaults in the Text Import Wizard

2. Insert the picture file **Tulips.jpg** into the **Itinerary worksheet**, then size and position it as shown in Figure EP 8-1

3. Import the **E-Commerce Sessions table** from the Access database **EE_Project8C.mdb** into cell **A3** of the **Sessions worksheet**

4. Connect to the Internet, start your Web browser, type *http://www.maptown.com/geos/netherlands.html* in the Address text box, then press **[Enter]**
   If the Web site is not available, use the search engine of your choice to find a map of the Netherlands that you can copy without violating copyright restrictions.

5. Arrange the Excel workbook window and the browser window so they appear side by side on the desktop, then drag the map of the Netherlands from the Web page into the Map worksheet and position it as shown in Figure EP 8-2

6. Publish the **Itinerary worksheet** from the EE_Project8A.xls workbook as a Web page called **Itinerary.htm** that includes interactivity

7. Close the Web browser, then save and close the workbook

8. Start Access, open **EE_Project8C.mdb**, then import the **Costs worksheet** from **EE_Project8A.xls** into the database, accepting all defaults
   The Costs worksheet appears as a table called Costs in the Access database.

 close EE_Project8C.mdb

Project 8

Figure EP 8-1: Itinerary worksheet

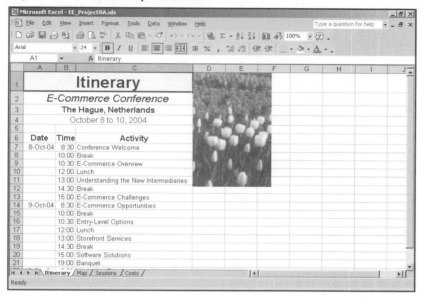

Figure EP 8-2: Map worksheet

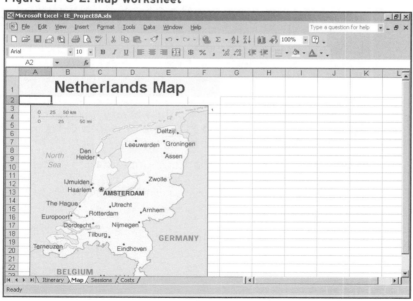

Project for Skill Set 9

Managing Workbooks

Expense Reports for Quito Imports

Quito Imports is a small retail outlet based in San Francisco that sells craft products from Ecuador, Peru, and Colombia. Several times each year, three employees travel to South America to purchase products for the store. As the new office manager, you want to streamline the reporting of travel expenses by creating and modifying a template for the expense reports and then creating a workspace containing each of the expense reports submitted by the three employees. Finally, you want to consolidate inventory data from three worksheets containing data about three of the product lines sold by Quito Imports.

Activity Steps

 open EE_Project9A.xls

1. Save the current workbook as a template called **EE_Project9B.xlt** to the location where you save your project files

2. Open the **EE_Project9B.xlt** template file, remove the **Fuel** column, then save and close the template file

3. Create a new expense report based on the revised template, then enter data in the expense report for **Marianne Bennett**, as shown in Figure EP 9-1

4. Save the workbook as **EE_Project9C.xls**, open **EE_Project9D.xls**, then open **EE_Project9E.xls**
   The Project9D file contains the expense report for Josh Ramirez, and the Project9E file contains the expense report for Yuri Gringko.

5. As shown in Figure EP 9-2, tile the three workbooks vertically, create a workspace called **Expense Statements**, then close all three workbooks

6. Open **EE_Project9F.xls**, then consolidate in the Totals worksheet cells **A3** through **D8** in the **Pottery worksheet**, the **Blankets worksheet**, and the **Jewelry worksheet** using the SUM function and using labels in the top row

7. Click cell **D11**, then use the **AutoSum button** to calculate the grand total
   The grand total for all the consolidated worksheets is $15,403.00.

 close EE_Project9F.xls

Figure EP 9-1: Data for Marianne Bennett

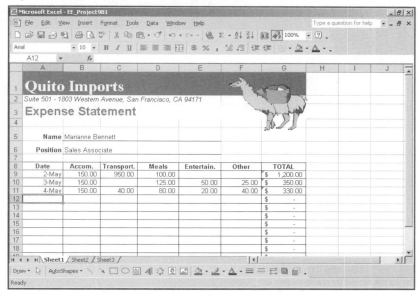

Figure EP 9-2: Workspace with three vertically tiled workbooks

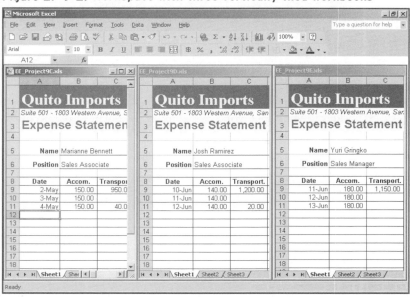

Project for Skill Set 10

Formatting Numbers

Extreme Adventures Tours Sales

You work for Extreme Adventures, a company based in Calgary, Alberta, that specializes in taking clients on physically challenging tours that include activities such as ice climbing, ski touring, and snowshoeing. An Excel workbook contains information about the tours sold on February 15, 2004, along with information about tour distances and durations. In this project, you will format the worksheet by creating, modifying, and applying a variety of custom number formats. You also will apply conditional formatting to highlight tours that generated income over a certain amount.

Activity Steps

 open EE_Project10.xls

1. In the **Tour Durations worksheet**, click cell **D7**, then create a custom number format that matches the number format of the value contained in cell **D6**

2. Apply the new format to cells **D8** through **D11**

3. Click cell **A4**, then create a Custom Date format that appears as **mmmm d, yyyy**
   The Tour Durations worksheet appears as shown in Figure EP 10-1.

4. Display the **Current Tours worksheet**, then apply the custom date format from Step 3 to cell A4

5. Use conditional formatting to automatically apply **Bold** and the **Blue** font color to all values greater than **6** in cells **B6** through **B11**

6. Click cell **E6**, then create a Custom Number format with text that appears as **$0.00" Good";$-0.00" Poor"**

7. Format cells **E7** through **E11** with the new custom number format
   The Current Tours worksheet appears as shown in Figure EP 10-2.

 close EE_Project10.xls

Figure EP 10-1: Revised custom number and custom date formats applied

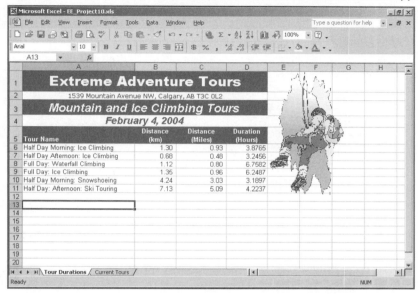

Figure EP 10-2: Conditional formatting and custom format with text applied

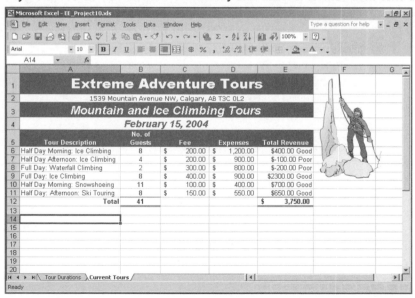

Project for Skill Set 11

Working with Ranges

Inventory Sheets for Vintage Records

You've inherited a great collection of vintage records in both 78 rpm and 33 rpm formats and are interested in trying to sell some of the records in online auctions. You decide to use Excel to create an inventory sheet that organizes your collection into categories. You'll create some ranges, use named ranges in a formula to calculate the total worth of your collection, and then use the HLOOKUP function to calculate appropriate discounts for some of the records.

Activity Steps

 open EE_Project11.xls

1. Select cells **F7** through **F25**, then create a range using the label in cell **F7** as the range name

2. Select cells **G7** through **G25**, then create a range using the label in cell **G7** as the range name

3. Designate **rpm78** as the range name for cells **F8** through **F15**, then designate **rpm33** as the range name for cells **F16** through **F25**

Step 6
To complete the HLOOKUP function, you will need to use the table in cells F3 through G4. Remember to make the reference to this table absolute in the formula. The formula required for cell G8 is =HLOOKUP(E8,$F$3:$G$4,2).

4. In cell **D4**, use the named range **rpm78** in a formula that calculates the total worth of the 78 rpm records in the collection
The 78s are worth $100.00.

5. In cell **D5**, use the named range **rpm33** in a formula that calculates the total worth of the 33 rpm records in the collection
The 33s are worth $113.00.

6. Enter an **HLOOKUP function** in cell **G8** to determine the discount by format on each of the records

7. Copy the formula in cell **G8** through to cell **G25**
The discount percentages appear in columns as shown in Figure EP11-1.

8. In cell **H8**, use the **Price** and **Discount** ranges in a formula that calculates the total price of the first record in the list
The required formula is Price-(Price*Discount).

9. Copy the formula through to cell **H25**
The completed worksheet appears as shown in Figure EP 11-2.

 close EE_Project11.xls

Figure EP 11-1: Discounts entered

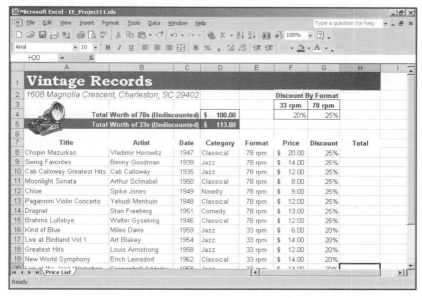

Figure EP 11-2: Completed worksheet

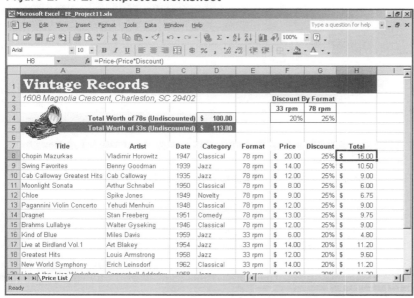

Project for Skill Set 12

Customizing Excel

Payroll Register for Tapestries Bistro

As the manager of Tapestries, a new Bistro in downtown Los Angeles, you have decided to use Excel to keep track of the monthly payroll for the five staff members who work in the restaurant dining room. Before printing all the payroll registers for the year, you decide to customize Excel so that you can format each payroll worksheet in the same way. In this project you will first customize a menu and then add a button to the Formatting toolbar so that you can perform specific formatting tasks quickly. Then, you will create a macro that will fill selected cells with a color and apply the Currency format to selected cells. Finally, you will edit the macro and run the revised version.

Activity Steps

 open EE_Project12.xls

1. Add a new menu called **Payroll** that appears to the right of the Help menu, then add the **Double Underline** command from the Format category and the **Pattern** command from the Format category to the Payroll menu

2. Click cell **A1**, then create a macro called **PayrollFormat** that uses the **Ctrl+F** shortcut key and performs the functions described in Figure EP 12-1

3. Click the **Undo button** several times to undo the macro steps, then click cell **A1** and use **Ctrl + F** to run the PayrollFormat macro

4. Edit the PayrollFormat macro in Visual Basic to change the fill color from **6 to 4**
   The code for the fill color is .ColorIndex = . The new color will be Bright Green.

5. Close Visual Basic, click cell **A1**, then press **Ctrl + F** to run the revised macro

6. Add the **AutoFormat button** to the Formatting toolbar

7. Use the AutoFormat button on the Formatting toolbar to apply the **List 2** AutoFormat to cells A5 through L11

8. Use the Pattern command on the Payroll menu to fill cell A1 with the Thin Horizontal Crosshatch pattern that appears in the bottom row of the pattern pallete, as shown in Figure EP 12-2
   The formatted worksheet appears as shown in Figure EP 12-3.

9. Open the Customize dialog box, then remove the AutoFormat button from the Formatting toolbar and the Payroll menu from the menu bar

 close EE_Project12.xls

Step 1
In the Customize dialog box, you will need to scroll down the Commands list box to find the Double Underlining and Pattern menu items.

Figure EP 12-1: Macro steps

1. Use the Ctrl key to select cells A1, B3, and D3
2. Use the Payroll menu to add Double Underlining
3. Fill the selected cells with the Yellow fill color
4. Select cells D7 to D11, then apply the Currency style
5. Stop the macro recording

Figure EP 12-2: Pattern selection

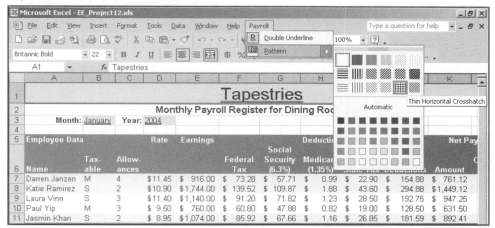

Figure EP 12-3: Formatted payroll worksheet

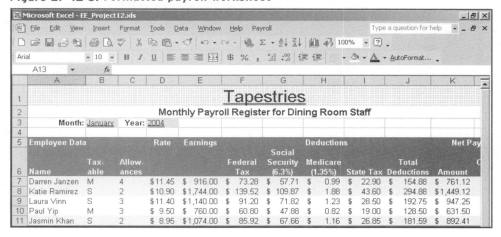

Project for Skill Set 13

Auditing Worksheets

Purchase Orders for Saguaro Art Academy

The Saguaro Art Academy has recently started using Excel to generate its purchase orders. You have been asked to use the formula auditing tools to verify the formulas in two of the purchase order worksheets that are ready to send out.

Activity Steps

 open EE_Project13.xls

1. In the **July 10, 2004 worksheet**, use the Trace Dependents feature to determine which cells are dependent on cell **L24**

2. In the **July 10, 2004 worksheet**, use the Trace Precedents feature to determine which cells are used by the formula in cell **L27**
   The worksheet should appear as shown in Figure EP 13-1.

3. Remove all the arrows

4. In the **August 12, 2004 worksheet**, use the Trace Error feature to identify the cell causing the error in cell **L28**
   The error should appear as shown in Figure EP 13-2.

5. Correct the error by changing the incorrect value in cell J16 to **7.25**

6. Verify that the total is now $412.50, then remove all the arrows

 close EE_Project13.xls

Figure EP 13-1: Traced dependents and precedents

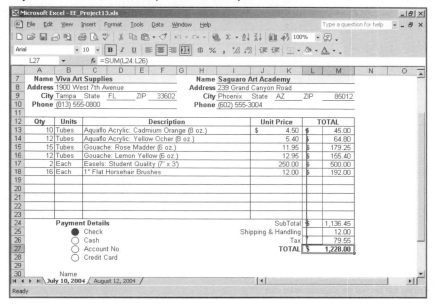

Figure EP 13-2: Error traced

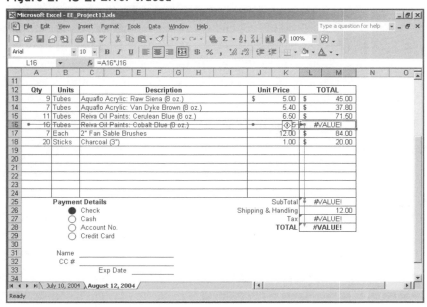

Project for Skill Set 14

Summarizing Data

Guest Information for Glacier Cruises

Each summer, the Glacier Cruises fleet of cruise ships heads north from Vancouver, BC through the scenic Inside Passage to the glaciers of Alaska. At the end of each month, one of your duties in the business office is to use Excel to summarize data related to revenue generated from each cruise. For this project, you will use subtotals, filters, grouping, and data validation to summarize data in three worksheets containing guest information, and then you will create a Web query using data from a weather site, save a worksheet as an XML spreadsheet, and create an XML query.

Step 3
The criteria for the filter appears in cells A21 and A22.
Step 6
From *www.weather.com*, you'll need to search for each city in turn (Juneau and Sitka) and then select the table that shows the current temperature.
Step 7
Enter the exact location of the Tour Revenue.xml file in the Address text box in the New Web Query dialog box. For example, if you have stored the file on a disk in your A:\ drive, the address is A:\Tour Revenue.xml.

Activity Steps

 open EE_Project14.xls

1. In the **June Room Revenue workshseet**, apply data validation to **E4:E27** to allow only whole numbers between **2000** and **8000**, enter **1500** in cell **E5**, click **Retry**, then enter **2000**

2. Sort cells **A3** through **G27** in ascending order by the data in the Cruise Date column and then the data in the Rooms Available column, then use the Subtotal function to calculate the revenue by **Cruise Date** added to **Revenue**
   The top portion of the list should appear as shown in Figure EP 14-1.

3. In the **June Fitness worksheet**, create a custom filter to extract the data from the list range A3 through D19 that contains the value **Massage** in the Assignment column, then copy the extracted data to cell A24

4. In the **June Tours worksheet**, apply the advanced filter to list only the guests who went on kayaking tours (filter in place)

5. In the **June Guests worksheet**, apply Auto Outline to create the groups in cells A4 through C29, hide all the detail so that the worksheet shows only the totals for each location, click cell **C30**, then calculate the total number of guests

6. Display the **Temperatures worksheet**, click cell **A5**, create a new Web query that enters current temperature data for Juneau from *www.weather.com*, then click cell **C5** and create a new Web query that enters current temperature data for Sitka
   Figure 14-2 shows the table selected for Juneau, Alaska and Figure 14-3 shows the completed Temperatures worksheet.

7. Switch to the **Tour Revenue worksheet**, then import the **Tour Revenue.xml** file located from your Project Disk as a Web query

 close EE_Project14.xls

Figure EP 14-1: Subtotals list

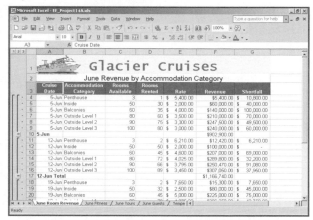

Figure EP 14-2: Web Query table selected

Figure EP 14-3: Completed Temperatures worksheet

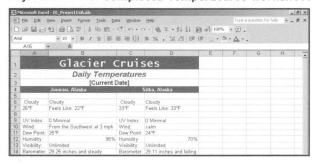

Project for Skill Set 15
Summarizing Data

Analysis of Web Design 101 Class Grades

You are assisting the instructor of Web Design 101 to analyze data related to the marks earned by students in the 2004 class. In this project, you will create a PivotTable to determine the breakdown of grades, and then you will create a PivotChart that displays the results in a pie chart. Next, you will create two scenarios to determine how best to weight the marks earned by students. Finally, you will add a trendline to a chart you created earlier that compares the overall marks earned by students in each of five classes over five years.

Activity Steps

 open EE_Project15.xls

1. From the data in the range **M3:M18** in the Grades worksheet, create a PivotTable in a new worksheet and use the **Grade** data for the Row area and the Data area

2. Click the Chart Wizard button on the PivotTable toolbar to create a PivotChart from the PivotTable
   The chart should appear as shown in Figure EP 15-1.

3. In the **Grades worksheet**, create a scenario called **High Assignments** from the values currently entered in cells **I21** through **K21**

4. Create a second scenario called **Low Assignments** from the values in cells **I21** through **K21** and change the value in cell **I21** to **25** and the value in cell K21 to **50**

5. Show the **Low Assignments scenario**, refresh the PivotTable data (in Sheet1), then view PivotChart shown on the Chart1 sheet
   The revised chart appears as shown in Figure EP 15-2.

6. In the **Class Comparison worksheet**, add a **Logarithmic trend-line** to the column chart

 close EE_Project15.xls

Figure EP 15-1: Completed PivotChart

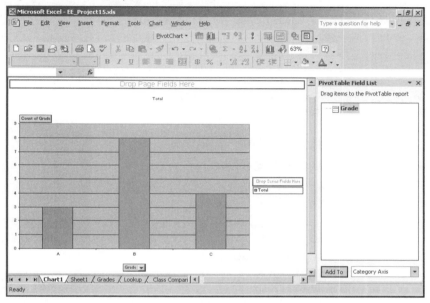

Figure EP 15-2: Revised PivotChart

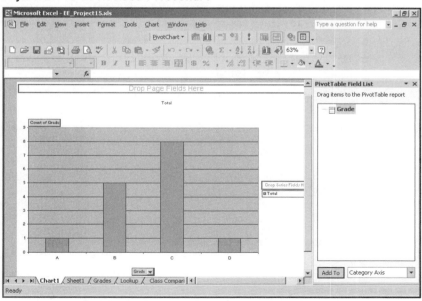

Project for Skill Set 16

Sales Projections for Big Sky Campgrounds

Big Sky Campgrounds operates four campgrounds in the state of Montana. To prepare for the Summer 2004 season, you and two colleagues are creating a sales projection worksheet that will show projected sales in July, August, and September. In this project, you will first use the track changes and merge features to develop a final version of a workbook from the worksheets prepared by your colleagues. Then you will open a new workbook containing sales projections for October, November, and December, and set it up for sharing.

Activity Steps

 open EE_Project16A.xls

1. Set the Track Changes option to track all changes and to highlight changes on the screen

2. Change the value in cell **B6** to **35**, then save and close the workbook

3. Open **EE_Project16B.xls**, open the Accept or Reject Changes dialog box, accept the tracked change to **B6**, accept the tracked change to cell **C6**, then reject the tracked change to cell **D6**
   The net revenue in cell F17 is $7,220.00.

4. Merge the current workbook with the files EE_Project16C.xls and EE_Project16D.xls
   Verify that the net revenue in cell F17 is $5,870.00, as shown in Figure EP 16-1.

5. Close the workbook, open **EE_Project16E.xls**, then unlock the cells in the **Sites range**

6. Protect the worksheet, change the value in cell **B11** to **400**, then try entering a new value in cell B12

7. Protect the workbook with the password **camping** to open and the password **bigsky** to modify, then save and close the workbook

8. Open the **EE_Project16E.xls** workbook using the **camping** and **bigsky** passwords, share the workbook by allowing changes to be made by more than one user at a time, then save the workbook when prompted

 close EE_Project16E.xls

Figure EP 16-1: Workbook with merged changes

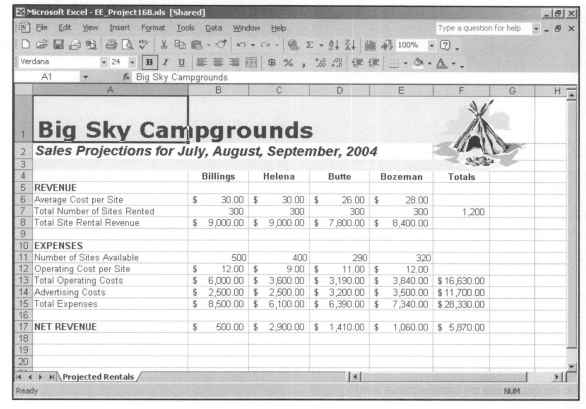

		Billings	Helena	Butte	Bozeman	Totals
5	REVENUE					
6	Average Cost per Site	$ 30.00	$ 30.00	$ 26.00	$ 28.00	
7	Total Number of Sites Rented	300	300	300	300	1,200
8	Total Site Rental Revenue	$ 9,000.00	$ 9,000.00	$ 7,800.00	$ 8,400.00	
9						
10	EXPENSES					
11	Number of Sites Available	500	400	290	320	
12	Operating Cost per Site	$ 12.00	$ 9.00	$ 11.00	$ 12.00	
13	Total Operating Costs	$ 6,000.00	$ 3,600.00	$ 3,190.00	$ 3,840.00	$ 16,630.00
14	Advertising Costs	$ 2,500.00	$ 2,500.00	$ 3,200.00	$ 3,500.00	$ 11,700.00
15	Total Expenses	$ 8,500.00	$ 6,100.00	$ 6,390.00	$ 7,340.00	$ 28,330.00
16						
17	NET REVENUE	$ 500.00	$ 2,900.00	$ 1,410.00	$ 1,060.00	$ 5,870.00

Glossary

#DIV/0! A worksheet error indicating that you have attempted to divide a value by zero; to correct the error, change divisor so it refers to a number.

#N/A A worksheet error indicating that a value is not available to a formula, such as a missing function argument.

#NAME A worksheet error indicating that Excel does not recognize text used in a formula, such as a name that has not been defined.

#NUM A worksheet error indicating that formula numbers are incorrect, such as a function that has a text argument instead of a number.

#REF A worksheet error indicating that a cell reference is incorrect; can occur when you delete cells to which a formula refers.

#VALUE A worksheet error indicating that an operand, value, or argument in a formula is incorrect, such as one value in a function that requires a range.

.bmp The file extension on a Microsoft Windows Bitmap filename.

.emf The file extension on an Enhanced Metafile graphic filename.

.gif The file extension on a Graphics Interchange Format filename.

.jpg The file extension on a Joint Photographic Experts Group filename.

.png The file extension on a Portable Network Graphics filename.

.wmf The file extension on a Windows Metafile filename.

3-D Reference A cell or range reference in a worksheet formula that refers to a cell in another worksheet or set of worksheets, such as January:December!A6.

Absolute reference In an Excel formula, a cell reference that does not adjust when the formula is pasted to a new location; to make a reference absolute, select it, then press [F4] until there are dollar signs before both the row and column references. See also *Relative reference*.

Action menu A menu that appears when you click a smart tag. See also *Smart tag*.

Active cell The worksheet cell with a dark border; text or numbers you type appear in this cell and in the Formula bar; also called the *selected* or *highlighted cell*.

Alignment The placement of cell data in a cell; horizontally, cell contents can be left-, right-, or center-aligned; vertically, cell contents can be aligned with the top, middle, or bottom of a cell.

Area chart A line chart where the areas below the lines are shaded to emphasize their volume.

Argument ScreenTip As you type an Excel function, the yellow ScreenTip that appears to prompt you for each argument; click the function name in the ScreenTip to open a Help window describing the function.

Arguments Values, or cell or range references, usually in parentheses after the function name, on which an Excel function acts.

Arithmetic operators Operators, such as +, -, *, or /, representing addition, subtraction, multiplication, or division, that are used in formulas.

ASCII file Another name for a text file, which contains only data without any formatting.

Audit To analyze and check worksheet formulas and structure.

AutoCorrect Feature that automatically corrects common spelling errors; can be customized by each Excel user.

AutoFilter Data menu command that displays arrow next to field name in a list, allowing you to display a subset of list data.

AutoFit The Excel feature that lets you double-click a column heading to automatically resize the column to the width of its longest entry.

AutoFormat Predesigned combinations of shading, borders, fonts, fills, and alignment that you can apply to a worksheet or a range.

AutoShape Predrawn shapes such as brackets, stars, banners, or arrows that you can insert as objects on any worksheet or chart; insert using the AutoShapes menu on the Drawing toolbar.

AutoSum A button on the Standard toolbar that automatically inserts the SUM function in a cell; also lets you drag to select cells containing the data you want the function to calculate.

Bar chart A chart type that portrays data points as horizontal bars.

Border A line you can place on any or all sides of a worksheet cell using the Border button on the Formatting toolbar or the Border tab in the Format Cells dialog box.

Callout Text boxes with attached lines that you can add to call attention to chart or worksheet features.

Cancel button The X button in the Formula bar that you click to cancel an unentered cell entry and redisplay its original value.

Category axis The x-axis in an Excel chart; usually represents the categories into which data is divided, such as years or stores.

Cell In a worksheet, the intersection of a column and a row, where you enter text or numbers.

Cell address The column letter and row number that describe the exact location of any worksheet cell, such as C5.

Cell range See *Range*.

Cell reference The address of a cell, composed of its column letter and row number, such as C15 or D6; used in formulas to indicate the formula should use the value in the referenced cell.

Change history A worksheet you can have Excel create that lists all changes made in a shared workbook and notes the users who made them.

Chart Sometimes called a graph, a pictoral representation of numeric information; in Excel, you can chart data using presupplied pie, column, bar, line, and scatter charts, in addition to many custom chart types.

Chart sheet A worksheet that includes only a chart.

Chart Wizard A series of dialog boxes that lets you create a chart and customize it as you create it; to start the Chart Wizard, click the Chart Wizard button on the Standard toolbar.

Clear To delete; in Excel, you can clear a cell's content, format, comments or all of these using the Clear command on the Edit menu.

Clip Art Presupplied art organized by topic, that you can insert in your workbooks.

Clipboard See *Office clipboard*.

Close A File menu command that removes a file from your computer's temporary memory but leaves it on your disk; leaves the Excel program running.

Code Text and programming commands written in a programming language, such as **Visual Basic for Applications**.

Column chart A chart that portrays data points as vertical columns.

Column headings The boxed letters at the top of columns that uniquely identifies each one.

Column labels Text or numbers you enter above column data to identify the data in each column, such as "Salary" or "2003".

Comment indicator The small red triangle that appears in the upper right corner of a cell containing a comment.

Comments Electronic notes you can attach to any worksheet cell; useful when sharing documents with others in workgroups.

Comparison values In the VLOOKUP function, the values in a column that Excel compares to a specified value to determine whether it's the value for which you are searching.

Conditional format A format you can create and apply to numbers if a particular condition is true; for example, you can specify that any values over $100 in a selected range be displayed in red.

Consolidate To gather data from other worksheets in a summary worksheet.

Consolidate by category To combine data from multiple worksheets with different layouts and categories; in the summary sheet, Excel creates categories from all the worksheets referenced.

Consolidate by position To combine data from multiple worksheets with the same layout.

Constant A value that does not change; a range name can represent a constant such as a tax rate that you use frequently.

Criteria In an Excel list, conditions for displaying subset records, such as "zip>9000" or "income<20,000". See also *Subset* and *Record*.

Crop To cut off, usually part of a picture or graphic, using the cropping tool on the Picture toolbar.

Custom number formats Special formats you can create and apply to numeric data.

Data consolidation See *Consolidate*.

Data labels In an Excel chart, an option that displays the values, percentages, or other information for each data point.

Data marker In an Excel chart, a graphical representation of a single data point in a worksheet cell, such as a sales figure for a particular store.

Data point In an Excel chart, the representation of a single cell in a worksheet, such as the salary expense for one store for one month.

Data series A group of related data, such as store sales for several locations.

Data table A grid that appears under a chart and that contains the values on which the chart is based.

Data validation An Excel feature that lets you limit cell entries to acceptable values, such as whole numbers or a list of values you specify, such as "Yes" and "No."

Database file A file created in a database program; usually contains related data, such as customer and product information for one company. See also *Database file* and *Database program*.

Database program A program that lets you organize and analyze large amounts of information; see also *Field*, *Record*, and *Table*.

Delimiter In a text file, a character that separates columns of data, such as a tab, comma, space, semicolon, or a character of your choice.

Dependent In worksheet auditing, a cell that uses values in another cell, either directly or via another cell; in the formula =A5+A6, the cell containing the formula is a dependent of both cells A5 and A6. See also *Direct dependent*, *Indirect dependent*, and *Precedents*.

Destination document In object linking and embedding or in a database query, the location to which you link, embed, or export another file.

Direct dependent In worksheet auditing, a cell that uses a value in a selected cell.

Discussion comments Notes relating to a document that you share with others using a discussion server.

Document In the Visual Basic for Applications (VBA) programming language, to add and edit comment lines to describe who created and edited a macro.

Document Recovery task pane The window that opens on the left side of your screen in case your Excel session is interrupted by an unplanned computer shutdown, such as a power interruption; presents workbook version(s) the program "rescued" and prompts you to choose a version to save.

Drop areas In a PivotTable report, special areas representing rows, columns, data, and pages to which you can drag fields from the field list to produce summary information.

Embed To place a copy of a source object (text, graphic, or worksheet, for example) into another file (worksheet, word processing file, for example); changes to the source are not reflected in the destination document because there is no connection between the two.

Enter To accept a cell value; accomplished by clicking the Enter button on the Formula Bar, pressing [Enter], [Tab], or one of the keyboard arrow keys.

Exit To close a program such as Excel; you can use either the Exit command on the File menu, or the Close button on the Excel title bar, which closes both the program as well as any open documents, prompting you to save any changes you have made to them since you last saved them.

Explode To move a pie slice away from a pie chart.

Exponential trendline In an Excel chart, a line chart that projects future values assuming that the series will increase or decrease at an increasingly rapid rate over time.

Export To send data created in Excel to another program in a format it can read.

Extensible Markup Language (XML) A universal data-sharing format that Web designers and organizations use for structured data, such as the data in Excel spreadsheets; instead of being formatted, XML files are "marked up" with tags that describe the type of data they contain. Excel lets you save worksheets in XML format.

Extension See *File extension*.

External data range A range of worksheet data that originated outside of Excel that you can analyze, format, and update. See also *Refresh*.

External reference indicator The exclamation point that separates the sheet name from a cell reference in a 3-D reference. See also *3-D reference*.

Field In an Excel list, a column representing one type of data, such as Last Name. See also *Database file, Database program, Record,* and *Table*.

Field name The label above each column of field information in a list.

File extension The three letters after a filename that identify the program that created it, such as .xls for Excel files; to display or hide extensions on your screen, open any window at the Windows desktop, select Folder Options on the Tools menu, click the View tab, then select Show file extensions for known file types.

File format A file type that is readable by selected software; Excel can open files in the formats listed in the Files of type list in the Open dialog box, and can save files in the formats listed in the Files of type list in the Save dialog box.

Fill color The cell background color; to change, use the Fill Color list arrow on the Formatting toolbar.

Fill handle The small black square on the bottom right corner of a selected cell; drag it to copy cell contents to the dragged area.

Filter In an Excel list, to display only a selected amount of data, such as clients with 96820 showing in a zip code field, or suppliers showing prices less than $10 in a price field. See also *Field*.

Find An Edit menu command that helps you locate worksheet data.

Find and Replace An Excel feature that lets you find data you specify and replace it with other data you specify.

Folder A named storage location on a disk that lets you group and organize files.

Font A letter style, such as Arial, with formatting, such as boldface or italic.

Font size The height of a font, measured in points; one point equals 1/72 of an inch.

Footer Information that prints at the bottom of every worksheet page; can include text you type, the date, time, page number, sheet name, workbook name, or a picture.

Format To change the appearance of cell entries or cells to enhance their appearance and to make data more readily understandable to readers.

Format Painter The Excel feature that lets you click a button to copy a format from one cell and paste it to another.

Formatting toolbar The Excel toolbar that lets you change the font, font size, type style, alignment, number formats, fills, and colors of any selected cell(s); can appear on the same line as the Standard toolbar or below it.

Formula An equation or combination of values, cell references, and operators that calculate a result in the cell containing the formula; changing values or cell references in source cells causes formula to automatically recalculate.

Formula bar The bar that appears above the worksheet column headings; contains the name box, the box displaying formulas and contents of the active cell, and the Enter, Cancel, and Insert Function buttons.

Freeze To keep rows and columns in place while you scroll rows and columns in other parts of a worksheet.

Function An automatic formula supplied with Excel; consists of the function name and selected arguments, which are the cell references or values that the function uses to calculate a result.

Function Wizard A series of dialog boxes that lets you search for a function and then prompts you for each function argument; start the Function Wizard by clicking the Insert Function button on the Formula Bar.

Graphic A picture, photograph, or drawn object; picture formats include .jpeg, .tif, and .bmp. See *Table 8-1* for common formats.

Gridlines In a chart, horizontal or vertical lines that help a reader's eye align a data marker with an axis.

Header Information that prints at the top of every worksheet page; can include text you type, the date, time, page number, sheet name, workbook name, or a picture.

Help system The library of information you access using the Office Assistant, the Type a question for help box, or the Help menu; explains Excel features and commands.

Hide To keep from view, such as a cell formula.

Highlighted cell See *Active cell*.

HLOOKUP function An Excel function that searches horizontally across rows to locate a specific piece of information; for example, you could have Excel search a row of client names for the name "Jones," and then display the number for that client.

Hyperlink Words or graphics that you click to display (or "jump to") another location in a document, another document, or a location on the World Wide Web.

Hypertext Markup Language (HTML) A special file format that lets users view files using a Web browser.

I-beam pointer The I pointer that appears when you hold the pointer over a cell you are editing.

Import To bring data created in another program into Excel.

In-cell editing Double-clicking a cell to enable editing within the cell containing the formula, instead of editing in the Formula Bar.

Indented report formats In PivotTable reports, formats that apply shading and fonts, move column fields to the row area, indent each row field, and show data in a single column.

Indirect dependent In worksheet auditing, a cell that depends on cells, but only via other cells.

Input value In Excel data tables, a value that a formula uses to calculate a result; a data table calculates multiple results for multiple input values.

Insert Function button On the Excel Formula bar, the button that starts the Function Wizard, enabling you to search for, select, and enter any function.

Insertion point The blinking vertical line that appears in the Formula bar or in a cell when you edit cell contents; typed text or clicked cell addresses appear at this location.

Integrate To combine information from one program or document with information from another program or document. See also *Link* and *Embed*.

Interactive workbook An Excel workbook saved in HTML format that users can manipulate using their Web browsers.

Internet The world-wide network of computers and smaller networks.

Internet Explorer The Web browser developed by Microsoft Corporation that lets users explore the World Wide Web.

Intranet Computer networks within organizations used by a group of people, often employees of one company.

Keyword In the Excel online help system, a word you type on the Help tab to find a help topic.

Label See *Column labels* or *Row labels*.

Label prefix A character such as an apostrophe that you type before a number so Excel treats it as a label that will not be used in calculations.

Landscape orientation A worksheet print orientation in which the page is wider than it is tall.

Legend The color key that denotes the colors assigned to each point or data series in a chart.

Line chart A chart type where data points are portrayed as lines.

Linear trendline In an Excel chart, a line chart that projects future values assuming that the trend will continue at a steady rate.

Link To connect a source object (such as text, a graphic, or a worksheet) to a destination file (such as a worksheet, database, or word processing file) so that any changes to the source will automatically update in the destination file.

List A collection of data organized in columns and rows that you can filter or sort; the Excel equivalent of a database.

Lock To prevent cell changes; all Excel cells are locked by default, but locking only takes effect if you protect the worksheet.

Logical test The first segment in the IF function syntax, which states "IF a particular condition is true".

Look in list arrow In the Open and Save dialog boxes, the arrow that you click to navigate to different disks and folders on your computer to locate or save files.

Macro recorder An Excel feature that lets you name and save for reuse a set of worksheet actions you perform; Excel translates your actions into macro code using the Visual Basic programming language.

Macros Named command sequences that quickly and automatically perform common tasks.

Marquee The moving border that surrounds a cell when you click it to include it in a formula.

Menu bar The gray bar below the title bar; contains names of menus, which you click to view and select program commands to manipulate and analyze data.

Merge To combine the changes made by separate users to identical copies of a workbook.

Microsoft Access 2002 The database program that is part of Microsoft Office.

Microsoft PowerPoint 2002 A presentation graphics program that lets you create electronic slides to use as part of a presentation on a standalone computer or over the World Wide Web.

Microsoft Query A program that comes with Excel that lets you connect to a data source, specify the data location, then select the data you need.

Microsoft Word 2002 A word-processing program that lets you enter, edit, and format text, such as letters, reports, and books.

Mixed reference Used in an Excel formula when you need to keep one reference relative and one reference absolute, such as $A4 or A$4; in a mixed reference only the row or only the column reference remains the same when the formula is pasted to a new

location. See also *Absolute reference* and *Relative reference.*

Mode indicator Text on the left side of the status bar in the Excel window that tells which mode, or state, the Excel program is in, such as "Ready" or "Edit."

Module A storage area in a workbook where Excel stores macros.

Name box On the left side of the Formula bar, displays the address of the active cell or the cell name, if any.

New Workbook task pane The window on the right side of the Excel screen that lets you open new or existing documents, or start a new workbook using a template.

Normal Style The default number format, alignment, and font for text and numbers in Excel.

Object An item on a worksheet that you can move and resize, such as a chart or a graphic; a graphic object "floats" over the worksheet, and is not tied to a particular cell.

Object linking and embedding (OLE) A process that lets you import text, objects, or documents to other documents, either with (linking) or without (embedding) a connection between the source and the destination.

Office Clipboard An area in your computer's memory that contains up to 24 copied or cut items; view or select them in the Clipboard task pane.

Online help system The on-screen help capability in Excel that finds answers to your questions about using the program; each Microsoft Office program has an online help system.

Open A File menu command that reads the contents of a selected workbook into your computer's temporary memory, displaying it on the screen.

Operators See *Arithmetic operators.*

Order of precedence The order in which Excel processes operations in a formula with more than one operation, namely: 1) calculations inside parentheses; 2) exponents; 3) multiplication and division; then 4) addition and subtraction.

Page field The area at the top of the PivotTable report where you can place any field to filter the PivotTable data by that field; for example, placing the month field there would allow you to display data for one or more months.

Pane A section into which you can divide your worksheet using the split boxes at the top of the vertical and to the left of the horizontal scroll bars.

Password A word or word/number combination you can assign to a workbook, worksheet, or cell range that must be entered before use.

Pattern A design you can place in a worksheet cell or cell range, using the Patterns tab in the Format Cells dialog box.

Picture toolbar The toolbar that appears when you select a graphic object such as a picture; contains buttons for formatting the selected object.

Pie chart A chart that displays data series as pieces of a pie.

PivotChart report A specially formatted worksheet area to which you can drag fields to chart summary information for an Excel list.

PivotTable Field list In PivotTable reports and PivotChart reports, you can drag the window containing the data fields over the report to produce summary information.

PivotTable report A specially formatted interactive grid in a worksheet to which you can drag fields to produce summary information for an Excel list.

Plot area The area inside the chart axes, where a graphic representation of data appears.

Point A measurement unit equal to 1/72 of an inch; used to measure font height.

Pointer The shape that appears on the screen and moves around as you move the mouse; the pointer takes on different shapes as it moves over different objects—it can be an arrow or a cross, for example.

Pointing A method of including a cell address in formulas; instead of typing the address, you can point to the cell itself to insert its address.

Portrait orientation A worksheet print orientation in which the page is taller than it is wide.

Precedence See *Order of precedence.*

Precedents In worksheet auditing, any cells referred to and used in a formula. See also *Dependent, Direct dependent,* and *Indirect dependent.*

Preview To open the Print Preview window to see how your workbook will look as a printed document.

Primary key In a database such as Microsoft Access, the field that contains unique information for each record or row.

Print area An area you designate that prints when you click the Print button on the Standard toolbar.

Procedure In the Visual Basic for Applications (VBA) programming language, a sequence of statements that performs an action.

Project In the Visual Basic for Applications (VBA) programming language, a workbook.

Properties File features, such as the workbook author and when it was created or last modified, which identify the file and are updated automatically every time a workbook is saved; you can set some properties, such as the workbook author name or summary workbook information.

Protect To prevent locked cells from being changed, using the Protection tab in the Format Cells dialog box.

Publish In Microsoft Excel, to convert a file in Excel format to a file in HTML format that can be viewed on the World Wide Web.

Query In an Excel worksheet or in a database, a request you make to obtain specific data, such as data in particular fields or records; can include filtered and sorted data.

Query Wizard A series of Excel dialog boxes to help you select the fields you want to import from a data source.

Range A group of two or more contiguous worksheet cells, designated by the first and last cell, separated by a colon, such as A1:B6.

Range name A name you can assign to a cell range, such as Expenses or Revenue; you can then use the range names instead of cell references in formulas.

Range reference In a formula, a reference to a range of cells, consisting of the first and last cells in the range, separated by a colon; for example, A6:B6 is the reference for the range of all cells in row 6 under columns A and B.

Record In an Excel list, an individual item represented by a row, such as one customer in a customer list. See also *Database file*, *Database program*, *Table*, and *Field*.

Refresh To update Excel data that has been imported from an external source, such as a database, when the source data changes.

Regression analysis In statistics, a method of analyzing data trends that attempts to project future data based on past trends.

Relative reference In an Excel formula, a cell reference that adjusts when the formula is pasted to a new location; the Excel default. See also *Absolute reference.*

Report formats See *Indented report formats.*

Return To find and display; Excel functions return values you can view and manipulate in the worksheet.

Row headings The boxed numbers to the left of each row that uniquely identify each one.

Row labels Text or numbers you enter to the left of row data to identify the data in each row, such as "Expenses" or "3rd Quarter".

Run To have Excel perform the steps of a macro.

Save The File menu command that you use to save an already-named worksheet under the same name.

Save As The file menu command that you use to save a new or existing document under a different name, in a different format, and/or in a different location.

Scenario A named set of formula input values you can name and save so you can apply them to your worksheet and view their effect on formula results.

Scenario Summary A worksheet Excel adds that shows the results of a set of scenarios simultaneously.

ScreenTip A feature of the Excel help system, a yellow box that appears when you point to a toolbar button or a chart element and that contains the name of the element.

Selected cell See *Active cell.*

Sheet tab scroll buttons The buttons to the left of the sheet tabs that let you display sheet tabs that are hidden from view.

Sheet tabs The small tab at the bottom of each worksheet that you click to display that worksheet; double-click then type to rename.

Sizing handles Small black squares that surround a selected object; drag them to resize the object.

Smart tag An icon that automatically appears adjacent to cells after certain Excel actions, such as pasting; click a smart tag to display an action menu that presents options you can take relating to the action, such as retaining source formatting.

Sort To reorder list or database data according to one or more columns of data, such as by Last Name; a multi-level sort reorders first on one column (such as State) then within each state, reorders data on another field (such as Last Name).

Source document In object linking and embedding or in a database query, the original data that you link to, embed in, or import to another file.

Source program The program that originally created data that you import to Excel.

Spell check An Excel feature that lets you automatically check the spelling in your worksheet.

Split To unmerge cells into their original component cells.

Spreadsheet A program that lets you organize and analyze information using a grid of columns and rows, in conjunction with analysis tools, including simple and advanced mathematical and statistical calculations and charting.

Spreadsheet functionality In the Publish as Web Page dialog box, an option that lets users enter, format, calculate, analyze, sort, and filter all kinds of data.

Standard toolbar The Excel toolbar, usually beneath the menu bar, that lets you perform standard Excel program tasks, such as opening, saving, printing, totaling, and charting data.

Start To open a program such as Excel, usually using the Programs subcommand on the Start menu, which is on the left side of the Windows taskbar; procedure may differ for networked computers.

Start menu The button on the far left side of the Windows taskbar; click it to see the Programs submenu, which you click to start any Microsoft Office program.

Statement In a macro, a line of Visual Basic for Applications (VBA) code.

Status bar The bar at the bottom of the Excel screen that displays information such as the program status and the total of selected cells.

Style A named collection of cell or number formats that you can apply to other cells for conveniently formatting worksheets; if you change a style definition, all cells with that style applied are also changed.

Stylesheets Documents that Web developers apply to XML files to specify formatting.

Sub procedure In the Visual Basic for Applications (VBA) programming language, a series of statements that performs an action.

Subset In an Excel list, a group of records that has been filtered to display only selected records. See also *Record* and *Filter*.

SUM The most commonly used function in Excel; sums a range of numbers.

Syntax The arrangement of elements within a function.

Tab split bar The small bar on the left side of the horizontal scroll bar below the worksheet; drag to enlarge tab area or double-click to return to original position.

Tab-delimited text file A text file containing only data but no formatting, in which data columns are separated by a character called a delimiter (such as a tab), and in which lines of data are separated by return characters.

Table In a database, a grid of rows and columns containing all the information for a particular part of a database, such as a company's customers or suppliers; See also *Database file, Database program, Record and Field.*

Table formats In PivotTable reports, sets of formatting features you can apply; table formats leave the PivotTable report data with its original organization.

Target The destination of a hyperlink; the location a hyperlink displays, or "jumps to," when you click the hyperlink.

Task pane A window that opens on the right side of the Excel screen at selected times as you use the Excel program; Excel task panes include the New Workbook, Clipboard, Search, and ClipArt task panes.

Template A workbook file with an .xlt file extension that you use as a basis for creating a new workbook using the same design; can contain text, formatting, formulas, macros, charts, or data.

Text annotations Text in shapes, boxes, or callouts that you can add to a worksheet or chart in Excel.

Text file A file that contains unformatted data.

Threaded Placed one after another, such as discussion comments, so a reader can follow the discussion "thread" or path.

Tick marks Small lines on chart axes that denote measurement intervals.

Title bar The blue bar at the top of the program window; contains the workbook and program titles on the left and the Minimize, Maximize, and Close buttons on the right.

Toggle A button or menu command that works like an on/off switch; click once to activate, then click again to deactivate the feature it represents.

Trace To find, as in tracing dependents when auditing a worksheet.

Tracer arrows In worksheet auditing, blue arrows that connect a selected cell to its dependents or precedents. See also *Dependents* and *Precedents.*

Track To keep a record of workbook changes; to track changes, use the Track Changes command on the Tools menu.

Trendline A special Excel line chart that projects future values based on past trends.

Typeface A style of letters such as Arial or Times New Roman, available from the Fonts list on the Formatting toolbar.

Up One Level button In the Open and Save dialog boxes, the icon that lets you move up one level in the disk structure as you locate disks, folders, and files.

Updating In object linking, the process that replaces the information in the destination object with more current information from the source object.

Value axis The Y axis on an Excel chart; usually contains the values, such as dollars.

Values The numbers in a cell; can be used in calculations.

Variable A value that changes; data tables calculate results based on different possible values for a variable, such as an interest rate.

Visual Basic Editor The Visual Basic program window in which you can enter and edit code to create macros. See also *Macro.*

Visual Basic for Applications (VBA) A programming language Excel uses to create macros.

VLOOKUP function An Excel function that searches vertically through columns to locate a specific piece of information; for example, you could have Excel search a column of client names for the name "Jones," and then display the number for that client. See also *HLOOKUP function.*

Watch window A window you can have appear at the bottom of your screen displaying a cell's address, value, and formula.

Web browser A program that lets you view documents on the World Wide Web, such as Internet Explorer.

What-if analysis An analysis method that lets you explore how changing worksheet values will affect formula results; trendlines are another form of what-if analysis that project values based on trends.

Wildcard In searching worksheets or workbooks, a character that represents one or more characters; the * wildcard represents one or more characters, while the ? wildcard represents any single character.

WordArt Shaped, formatted words that you can add to any worksheet or chart using the Insert WordArt button on the Drawing toolbar.

Workbook An Excel file with an .xls file extension; contains one or more worksheets, which contain columns and rows that enable you to organize and analyze numeric information.

Workgroup A group of people in an organization who work together and who share documents, often electronically.

Worksheet An electronic ledger within an Excel workbook, containing a grid of rows and columns you use to store and analyze data.

Worksheet area In the Excel window, the grid of columns and rows that holds text, values, and formulas you enter.

Workspace An Excel file with an .xlw file extension that contains the location, window sizes, and display settings of workbooks you specify; instead of opening each individual file, you open the workspace file, which automatically opens the workbooks in the arrangement and settings you specified.

World Wide Web (WWW) A series of documents called Web pages, in HTML format, connected by hyperlinks over the Internet.

XML parser A program with the ability to open and display XML code; Internet Explorer 5.5 has an XML parser.

Zoom In Print Preview, the ability to get a closer view of your worksheet.

Index

.dbf file extension, 63
deleting
    cell, 22, 34
    compared to clearing, 34
    hyperlinks, 162, 164
    range names, 222
    rows and columns, 72
    worksheet, from workbook, 102
delimiter, 170
dependencies
    direct dependents, 246
    indirect dependents, 246
    locating in formulas, 252
        remove all tracer arrows, 254
    trace, 246
    tracer arrows, 246
destination document, 182
Dictionary, 40
discussions, Web Discussions, 167
.doc file extension, 6
.dqy file extension, 174

E

editing
    with AutoCorrect, 31
    cell, in-cell editing, 30, 118
    cell comments, 166
    formulas, 36, 118
    macro, 242
    numbers, 30
    text, 30
embedding. *See also* object linking and embedding
    chart, in Word document, 180
equal sign (=)
    formula operator, 37, 116
    functions, 38
error checking, 38. *See also* spell checking
    auditing, 245
    locate and resolve formula errors, 250
Excel
    exiting, 2
    starting, 2, 3
Excel window
    menu bar, 4
    title bar, 4
    toolbars, 4
    worksheet, 4
exclamation point (!), external reference
  indicator, 110
exponential trendline, 292
exporting. *See also* importing
    data, 169

chart, 180, 182
    to PowerPoint, 182
Extensible Markup Language (XML), 257. *See also* Hypertext Markup Language
    data sharing, 276
        stylesheets, 276
        tags, 276
        XML parser, 276
    XML Web query, 278
external reference indicator, 110

F

field, 172
    definition, 48
    field names, 184
    list sorting by one field, 258
    list sorting by two fields, 260
    page field, 284
    primary key, 184
    sorting by multiple fields, 261
file. *See also* folders; workbook
    copying, to folders, 58
    database file, 172
    destination file, 180
    locating, 52
    naming, 54
    opening, files created in other programs, 171
    text file, 170
file extensions, 6
    displaying, 7
fills, 86. *See also* graphics
    cell, 65, 68
filter
    creating
        advanced, 266, 267
        custom, 264
    list, 257
        with AutoFilter, 48
    query, 174
    wildcards with, 265
Filter dialog box, 174
Find and Replace. *See also* sort
    using in cell, 42, 46
folders. *See also* file
    copied, names for, 13
    files and, 52
    for saving workbook, 54
        workbook storage, 58
fonts, 86. *See also* text; typeface
    formatting, 66
    Increase Font Size button, 232
    modifying, 78

hiding, rows and columns, 74
.htm file extension, 186
HTML. *See* Hypertext Markup Language
hyperlinks, 159, 178. *See also* links
   creating, 162
   deleting, 162, 164
   destination, 162, 163
   modifying, 164
   pointer over, 10
   target, 162
Hypertext Markup Language (HTML), 160. *See also*
  Extensible Markup Language

I

IF function, formula creation, 134
Import Data dialog box, 272
importing. *See also* exporting
   Access database tables, 172
   data, 169
      from World Wide Web, 178
      with query, 174
   graphics, 176
   text file, 170
   Web data, 272
      Web query, 274
integration, data, 182
interactivity
   spreadsheet, 189
   workbook, 190
Internet, 159
Internet Explorer, 160
intranets, 159
.iqy file format, 272

K

keyboard
   navigation tools, 9
   for worksheet navigation, 29

L

labels
   cell, 28, 99
   data labels, 146, 152
   range names creation, 222
linear trendline, 292
links, 182. *See also* hyperlinks
   data consolidation, 207
   updating linked data, 183
list
   converting to Access database table, 184
   creating, guidelines, 259

definition, 257
filtering, 257
   with AutoFilter, 48
finding values within, 226
name list, 225
sorting
   multiple fields, 261
   one field, 258
   two fields, 260
subtotal, 262
   modifying, 263
using range within, 219
locking. *See also* cell
   cell, 302, 304
logical text. *See also* functions; text
   functions, 134

M

macro. *See also* macro code
   custom, 230
   definition, 229
   editing, 242
   recording, 234
   running, 236
      header and footer macro, 238
macro code
   viewing, 240
      module, 240
      procedure, 240
      statement, 240
macro recorder, 229, 234
Margins and Sheet tabs, 92
marquee, 116
MAX function, 38
   formula creation, 128
menu, custom, 230
menu bar, 4. *See also* toolbars
Merge and Center button, 24
merging
   cells, 24, 25
   workbook, 318
method, 240
Microsoft Query, 174. *See also* query
MIN function, formula creation, 128
minus sign (-), formula operator, 37, 116
mixed reference, 124. *See also* cell reference
module, 240

N

name list. *See also* list; range names
   creating, 225